DATE			

Puppy's First Steps

Puppy's First Steps

THE WHOLE-DOG APPROACH TO RAISING A HAPPY, HEALTHY, WELL-BEHAVED PUPPY

By the Faculty of the Cummings School of
Veterinary Medicine at Tufts University

EDITED BY *Nicholas Dodman, BVMS*

WITH *Lawrence Lindner, MA*

HOUGHTON MIFFLIN COMPANY · Boston New York 2007

For information about permission to reproduce selections from this book, write to Permissions, Houghton Mifflin Company, 215 Park Avenue South, New York, New York 10003.

Visit our Web site: www.houghtonmifflinbooks.com.

Library of Congress Cataloging-in-Publication Data

Puppy's first steps : the whole-dog approach to raising a happy, healthy, well-behaved puppy / Faculty of the Cummings School of Veterinary Medicine at Tufts University ; edited by Nicholas Dodman with Lawrence Lindner.
    p. cm.
  Includes index.
  ISBN-13: 978-0-618-66304-0
  ISBN-10: 0-618-66304-5
  1. Puppies. I. Dodman, Nicholas H. II. Lindner, Lawrence.
III. Cummings School of Veterinary Medicine.
  SF427.P87 2007
  636.7'0887—dc22   2006029513

Book design by Lisa Diercks
The text of this book is set in Celeste.

Printed in the United States of America

MP 10 9 8 7 6 5 4 3 2 1

This book is going to the dogs.

Contents

A Note to the Reader

WE TRY VERY HARD IN *PUPPY'S FIRST STEPS* NEVER TO REFER TO A DOG AS an "it." Your canine companion is not an "it," but rather a "he" or "she." Which pronoun to use, however? The exclusive use of either one leaves out half the canine population. And constant use of "he or she"/"him or her" language construction makes reading cumbersome. To get around the problem, we alternated. In the odd-numbered chapters, puppies are referred to with female pronouns; in the even-numbered chapters, with male pronouns.

Tufts Faculty Contributors

By virtue of their ongoing clinical and research work with puppies and older dogs and the information they help us to accumulate on the best options for canine care, *all* the faculty at the Cummings School of Veterinary Medicine at Tufts University are contributors to *Puppy's First Steps*. Certain faculty members, however, are direct contributors, having overseen the writing of whole chapters or large segments of information presented in the book:

John Berg, DVM, chair of the Department of Clinical Sciences at Tufts Cummings School of Veterinary Medicine, is a board-certified surgeon specializing in small animal soft tissue who has taught and practiced for more than twenty years. Dr. Berg's special interest is surgical oncology—the application of surgery to the treatment of cancer. His research has been published in the prestigious *Journal of the American Veterinary Medical Association, Journal of Veterinary Surgery, Journal of Veterinary Internal Medicine,* and *Cancer* (the journal of the American Cancer Society). He lives in Westborough, Massachusetts, with his wife and two daughters.

Lisa M. Freeman, DVM, PhD, an associate professor in the Department of Clinical Sciences at Tufts Cummings School of Veterinary Medicine, is chair of the board of the American College of Veterinary Nutrition. As a board-certified veterinary nutritionist, she has a special interest in nutritional modulation of heart disease and critical care nutrition. Dr. Freeman lectures both nationally and internationally on clinical nutrition and has published numerous articles and book chapters on her work.

ALICE MOON-FANELLI, PhD, CAAB, a clinical assistant professor in the Department of Clinical Sciences at Tufts Cummings School of Veterinary Medicine, is certified by the Animal Behavior Society as an applied animal behaviorist. A frequent lecturer on animal behavior both nationally and internationally, she focuses her research on the development of animal models for human compulsive disorders and the genetic basis for these disorders. Prior to joining the Tufts faculty, Dr. Moon-Fanelli researched the social and genetically based behavior of wolves and coyote-beagle hybrids; she maintains her interest in wild canids by volunteering her expertise to the New Guinea Singing Dog Conservation Society. Dr. Moon-Fanelli lives in Eastford, Connecticut, with her husband, New Guinea singing dog, five cats, and yearling colt.

SCOTT SHAW, DVM, an assistant professor in the Department of Clinical Sciences at Tufts Cummings School of Veterinary Medicine, is board-certified in emergency and critical care medicine. He is a frequent lecturer at veterinary meetings across the country, including the annual Veterinary Emergency and Critical Care Symposium and the American College of Veterinary Internal Medicine Forum. Dr. Shaw's research interests include the treatment of life-threatening infections and the blood coagulation system. Along with his wife, he is a breeder of Labrador retrievers. They live in Oxford, Massachusetts, with six dogs and two cats.

About the Editor

NICHOLAS DODMAN, BVMS, MRCVS, is one of the world's most noted and celebrated veterinary behaviorists. Born in England and trained as a veterinarian in Scotland, he joined the faculty of the Glasgow Veterinary School at age twenty-six, making him the youngest veterinary faculty member in all of Great Britain. Dr. Dodman emigrated to the United States in 1981, when he became a faculty member at the Cummings School at Tufts. Originally specializing in surgery and anesthesiology and then in behavioral pharmacology, he founded the Animal Behavior Clinic at Tufts in 1986.

Since the mid-1990s, Dr. Dodman has written four acclaimed best-selling books: *The Dog Who Loved Too Much, The Cat Who Cried for Help, Dogs Behaving Badly,* and *If Only They Could Speak.* He has also coauthored two textbooks and more than a hundred articles that have appeared in scientific books and journals.

A columnist for *Life* magazine and *Family Dog* (a quarterly publication of the American Kennel Club), Dr. Dodman has appeared on many television and radio shows, including *20/20, Oprah, Today, Good Morning America, Dateline, World News Tonight,* the Discovery Channel, *NOVA, Animal Planet, Inside Edition, CNN's Headline News,* and the BBC and CBC. He has been interviewed for NPR's *Fresh Air, Talk of the Nation,* and *The Connection* and has had a regular segment on WBUR's *Here & Now.*

Dr. Dodman is a member of the American Veterinary Medical Association and the Royal College of Veterinary Surgeons, and he is board-certified by the American College of Veterinary Anesthesiologists and the American College of Veterinary Behaviorists. He lives near Tufts University with his wife, Linda Breitman Dodman, DVM, and the younger two of his four children

About the Writer

LAWRENCE LINDNER is a *New York Times* best-selling author who has also had regular columns in the *Washington Post* and the *Boston Globe.* His writing on health, travel, and humor has appeared in a wide range of publications, including *Condé Nast Traveler,* the *International Herald Tribune, Arthritis Today,* and the *Journal of Gastronomy.* He lives with his wife and son in Hingham, Massachusetts.

Preface

EACH YEAR, 13 MILLION HOUSEHOLDS IN THE UNITED STATES ADOPT A DOG, often a puppy. They love dogs and, like you, finally make the decision to raise one and enjoy the special kind of companionship only a dog can bring.

The next year, half of those households surrender their young canine charges to shelters and pounds, where most of them are put to sleep. Clearly, there's a gap between the wanting and the doing, a hole that needs to be filled.

That's why we wrote this book—to get you and your puppy off to the best start so that you'll enjoy many happy years together, developing the kind of bond you always hoped for and that your puppy deserves. Our experience has shown us that the first twelve months of a dog's life is the time her owner(s) most need recommendations and guidance on health and deportment.

We're in a good position to know—and to know what new dog owners need to hear. Each year, nearly twenty thousand people bring their dogs to see us at our hospital for small animals, providing us with one of the largest canine caseloads in the country, which in turn affords us an incredible opportunity to learn exactly the kind of advice puppy owners need and how best to communicate it.

We have among us some of the world's most celebrated veterinarians doing the communicating. Housed in various facilities on our 585-acre campus in Grafton, Massachusetts, is a team of patent-winning, premier vet-

erinary practitioners and investigators who combine practical clinical pro-
grams with cutting-edge research to bring together the best in health care
and behavior.

Consider, for instance, that our nutrition faculty is often consulted by the
pet industry in designing new diets for dogs—in health, in the face of disease, during growth, and during maintenance. Our emergency critical care
program is the largest residency training program in the country. And we
use some of the most refined equipment anywhere for diagnostic imaging
of puppies, including an MRI, a spiral CT scanner, quantitative EEG, ultrasound, and nuclear imaging technology. All of these advances allow us to
understand as much as possible about the conditions we treat. We also practice preventive medicine so that painful, debilitating, and costly diseases can
be avoided, or at least attenuated, down the line.

But Tufts doesn't specialize only in expensive medical diagnostics and
preventive medicine techniques. We have also identified the best choices
for general health care maintenance—everything from spaying and neutering to vaccinations, grooming, and flea and tick prevention.

Then, too, *humane* care of small domestic animals is our priority. Tufts is
one of the few institutions in the country that study human-animal relations
(we even run a bereavement hot line for pet owners), so we know what
works for the best people-dog relationships. And we have a behavior clinic
that's second to none. Its approach is not hard-line or punishment-based.
Rather, it is holistic, based on understanding, canine lifestyle enrichment,
and positive reinforcement of desired deportment. Our experience has
demonstrated that dogs behave better—and more consistently—when they
are rewarded for their good actions rather than punished for their bad ones.

It's a paradigm shift from the approach still put forth by a number of popular schools of dog training and espoused in numerous dog care books—even
though that shift should have taken place throughout the training commu-
nity a hundred years ago. At the beginning of the 1900s, psychologist Edward
Thorndike showed that you could teach a dog (and a number of other
species) a lot more by rewarding the right response than by punishing the
wrong one. Positive reinforcement works more quickly and more effectively
over the long term. Nonetheless, nine out of ten dogs whose owners bring
them to us to help correct behavior problems have been through hard-knocks
training in their puppy classes—punishment-based tactics using choke or
prong collars, or worse, methods that were first employed to get military dogs
to perform essential maneuvers during World War II and then, unfortu-

nately, brought into the civilian dog-training arena. A lot of people bring their dogs to our offices in those very instruments of torture, meaning to do the right thing yet feeling bad about the pain they have been inflicting.

Owners don't have to feel bad any longer. Punishment, aside from making a puppy anxious and miserable, teaches a dog nothing other than how to avoid punishment. There's nothing learned about what goes into positive interactions between a person and a pup and how the two can get a mutually beneficial relationship going. In fact, once you begin with punishment tactics, you have to keep punishing to keep getting the desired response, which only breaks down the human-canine bond even more.

The bottom line here: you can get a lot more out of a puppy with a carrot than with a stick. Thus, if hitting a dog with a newspaper, pinning him on his back, or bopping him under the chin as methods of training all feel wrong to you, your instincts are right, and you've come to the right place.

We're not saying your pup doesn't need firmness. But inflictions of physical pain are not simply "corrections," as they are sometimes euphemistically called. They are abuse. We'll tell you, instead, what you need to do to keep your dog happy as you teach him to be well behaved.

Follow our recommendations and your canine companion will go through life not only healthy and content but also easy to get along with the kind of pet you like having around and that others will be well disposed toward, too. Good feelings from others will only enrich the relationship between you and your dog that much more.

Your role will not be insignificant; proper puppy rearing takes commitment. But the return on what you put into the process during that first year will be immeasurable—for years and years to come.

PART 1

Before the Puppy Comes Home

1
How to Select a Puppy

Why get a puppy? There are at least as many reasons as there are stages of life. Empty nesters may want to care for a cute little creature in the absence of their children. A young couple wanting to delay starting a family might act on their nurturing instinct. A young—or older—adult who's single may seek the companionship afforded by a canine friend. And parents of small children may decide to give in to "Mommy, Mommy, I want a puppy" entreaties. They're all valid reasons, and there are plenty of others.

But why a *puppy?* One reason is that with a pup, you're getting raw material, so to speak. You are part of the molding experience. Also, if you're the puppy's primary caretaker pretty much from the beginning, your relationship will have an intimacy, a specialness, that you can't quite get with a dog that has been in someone else's home for much of her life. Your home-grown bond of understanding and communication will be as deep as possible.

Then, too, there's no denying that puppies are adorable—eyes bigger than a teddy bear's, tiny bodies, round, flattish faces. Who doesn't love holding a "baby"?

The thing is, that little puffball is going to turn into a real dog one day, and your aim is to be in it for the long haul, so you want to base your choice on more than initial attraction.

Unfortunately, a decision based solely on superficial beauty is the way many people choose their dogs. It often comes down to not much more than qualities like soulful, chocolate-pudding eyes or soft hair. But bringing home a puppy is not like casual dating, where people often choose who to go out with based largely on their blond hair or dark eyes or good physique, knowing they can easily move on if it doesn't work out. Choosing a dog is a decision that's going to stay with you for the next ten to fifteen years.

You need to consider who the dog is inside—warm or aloof, calm or jittery, easygoing or domineering. That is, you need to give some thought to the puppy's temperament and to whether she would get along with children, whether she looks as though she is going to develop a high-maintenance personality, and so on. After all, you wouldn't spend ten to fifteen years—or longer—with somebody simply because the person had the "right" look.

Beautiful, yes, but are you prepared for frequent grooming sessions?

Don't get us wrong. Big, longing eyes and a pretty coat are great qualities in a dog. They're just not enough on their own to carry the two of you through the next decade and a half together. There's much more you need to consider—not just about the dog but about yourself. For instance, are you outdoorsy or indoorsy? Do you have young children? Would you be bothered by having to brush a dog often, both for her own sake and your furniture's? Do you want a dog who will wait calmly for you in your small apartment all day while you go off to the office or one who would prefer riding around with you in the back of a pickup truck and then romping around on your job site—a lumberyard, perhaps, or a landscape garden nursery? And just how exuberant a creature do you want your canine friend to be?

There are even more questions than these—and more than 150 breeds recognized by the American Kennel Club, plus mixed breeds, making the task of selecting a dog seem daunting. It's not.

There is a distinct and systematic series of considerations to go through when choosing your new puppy, including *where* to get the dog and what questions to ask of the people who have been taking care of her; the cost of upkeep; potential medical problems that might crop up down the line; exercise requirements of particular types of dogs; and grooming requirements.

PUREBRED OR MIXED BREED?

One of the first decisions you'll need to make is whether to get a purebred dog or a mixed breed, commonly referred to as a mutt.

Buying a purebred assures you that your puppy will grow up to look a certain way. Think collie or Dalmatian or poodle and a certain picture immediately comes to mind.

It's also relatively easy to buy a purebred dog as a brand-new puppy, so you know where the dog has been and can assess how she has been treated from the start. Then, too, many breeds tend to have certain personality traits, which help predict what they will be like as they grow older. For instance, there's a fair chance that an Akita will be on the naturally protective side, while terriers are often strong-minded, highly focused, and of

Dog Ownership Brings Better Health

It has been proven that bonding with a puppy doesn't only bring companionship. It also lowers blood pressure, thereby reducing the risk for heart disease.

By taking the dive and going from thinking about buying a new puppy to opting to bring one home, you're joining the ranks of more than one in three American households that currently enjoy all the benefits dog ownership can bring. Those benefits don't include just close companionship and unqualified love. There are physical advantages, too. It has been shown that people who own a dog walk more than others, for obvious reasons, and that dog owners enjoy lower blood pressure (between petting episodes as well as during), which can reduce the risk for heart disease. By one estimate, owning a pet can decrease heart disease mortality by 3 percent, which translates to tens of thousands of lives saved annually.

Not surprisingly, acquiring a dog also decreases feelings of loneliness and isolation and works as both a preventive and therapeutic measure against everyday stress. In fact, dog owners report better psychological well-being in general.

medium trainability, and Labrador retrievers generally will get along well with children but need a fair amount of physical activity.

But there's a lot of variation within any breed. It's like ethnicity. You might assume that someone from a Latin culture has a hot and fiery temperament, and that someone from Scandinavia is certain to be reserved and aloof, but there are plenty of shy and retiring Argentinians, just as there are warm and bubbly Norwegians.

At the same time, "pure" does not automatically equate with better. No humans are more purebred than royalty—we can trace their lineage back hundreds of years. But despite their impeccable papers, plenty of royalty would make for lousy loved ones. They cheat on their spouses, engage in profligate spending, and exhibit a willful disregard for others.

So it goes with dogs. Buying a certain breed offers no guarantee that the dog will be a suitable companion. Take the German shepherd. Most German shepherds make great family pets, but anxious lines exist, and perhaps because of this trait, the breed is frequently ranked number one for bites. Conversely, chows (who also rank high on the bite parade) can be indifferent and independent, reluctant to play. But with the right training, you can jolly a lot of chows out of their funk, making them much more amiable and even bringing out in them a veritable joie de vivre.

Consider, too, that what a breed is like is something of a moving target. Cocker spaniels, originally a reliably sweet breed, have been so overbred that many now have a nippy, unfriendly streak, making a number of them less than ideal family dogs. Conversely, Doberman pinscher breeders have been successful at breeding away from aggressiveness over the last fifteen years.

Just as buying a purebred puppy isn't the sure bet many people assume it is, getting a mixed breed comes with benefits that often go underappreciated. Granted, if you get a dog at a shelter, it can be hard to find out what her life was like before you met her, so you're a bit in the dark on nurture as well as nature. But unlike purebred dogs, "mixes" are generally less prone to particular diseases. For instance, German shepherds are at increased risk for hip dysplasia, dachshunds struggle with herniated disks in the lower back, and Pomeranians are prone to collapsing tracheas. (See box on page 17.) A Heinz 57 of a dog has less chance of inheriting a predisposition toward any one illness or condition.

To use an automobile analogy, a purebred is akin to a Ferrari and a mutt is more like a commonplace sedan. The fancy sports car may look great and may tear down the road with amazing speed and control, but it's more "tem-

Mixed breeds can win your heart as well as purebreds— and may be less prone to various illnesses.

peramental," if you will. Things tend to go wrong rather frequently, and when something does, it's hard to find a mechanic who can deal with it. The car may also prove very expensive to fix. A middle-of-the-road sedan, on the other hand, might not be as flashy or fast, but it could be more dependable and more easily fixed in the event of a problem, and it will probably get better mileage.

Aggressive or predatory tendencies may also be attenuated in a mixed breed. A dog who comes from diverse genetic stock has a reasonable shot at not being terribly jittery or distant or willful, because there are too many competing personality traits for any one of them to necessarily take center stage.

The up-front cost of a mix versus a purebred dog counts, too. Mixed breeds are generally free, or close to it, while purebreds often run as high as $500 to $1,000, and sometimes higher. In other words, there's a lot to be said for mixed breeds, which makes for a lot of high-quality, adoptable pups (*and* older dogs) at local shelters and pounds.

That said, some people still have their heart set on a certain breed. Here's a rundown, so you can at least get a sense of whether a particular breed has a reasonable chance of being a good fit in your home.

The Breed Groups

There are, by some accounts, roughly 400 dog breeds altogether. But the American Kennel Club currently recognizes only 160 breeds (the number tends to fluctuate a bit). While even that may sound like a lot, there are only seven breed *groups*. And the breeds within each group frequently share general characteristics, based on the traits for which the dogs in the group were originally bred. So you don't need to memorize 160 sets of character traits to choose a puppy. Just getting a sense of which breeds belong to which groups in the following American Kennel Club list will give you an idea of what the breeds are like on the inside.

Along with going over general breed characteristics, we include here some notes about certain specific breeds. The length of this book precludes our commenting on each and every breed listed, but you'll get a close-up sense of some of the popular breeds available.

Note that in general, small breeds live longer than medium-size breeds; medium-size breeds live longer than large ones; and large breeds live longer than giant breeds. For instance, a toy poodle might live as long as fifteen years, while a Great Dane may live for only about six years and a Saint Bernard, for eight. That's true for mutts, too—the larger the dog, the shorter her life span will tend to be. Thus, one of the things you want to think about is how often you can bear the pain of losing a beloved pet. Those who choose very large dogs are going to grieve more often.

Sporting Group

Generally low on aggression and reactivity and high on trainability, it's no surprise that dogs from the sporting group are generally said to make good family pets and faithful companions. Sporting dogs also tend to be physically insensitive, relatively speaking, which makes them good bets if you have small children who might pet them too hard or otherwise treat them too aggressively.

But they also do best with a high level of physical activity. (They were originally bred to work alongside people, hunting down prey and so forth.) Making them sit around alone at home all day while the family goes off to work and school is akin to making an Olympic athlete spend his or her life at a desk job.

NOTES ON SPECIFIC BREEDS: Chesapeake Bay retrievers should in general be thought of more as guard dogs than easygoing family dogs. They require strong leadership. And both Labrador retrievers and golden retrievers are bigtime shedders who require a lot of grooming. You'll either be spending a lot of time brushing out the dog or washing your slipcovers — and avoiding dark clothing. Be aware that there are some aggressive strains of golden retriever around these days, and they appear on some bite lists. The old fashioned, all-American golden is by no means a thing of the past,

Vizsla — sporting group.

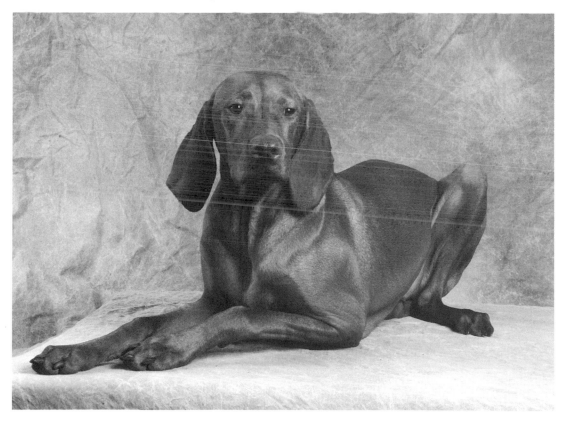

but choosing a golden does not guarantee an easy pet to have around. Springers (as well as cockers) come in aggressive flavors, too. Temperament testing is crucial.

American water spaniel	Golden retriever
Brittany	Gordon setter
Chesapeake Bay retriever	Irish setter
Clumber spaniel	Irish water spaniel
Cocker spaniel	Labrador retriever
Curly-coated retriever	Nova Scotia duck tolling retriever
English cocker spaniel	Pointer
English setter	Spinone Italiano
English springer spaniel	Sussex spaniel
Field spaniel	Vizsla
Flat-coated retriever	Weimaraner
German shorthaired pointer	Welsh springer spaniel
German wirehaired pointer	Wirehaired pointing griffon

Hound Group

Whereas a sporting dog would play Frisbee back and forth with you, dogs from the hound group would rather *find* the Frisbee. They're hard-wired for chasing via movement (sight hounds) or smell (scent hounds). They're also less interested in the human family structure than sporting dogs, and less likely to look to their leaders for approbation.

That makes them relatively tough to train. If a sight hound sees movement, she's off and running. If a scent hound smells something interesting, she'll be much more inclined to follow the scent than to listen to your command to get back to the car.

But because of hounds' relatively independent nature, they might have an easier time staying home alone than sporting dogs, especially if you're willing to own two of them. A dog's dog, a hound particularly enjoys being in a pack with members of her own species. Hounds also often make good fits with strong leaders who like outdoor activities—hiking and so forth—and less than perfect fits for those interested in a cuddly, clingy relationship.

NOTES ON SPECIFIC BREEDS: Retired greyhounds often make great family pets. They tend to be gentle and obedient and, contrary to popular belief, don't require much exercise. Afghans have mega-grooming requirements, and beagles need a fair amount of grooming as well. Don't consider getting either of these breeds unless you're prepared for a lot of brushing. And except for basenjis, hounds in general can do a fair amount of yodeling or barking. If your upstairs neighbor is finicky about noise, a hound may not be the way to go.

Afghan hound	Harrier
American foxhound	Ibizan hound
Basenji	Irish wolfhound
Basset hound	Norwegian elkhound
Beagle	Otterhound
Black and tan coonhound	Petite basset griffon vendeen
Bloodhound	Pharaoh hound
Borzoi	Rhodesian ridgeback
Dachshund	Saluki
English foxhound	Scottish deerhound
Greyhound	Whippet

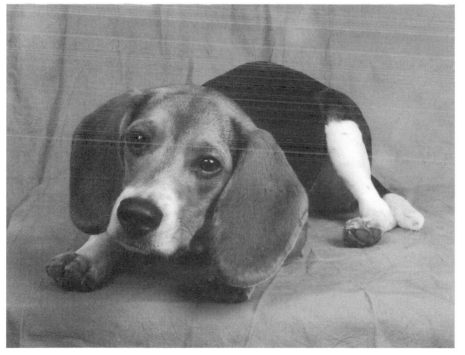

Beagle— hound group.

Working Group

If you want a huggy, kissy dog who's going to sit in your lap, a canine from the working group is not it. Akitas were bred to hunt bears, deer, and wild boar. Alaskan malamutes were bred to drag sleds. Rottweilers are among the top three breeds for lethal attacks. And boxers, who have super-high energy, are particularly hard to get under control (all made worse by the fact that boxers are generally clumsy). Chows and Siberian huskies, too, are hard to train; they can be somewhat aloof. In other words, working dogs are tough—and potentially very aggressive.

Bernese mountain dog —working group.

It's fair to say that having a dog from the working group is a bit like having a small pony. Her sheer size makes grooming no small task, so you have to have the patience for it. Working dogs can also be expensive to keep if for no other reason than that they require more food than smaller dogs. Very tall human adults are only about 30 percent larger than short ones; restaurants don't need to serve two different-size portions. But the difference between a large dog from the working group and a small one from another group would be like the difference between a person who is two feet tall and one who is nine feet tall. The difference in dog food money could easily add up to hundreds of dollars per year—an important consideration for a dog owner on a tight budget.

At the same time, dogs from this group make great guard dogs and tend to be loyal. But you've got to be a strong leader. If you don't lead, the dog will. These pets are not for novice dog owners.

NOTES ON SPECIFIC BREEDS: Saint Bernards are the biggest droolers of all breeds, with Great Pyrenees and Newfoundlands not far behind. The slobbering can be unpleasant. And Portuguese water dogs need frequent grooming. They don't shed much, which is nice, but *because* they don't shed a lot, their hair becomes matted, smelly, and itchy, causing them discomfort unless they receive professional grooming care.

Akita
Alaskan malamute
Anatolian shepherd dog
Bernese mountain dog
Black Russian terrier
Boxer
Bullmastiff
Doberman pinscher
German pinscher
Giant schnauzer
Great Dane
Great Pyrenees

Greater Swiss mountain dog
Komondor
Kuvasz
Mastiff
Neopolitan mastiff
Newfoundland
Portuguese water dog
Rottweiler
Saint Bernard
Samoyed
Siberian husky
Standard schnauzer

The difference in size between a very large and a very small dog could be as much as the difference between a two-foot person and a (theoretical) nine-foot person. Food bills vary by hundreds of dollars a year depending on the size of the dog.

Terrier Group

Terriers are smart, highly energetic, and highly reactive. They're also strong-minded, focused, and persevering, which means they're only of medium trainability. But they tend to be extremely loyal to their human owners. At the same time, they're known for dog-on-dog aggression. With their huge muscles and great strength (they can take on animals twice their size), they're the gladiators of the canine world.

Without proper training, terriers can become great barkers, making many unsuitable for apartment living. The Parson Russell terrier on Kelsey Grammer's *Frasier* appeared to be the exception (although off the set, away from expert trainers, he was said to be a bit of a handful).

Terriers in general are not bigtime shedders—all in all a good thing, but frequent grooming is still called for or they will look unkempt.

NOTES ON SPECIFIC BREEDS: Some American Staffordshire terriers, like their close cousins the pit bulls, can be unpredictably aggressive toward humans, going for years without an incident and then attacking a child seemingly out of the blue. Both breeds may also attack other pets, including other dogs.

Parson Russell terriers — terrier group.

Airedale terrier
American Staffordshire terrier
Australian terrier
Bedlington terrier
Border terrier
Bull terrier
Cairn terrier
Dandie Dinmont terrier
Glen of Imaal terrier
Irish terrier
Kerry blue terrier
Lakeland terrier
Manchester terrier
Miniature bull terrier

Miniature schnauzer
Norfolk terrier
Norwich terrier
Parson Russell terrier (also known
    as Jack Russell terrier)
Scottish terrier
Sealyham terrier
Skye terrier
Smooth fox terrier
Soft-coated wheaten terrier
Staffordshire bull terrier
Welsh terrier
West Highland white terrier
Wire fox terrier

Toy Group

While the other breed groups are based largely on the functions for which the dogs in the group were originally bred (terriers were meant for varmint control, hounds for hunting), dogs in the toy group are lumped together solely because of their size. Many are small versions of dogs in the other breed groups, but some, like the chihuahua, are simply small dogs — they have no larger counterpart.

That makes the toy group very eclectic. A toy terrier will tend to have terrier qualities; a toy spaniel, sporting qualities; a chihuahua, qualities of her own.

For obvious reasons, toy dogs make great lap dogs. Also for obvious reasons, they do well in small apartments, and tend to have low feeding and veterinary bills and easy grooming requirements.

Toys are *not* great for active families, and they tend not to be the best choice for families with children, particularly small children. If a child falls on a toy dog or isn't careful about treating it gently, the dog can easily end up with fractures — or worse. Also problematic for households with youngsters: some toys will defend themselves against what they perceive as aggression rather than try to run and hide, and that, in turn, can be dangerous for a small child.

Note that toys are good for novice dog owners. It's easier to control a ten-pound dog than a hundred-pound one.

Havanese—
toy group.

NOTES ON SPECIFIC BREEDS: Cavalier King Charles spaniels, bred as lap dogs in the days of England's King Charles I in order to attract fleas away from unwashed, parasite-ridden nobles, tend to be super-friendly and sociable but can be a bit compulsive. For instance, some bite at imaginary flies, and some lick compulsively. Pugs are sweet dogs, too, but are low on trainability. Yorkshire terriers, while very cute and cuddly-looking, can be, well, holy terriers. If you need to let a Yorkshire terrier know she's not a big dog, you must write her a letter. They bark a lot and chase things and can be aggressive, too—snappy with children.

Affenpinscher	Miniature pinscher
Brussels griffon	Papillon
Cavalier King Charles spaniel	Pekingese
Chihuahua	Pomeranian
Chinese crested	Poodle
English toy spaniel	Pug
Havanese	Shih Tzu
Italian greyhound	Silky terrier
Japanese Chin	Toy fox terrier
Maltese	Yorkshire terrier
Manchester terrier	

Nonsporting Group

Like the toy group, the nonsporting group is diverse—hard to pin down as far as temperament and other characteristics go. A Dalmatian and a poodle, after all, are pretty different.

The best generalization that can be made about nonsporting dogs is that they can be aggressive. Consider that bulldogs were originally bred to attach themselves to the nose of a bull (for entertainment purposes). They are also generally independent and tough-minded. Don't adopt a nonsporting dog if

Certain Breeds Predisposed to Certain Illnesses

Dogs, like humans, get all kinds of diseases and conditions that can compromise their quality of life. But some breeds have a particular predilection for one or another illness that greatly affects the course of their lives—and their owners' lives as well. Thus, people should give serious consideration to these breeds, no matter how much they may want one, before making a final choice. Falling in love with a certain breed can cause premature heartache, not to mention a drain on your pocketbook.

Note that the following list is not all-inclusive, but it gives a sampling of the major predilections.

Hip dysplasia: German shepherds, golden retrievers, Labrador retrievers

The hip is a ball-and-socket joint, but the socket component in these breeds is more shallow than it should be, so the ball isn't held firmly in place. That laxity can lead to severe arthritis in dogs as young as a year old. Affected dogs

The drapelike folds in the skin of Shar-Peis makes them prone to skin infections, causing some of these dogs to itch—and scratch—incessantly.

have trouble walking, running and playing, getting up, going up and down stairs, and jumping in and out of the car.

The majority of dogs with hip dysplasia (and really, almost *any* large breed could end up dysplastic) can be managed with physical therapy and medications rather than with surgery. Still, the condition can greatly diminish mobility and comfort.

Atopy (skin condition): West Highland white terriers, Dalmatians, Shar-Peis

Atopy is a heritable condition of susceptibility to allergies that manifests itself in skin. The allergies can be to everything from foods to carpets to inhaled allergens, leaving dogs terribly itchy and scratching incessantly, to the point that the scratching becomes constant background noise.

While easy to diagnose, atopy is hard to treat. Medications can help manage but do not cure the disease. The dog will tend to be in at least some discomfort for her whole life.

Note: In addition to putting up with atopy, Shar-Peis can end up afflicted with other skin conditions. The wrinkly nature of their skin, in combination with their bristly hair,

continued on page 19

Dalmatian—nonsporting group.

you don't want to devote a fair amount of energy to training, or if you feel that such a pet would be too much dog for you.

NOTES ON SPECIFIC BREEDS: Chow chows have been ranked number 2 for biting. Dalmatians truly were originally bred to guard fire trucks—as well as carriages. These usually smart dogs can also be difficult to handle, and about one in five is deaf (it's related to their whiteness). Poodles are nonshedders (they are unique in their continuous hair growth), so they require frequent professional grooming if you want them to look chichi. But as a breed, they tend to be smart and highly trainable and, unlike many other nonsporting dogs, they usually make wonderful family pets.

American Eskimo
Bichon frisé
Boston terrier
Bulldog
Chinese Shar-Pei
Chow chow
Dalmatian
Finnish spitz
French bulldog

Keeshond
Lhasa apso
Lowchen
Poodle
Schipperke
Shiba Inu
Tibetan spaniel
Tibetan terrier

Herding Group

Bred to herd (they will often try to corral children playing, out of concern, not aggression), dogs from the herding group can make terrific family pets. These very smart animals are also very trainable.

But they are relatively exuberant, high-strung sorts and need activity, direction, and acknowledgment. That is, they often must have a job to do, they must have clear leadership from you to tell them to do it, and they must have your attention and praise. If your herding dog doesn't have a job and is instead forced to sit around all day, she might well invent one—like chew-

Certain Breeds Predisposed to Certain Illnesses, continued from page 17

makes them susceptible to skin infections (compounded by their tendency toward hypothyroidism). Bacterial infections thrive in their skin folds, causing them to itch like crazy. Touching a Shar-Pei can even make some humans itch.

These dogs' skin problems can be managed with medications and medicated shampoos, but they will never go away.

Intervertebral disk disease (spinal problems): Dachshunds

It's intuitive to assume that dachshunds, with their long backs and short legs, would be prone to back problems. But their frankfurter shape is not what causes their troubles. Rather, they tend to be chondrodystrophic. That means the jellylike component of the disks in a dachshund's spine calcifies early in life, so the disks lose their resiliency. The disks can then rupture, causing the calcified material to press on the spinal cord. This, in turn, leads to weakness or paralysis.

The condition is treatable but often requires major surgery to remove the ruptured, or herniated, disk. Some dogs, even after back surgery, never walk again.

Brachycephalic breeds (squished-in faces): Pugs, bulldogs

Some of these dogs have so much trouble breathing that they can't exercise for more than thirty seconds without experiencing oxygen deprivation and gasping for breath. It makes sense. Their nostrils and trachea (windpipe) are too narrow, and the soft palate at the back of their mouth is too long and floppy.

The trouble, which can arise as early as age one, can be treated very effectively with surgery. But like any canine surgery, it's expensive, involving both anesthesia and intensive postoperative monitoring.

Note: Bulldogs can have difficulty giving birth naturally, so cesarean section is the usual method of delivery. C-sections are not without risk to Mom and pups and, once again, are costly.

Collapsing trachea (windpipe): Pomeranians, pugs, Maltese terriers, Yorkshire terriers

A collapsing trachea makes it difficult to breathe. The weakness occurs in that part of the windpipe that's in the neck (it's usually less severe in the lower part of the chest), often creating a "goose honk cough."

The afflicted dog is born with it, although people tend to come to the veterinarian with the problem anywhere between the dog's first and fifth birthday. Medication can help owners manage the condition, and surgery can also work quite well.

Ear infections: Cocker spaniels

Severe infections in the ear canal can cause cocker spaniels (and other breeds, too) to itch very badly and shake their head. These dogs can end up extremely uncomfortable, and they very often require surgery.

continued on page 21

ing the siding off your house. The dog's smarts, coupled with her need for activity, drive her crazy if she's left home alone for hours on end with nothing to occupy her. That makes a herding dog a poor choice for those whose houses are empty all day but great for, perhaps, a young couple with a lot of energy, at least one of whom works from home and likes to spend part of the day walking or otherwise checking out the world. The dog has to be able to run and chase.

Notes on specific breeds: Border collies have been said to be *the* smartest dogs. But that makes having one like living with a genius on too many cups of coffee. If she doesn't have activities to release her energy, she's going to be very anxious and unhappy—and so are you.

German shepherd— herding group.

Certain Breeds Predisposed to Certain Illnesses, continued from page 19

Mitral endocardiosis (a heart condition): Cavalier King Charles spaniel

Virtually all Cavalier King Charles spaniels are susceptible to this condition. The mitral valve in the heart becomes thickened and misshapen, causing it to leak blood backward. This eventually leads to heart failure. The problem usually causes a heart murmur by the time the dog is four, with death ensuing a couple of years later.

Surgery can fix the problem, but there are only three or four places in the world (including Tufts Cummings School) where it is performed.

Malignant histiocytosis: Bernese mountain dogs, flat-coated retrievers

Many dogs, like many humans, die of cancer in old age, but this often fatal, cancerlike syndrome of the lymph system attacks these two breeds more than others, when they are as young as five years old.

Australian cattle dog	Canaan dog
Australian shepherd	Cardigan Welsh corgi
Bearded collie	Collie
Belgian Malinois	German shepherd
Belgian sheepdog	Old English sheepdog
Belgian Tervuren	Pembroke Welsh corgi
Border collie	Polish lowland sheepdog
Bouvier des Flandres	Puli
Briard	Shetland sheepdog

Miscellaneous Class

What distinguishes dogs in the miscellaneous group is simply that they are newly recognized breeds. There is no one general characteristic, either in function or form, that unites them. The Redbone coonhound is a hound (enough said), and the Tibetan mastiff is a potential drooler. Also, if she's aggressive, she's *very* aggressive.

Beauceron	Swedish Vallhund
Plott	Tibetan mastiff
Redbone coonhound	

WHERE TO GET YOUR DOG

Professional breeder or backyard breeder? Pound or shelter? Through a newspaper ad? Over the Internet? There are almost as many places to procure a dog as there are kinds of dogs. But the guidelines for what to look for in a puppy's first home are pretty straightforward, and they don't differ, whether you're getting a purebred with papers going back five generations or a mixed breed from a neighbor down the street whose bitch just had a litter.

Where a dog should generally *not* come from is a pet store. Dogs you see in a store frequently come from puppy mills—massive kennels functioning as huge dog slums where puppies are raised, like so many units, purely for profit. There is little to no compassion for them in their first days and weeks and little or no training, which severely limits the chances that they will grow into companionable pets. You can take even purebreds of the very best genetic material and ruin their chances of becoming desirable animal com-

Can You Truly Choose a Hypoallergenic Dog?

There's a belief among dog lovers that if a dog doesn't shed a lot of hair, she's hypoallergenic and therefore will not cause the watery eyes, itching, and sneezing that go with pet allergies. If only that were true.

The substance that makes people allergic to dogs is not in their hair but in their *skin*. And all dogs slough off skin cells, also known as dander. There's constant turnover. So no breed comes with a guarantee of being hypoallergenic, despite the lists that proliferate on the Internet.

Granted, sometimes skin cells can get into a dog's hair, so a dog who sheds hair relatively frequently could conceivably cause more of an allergic reaction in people who are allergy prone. And, of course, big dogs are going to slough off more skin than smaller ones. But—and this is very impor-

tant—**you can't make a general statement.** One man's (or woman's) allergen is another's nonissue. In some cases it takes just a very small amount of dog dander to get somebody sneezing, so that even frequent bathing of a small dog may not do much good. It's all on a case-by-case basis.

To make matters more complicated, a human might not build up antibodies to a dog's dander for a year or so until after the dog comes to live with him. That's right. You could have no allergic reaction for a long time and then find yourself constantly reaching for a box of tissues.

We don't want to dissuade potential dog owners, but if you or someone in your family is prone to airborne allergies (the offending substance is breathed in), this is something you should know.

panions by putting them through the school of hard knocks that puppy mills represent in the canine world.

Once you rule out pet stores, you need to decide between getting a very young puppy who is still with her mother or an older one who has ended up in a shelter or pound. Depending on which way you go, there are different things you need to consider.

Choosing a Puppy from a New Litter

An advantage of choosing among newly born puppies, whether from someone who raises purebreds professionally or someone whose bitch became pregnant without regard to breed, is that you will be able to learn the temperament of her parents, or at least her mother. You will learn something about her *line*. Remember, even for a purebred puppy, far more important than the genetically hard-wired personality proclivities of her breed are the temperaments of the bitch and male dog who sired her. To borrow from the metaphor we used earlier, you can tell much more about someone from Argentina or Norway by knowing something about his parents than simply by knowing his native stock.

So where do you find a puppy whose owners can tell you something about the personality of her parents? And how can you make sure the puppy was raised with compassion and appropriate socialization right from the beginning—in a family arrangement rather than a large operation? After all, nurture is at least as important as nature. It's during a puppy's first eight weeks, in fact, that a lot of her personality is shaped.

Making sure you've gone to the right place takes a little digging, but by asking the right questions, you'll get the answers you need to make a decision.

Whether you see an ad in the local paper for newborn mutts or identify on the Internet a breeder, professional or amateur, who raises a particular breed of dog you are looking for, start with a phone call and ask the following:

    1. *How many bitches do you have?* Someone with two to three bitches who handles two to four litters a year is probably going to be able to give each new pup the attention and care she needs. Someone who has eight to ten bitches and handles eight to ten litters a year is starting to sound more like the proprietor of a mill than a concerned dog lover.

2. *Where does the whelping (birthing) take place?* The wrong answers are, "Well, we have a garage/barn" or "Down in the cellar." The right answers: "We have a whelping area right off the kitchen" or "We let her choose her location in the house. Whenever she's near term, she starts brooding and begins to build a nest with rag strips or pieces of paper that we provide for her." The whelping area should be fairly central in the home because puppies should be born right into the human family. It's the beginning of their acclimation to living among a species other than their own.

3. *What are the puppy's mother and — if it's possible to find out — father like?* Is either high-strung? Fearful? Dominant? Indifferent? Playful? Independent? Feisty? Lovey-dovey? Compare the answers with your expectations for what you want in a relationship with a dog. Also, listen for hesitation and incomplete answers from the puppy raiser. These are not good signs. The person should be very open and willing to volunteer information. Let's say he or she has a sense, based on a dog's lineage, that the puppy will grow up strong-willed and needing firmness. That should come through rather than be hidden just because it doesn't appear to jibe with what *you* seem to want in a dog.

4. *Do people come and go? Is there active interaction with the pups?* You want a dog to get used to being socialized with both men and women, and perhaps children, cats, and other animals — whoever is going to end up interacting with the dog in your own home.

5. *Does the puppy have littermates?* A singleton puppy is at a social disadvantage. Through interactions with siblings who correct and cajole them, pups learn such social necessities as how not to bite too hard and when and how to defer.

Along with asking these questions, you want to get a sense that the puppy raiser is scrutinizing *you.* He or she might ask, for example, whether you travel a lot and may try to ascertain whether you plan to raise a dog with true concern and empathy.

If you get the feeling that this is someone who truly cares about the welfare of dogs and isn't raising them purely for profit, the next step is to go see the place. You want to be certain that it's set up the way it has been represented over the phone and that it's a clean operation. A dirty area for new pups is a bad sign.

Also, you want to get into more of the nitty-gritty about how the dog is being raised and exposed to her environment. You'll get a sense, for instance, of whether the puppy is being protected from anything scary or hurtful. If small children are allowed to come right up to the dog's face and taunt or otherwise bother her, the puppy is being disrespected—and learning to be turned off to children, making the prospect of acclimating the dog to a house with children that much harder.

In person you will also be able to learn whether the proper steps are being taken at the proper times to enhance the puppy's development. The right things have to happen during certain critical windows of opportunity in a puppy's first weeks to optimize the chances for healthy social interactions down the line. These times are not completely set in stone, and one phase of development overlaps another to some extent. But if you have a general sense of what should be going on when, you'll know whether the puppy you have your eye on is being raised in the right place.

Early Developmental Periods

FIRST SEVEN TO FOURTEEN DAYS: This is a puppy's infantile, or neonatal, period. Her eyes and ear canals are closed for most, if not all, of this time. But she should still be held by humans for a few minutes at a time, several times a day. The newborn puppy can experience tactile sensation and may even be able to pick up scents.

THIRD WEEK OF LIFE: This is the transitional period. Somewhere around the fourteenth day, the puppy's eyes and ear canals will open. By the sixteenth day, she will be able to tell where a sound is coming from, and between the fourteenth and eighteenth day, she is capable of being startled by an auditory stimulus. At the end of the transitional period, the puppy will pretty much have her sensory act together. She will take her first steps—literally—and start getting used to walking around, balancing, seeing, and hearing. She will be able to play rough-and-tumble with her littermates. You want to make sure that she has ample opportunities to use her senses in a secure, nonthreatening way during that time. She shouldn't be isolated, reprimanded, or disciplined in any way. She should, instead, receive a lot of human love and handling. (Petting the puppy for five minutes twice a day doesn't cut it.) Lots of positive attention is crucial, because a dog should appreciate from the inception of her newly acquired senses the comfort, safety, sights, and sounds of human guardianship.

WEEKS THREE THROUGH TWELVE: Near the end of the third week begins what is termed the sensitive period of learning. This is when the puppy

A puppy's first steps, literally.

starts to interact more with her littermates and with people. From the sixth week onward, the pup will start exploring her environment in earnest and become more independent. At the end of week seven, forty-nine days, the puppy can be subjected to temperament testing for fearfulness, willfulness, attachment, anxiety, and the like, the composite being a product of what nature intended and what the puppy raiser helped hone. (More on temperament testing in a bit.)

Should you take the puppy home at this point? Probably not. **Ideally, a pup will be with her mother and littermates for the first eight to ten** weeks. Officially, the best time for taking a pup home is considered to be anywhere from seven to twelve weeks, but seven is a little on the early side for most. And waiting eleven or twelve weeks is unnecessary. Better to get the pup into her new environment by around ten weeks.

While the pup is still with her mother and first human caretakers from weeks four through eight, she should continue to be protected from anything harmful. Neighbors who are too in-your-face for a puppy's good, adult dogs who are too assertive or aggressive, groups of loud teenagers horsing around—these should all be kept at a safe distance or banished.

The puppy's human caregivers would also do well to arrange puppy parties with all kinds of people—scheduled visits from men, women, children, the mailman, a few friends from work, and so on, in order to introduce the dog to life the way it's really going to be lived. That's one of the best ways to acclimate the puppy to life away from her mother and littermates. Introducing the dog to other animals in the house, such as cats, is also very important. Dogs outside the litter can be invited to a puppy party, too, as long as they have been deemed friendly and safe. Even though pups younger than nine or ten weeks haven't all had their vaccinations yet, they are usually protected by maternal antibodies up until that age.

Of course, to avoid undue risks, any visiting dogs should be free from infectious diseases and fully vaccinated. And meetings should take place in the safety of the house, not in the park!

Whoever is invited to a puppy party, the gatherings should occur under pleasant, positive circumstances during which the young pup receives praise and petting for agreeable behavior. This is crucial, as are all other aspects of the puppy's care. Get the wrong breeder/caretaker who doesn't put in the effort to throw even casual puppy parties or commit to other aspects of a positive upbringing, and even the best puppy in the world with the best pedigree will not develop a personality that will be easy to live with—or manage—for years to come. Get the right caretaker during that sensitive learning period, one who really follows through warm-heartedly with puppy parties and whatever else the pup needs to adjust, and your puppy will be able to reach her best, most compatible potential. Even negative genetic bias can be offset to some degree with proper raising practices. Remember the aloof chow we spoke of early in this chapter—a good caretaker's house is where a dog like that can learn that socializing is fun.

When it is time for you to finally take the puppy home, there should be a willingness, perhaps even an insistence, to take the dog back and return

Choosing a Puppy (or Older Dog) from the Pound

An older puppy may not have a teddy bear face anymore. And to some degree, at least, she has the mark of her previous owner. But she might still be the right dog for you.

Of course, it's important to be forthright here. There absolutely are unadoptable dogs at pounds. Often as the result of unfortunate nature or inappropriate nurture, they wind up there. But by no means is that always the case. Sometimes the most lovable dog in the world ends up in the pound because her owner has died. Or because she developed a behavior problem due to a lack of training or a life of hard knocks. Sometimes a dog simply hasn't been loved yet. Or she may have been a poor fit with her owner—perhaps she's independent and needs a fair amount of space when the owner was looking for a more clingy pet.

In other words, a lot of wonderful dogs—mixed breeds and others—are simply waiting to be adopted from a shelter into the right home: yours. Even dogs who might be something of a project deserve a second chance—and can find it in the right hands.

How can you tell which one to choose when you get there? After all, so many of them are clamoring for your attention. And so many have big, beautiful, yearning eyes—eyes that were meant to gaze longingly on you, it seems, and on you only.

As at someone's home, ask questions once you've set your sights on a particular dog:

1. *Why is the dog at the shelter?* You won't always be able to learn the truth, in large part because the people running the shelter don't always know it. They may have been told, for instance, that the owner lost his job and can no longer afford a dog, when the truth is that the owner just wasn't up for the responsibility. But you don't even have a chance of finding out if you don't ask.

2. *How old is the dog?* Again, you may not be able to learn for sure (although a veterinarian will at least be able to give you a rough idea). Keep in mind that a dog is a puppy until she is one year of age and a "juvenile" (think canine teenager) until her second birthday. After that, she is an adult. You *can* teach an older dog new tricks—it just takes more patience and stick-to-itiveness.

3. *What has the dog been like since she arrived at the shelter?* Scared? Bossy? Willful? Calm? (Ask the ward attendants. They're animal people who work around dogs all day, and they will know.)

Beyond the questions, talk to the shelter staff about the kind of temperament you're looking for in a dog. Also, tell them whether you have small children, are away a lot, do or don't have people over often, are active or relatively sedentary, and so on. They

your money if your new charge turns out not to be a good fit in your household. The puppy raiser shouldn't want the dog in a home in which, for whatever reason, she turns out not to be welcome. He should always have the pup's best interests, not his own, at heart.

TEMPERAMENT TESTING FOR YOUNG PUPPIES *OR* OLDER DOGS

It is often said that when a dog reaches seven weeks of age, or forty-nine days, you can begin to conduct certain tests to ascertain her temperament — see whether she is naturally aggressive or phobic or fearful, or has a tendency toward anxiety. By going through such tests, you can supposedly predict a dog's future behavior and get a handle on what to emphasize in the dog's training. An aggressive, willful dog will need a firmer touch to ratchet down the bravado; a scared, insecure one, more kid-glove handling to increase her sense of security in the world. (Later chapters will go into canine socialization training in depth.)

In truth, as ubiquitous as temperament testing is, the scientific jury is still

---

Choosing a Puppy (or Older Dog) from the Pound, continued from page 28

know dogs and love dogs, like you do, and trying to find the right home for each of their charges is a mission for them. They don't want a boomerang situation, with the dog returning to the pound.

Spend time with the dog outside the pound, too, fifteen minutes at a bare minimum. Will the dog take a food treat? Does she want to play? Will she roll over? Does she seem like fun? Is she having a good time? Does she pull on a lead? Growl or snarl at other dogs? Is she indifferent to you, staring instead at birds or other prey? You'll at least be able to get a sense of whether the two of you are simpatico.

You may even go the extra step of bringing a professional evaluator with you, preferably someone from the Association of Pet Dog Trainers (see "Resources" at the back of the book for more information). She or he will be better able to ascertain a dog's temperament and personality.

A professional will also engage the dog in temperament testing. If you don't bring a professional along, you should temperament-test the dog yourself. It's a good idea to temperament-test young puppies, too. Consider that **personality clashes between dogs and their owners are the number one reason dogs are returned, so temperament needs to be considered as carefully as possible.**

out on whether it really does predict behavior. There has been little clinical assessment for outcome. In other words, temperament testing is more art than science. A lot of subjectivity is involved, with the tester's interpretations very much in play.

Still, we believe there is something to it. Of course, the younger the puppy, the less reliable temperament testing will be—the dog's personality is still developing. But the benefit there is that you can use temperament testing to chart a good course for curbing what you perceive to be a pup's undesirable tendencies; a younger dog is more malleable.

Temperament testing will prove more reliable on an older dog you find at a shelter; you're not projecting future behavior so much as discerning a personality already in place. While that's good, it means it will take more consistent effort to take the edge off an undesirable behavior trait. You're more likely to have to keep at it, since the problem is more ingrained.

Temperament Testing's Nuts and Bolts

Try these seven temperament tests on a puppy who is between seven and ten weeks of age, whether she is still at her original caretaker's house or you have already brought her home. Then try the tests again a few weeks later. Temperament testing is likely to be more predictive of behavior at three months than at two months, and more so at six months than at three months. The older the dog, the less her personality is likely to change.

1. Cradle the puppy in your arms like a baby, on her back. Put a hand on her chest. Look right into her eyes and hold the look. A puppy who submits to this type of handling is said to have a low score for willful behavior. She does not seem to be naturally independent or aggressive. If she tries to flip up and resist, chances are you're holding a more independent-minded dog.

2. Take the puppy under her front armpits and lift her up, with her legs hanging down. Again, look right into her eyes for five to ten seconds. If she takes this treatment well, she is assumed to have a low score for willfulness or dominance. If she wriggles, paddling her back legs and fighting to gain control, chances are she likes to do things her own way.

3. With the breeder/caretaker out of sight, see how the puppy reacts when a stranger walks into the room. Does she go to greet the person?

Temperament testing: this struggling pup appears to have some willfulness in her.

Back away? Cower? Show little or no curiosity? Will she play with the stranger? The answers to these questions will give you a sense of the puppy's level of social interest.

4. While walking the puppy, test for noise sensitivity by dropping car keys or a tin pot behind her, or blow on a party noisemaker. Does she startle easily? Turn around to see what the noise was? Pay no attention whatsoever? You'll get a feel not only for how sensitive she is to noise but also how high-strung, how reactive.

5. Interact with the puppy, then stand up and move away. Does the dog totally shrug it off? Follow you? Pay attention but not follow? How the puppy reacts will provide a clue to her clinginess. Of course, what one person sees as clingy another sees as delightful. The answer depends in part on how cuddly or independent you want your pet to be.

6. Test sensitivity to touch by squeezing gently on the web between the puppy's toes. Does she gently pull away? Try to stop you and make a fuss? Somewhere in between? If you're looking for a dog to be able to hike with you through prickly bramble, you'll want one who is relatively insensitive to touch. The same dog should feel okay about being touched

Tufts Tests Temperament Testing

While clinical research into the value of temperament testing is limited, some evidence does shed light. Several years ago, investigator Margaret Shunick, who started out as a child psychologist and later went on to get a master's degree at the Tufts Center for Animals and Public Policy, selected a group of puppies who appeared to be slated for dominant, bossy, or willful behavior down the line. She divided the puppies into two groups. One group was given to their new owners without any comments. The other group was given to their owners with the advice that the pups should be made to work for treats and meals by sitting first and otherwise acting respectfully. (That helps establish the owner as top dog and the pet as just one of the pack rather than the leader.)

The first group of puppies—the ones whose owners went home without any particular instructions—did in fact go on to develop pushy, dominant-aggressive behavior. The second group grew up nonaggressive and more respectful. So it would appear that going through temperament testing—and then following up—has benefits.

Shunick also conducted a project on puppies using a test that was originally used to assess the temperaments of small children. Called the "Strange Situation" test, it

in a number of sensitive areas—her ear and muzzle, for instance. You should be able to open her mouth without a problem, too.

7. Introduce an unfamiliar animal, such as a cat or a rabbit, in a cage. How the dog reacts will give you an idea about her predatory instinct—whether you'll be able to let her off leash in a park and not have to worry that she won't come back easily because she's busy chasing other animals.

Don't feel compelled to stick to just these seven tests. You can rig temperament testing any way you want, depending on what you want to test for. For instance, if there are young children in your home, introduce the puppy to a child or two and see what happens. If you have a lot of visitors, introduce a number of strangers at different times—a big man with a booming voice; a petite woman with a high voice; a man in uniform with a package; and so on.

You can test, too, whether the puppy will come to you. Kneel on the floor, look excited, perhaps clap your hands, and say the pup's name. If she comes to you wagging her tail, you know this is a naturally cooperative, people-oriented dog.

Tufts Tests Temperament Testing, continued from page 32

simply involves putting children and their mothers in a room with new toys. Then the mother leaves the room and the children react.

Shunick found that the puppies fell into three categories:

1. Couldn't care less when their owners left the room or came back in. They just played with all the toys and had a blast, suggesting, perhaps, a tendency toward more independent, willful behavior or improper bonding.

2. Superneedy. These pups clung to their owners, whimpering and refusing to play with any toys, then ran to their humans for dear life when they reentered the room, suggesting overattachment and heralding separation anxiety.

3. Middle of the road. They paid attention to their owners' coming and goings but weren't traumatized by them and enjoyed the toys, suggesting an easygoing temperament that didn't need extra firmness or extra coddling and a healthy attachment to their humans.

If these study results are as analogous to children's strange-situation test results as they appear to be, a lot can be learned about a dog up front (but follow-up work is needed to confirm the findings).

There's also passive testing. Simply observe the puppy in her environment. Is she cowering in the corner? More of an in-your-face kind of dog? Aggressive toward the other dogs in the litter or more of a wallflowery follower? You'll intuitively begin to understand who the dog is on the inside.

Remember, none of this testing is foolproof. It's all just a rough guide as to what kind of leadership the dog is going to need. But it will help you get a handle, at least, on whether the leadership emphasis will need to be relatively firm or centered on confidence building. You'll know which tendencies will need to be encouraged or curbed.

With all of these tests, chances are you're probably looking for a pet who is not completely fearful and submissive and not completely dominant. After all, even if you want a rather clingy dog, you don't want one who's so scared she can't say boo to a goose. The dog should have *some* character, some exuberance. You also probably don't want one who's so independent or aggressive that her willfulness will make her difficult to have around. Think about the kind of companion you'd feel most comfortable with.

Temperament Testing an Older Puppy or Adult Dog

Essentially, temperament testing an older puppy or a dog who is no longer a puppy is the same as for a very young dog. For noise sensitivity, for example, you can use one of the strategies we mentioned above, or perhaps put pennies in a soda can, tape the top of the can, and then throw it behind the dog to see how she reacts.

The only thing is that you'll need to take some precautions when handling the dog. She has big enough teeth to bite—and hurt you—if you put her on her back. Her aggression can do you physical harm. So you'll want to find out from the shelter operators whether various temperament tests are *safe*. Most probably, you will not want to include children directly in the testing.

Bear in mind, too, that whatever undesirable proclivities you find in an adult dog—owner-directed aggression, stranger-directed aggression, phobias, separation anxiety—the longer it will likely take to train her out of them. You're not projecting possible future behaviors but instead assessing behavior that has already crystallized, so you'll have to keep at the training with consistency and purpose to take the edge off behavior you find unacceptable.

The advantage to testing a dog at the pound is that you can assess her temperament *before* adopting her. With an eight- to ten-week-old puppy, you've probably made your decision to adopt before the time for temperament testing is fully predictive.

NOW YOU'RE PREPARED

By taking the steps outlined in this chapter, you are much more ready to decide which kind of dog you will bring home—and whether to choose a puppy or an adult—than if you just went by looks, or a childhood dream of having a certain breed. You'll be much more likely to make the right match. Now you need to know how to set up your home so that when your new charge comes into your life, you will both make the most successful transition possible.

PART **2**
Upon Arrival

2

Getting Puppy Settled In

TUFTS HAS A TERM FOR CERTAIN PUPS — CHRISTMAS PUPPIES. IT HAS TO DO with how a dog is introduced into his new environs. Christmas puppies are dogs who are kept in the cellar for a couple of days in a box poked with holes and then brought into a room crowded with laughing and joking strangers as a gift to someone for a holiday or birthday. This kind of treatment, while it may look adorable from a human perspective, is inappropriate — even bordering on cruel — and is among the least successful ways of introducing a puppy to his new surroundings and new family. Crash introductions are about as appropriate as keeping a child in a box for two days would be.

Instead, your new puppy should be treated with kindness and consideration from the moment he enters your home. Remember, a dog is not a present. He's a family member. Imagine yourself in the pup's position and you'll be on the right track.

PREPPING FOR THE HOMECOMING

Introducing your new puppy to your environment begins even before you leave the house to pick him up. You'll want to get the place ready for his arrival so that you won't be scrambling to keep him — and your valuables — secure once you get him home. That done, you'll be able to focus entirely on making him feel comfortable in his new surroundings.

Things to Have on Hand

Make sure you have the following items:

Metal food and water bowls. Both the food and water bowl should be made of stainless steel rather than plastic or glass so he can't chew them, break them, or push them around the room too easily. It's fine for the food bowl and the water bowl to be identical.

The exact food the puppy has been eating. Too many changes all at once will make it harder for the pup to adjust.

Chew toys, squeaky toys, toys that roll. Let the games begin! It's never too early to distract the puppy from his anxiety about being thrust into a new situation, and it's never too early to enrich his environment with fun things to do.

Head halter or body harness. While a regular flat collar attached to a leash (also called a lead) is not a bad thing, a head halter (for long-nosed dogs) or body harness (for dogs with very short noses, like pugs) works better for training. Gentle tension applied to either of those will get the puppy to comply more easily than tugs on a collar around the pup's neck.

Dog bed. Every dog should have a nice soft dog bed for napping, sleeping at nighttime, or just plain hanging out. It adds to his sense of security.

Crate. Your puppy, and later on your adult dog, is going to want "a room of his own" to retreat to when he feels like it. Consider it his den. Thousands of years ago, your puppy's ancestors used dens largely for birthing and tending to newborns. But today's dogs use their crate dens as places of refuge, to remove themselves from the madding crowd, from invasive children, or from activities they'd just as soon not be a part of. Sometimes they simply need to get away from it all. That's okay; everyone, including your canine, deserves some space. Indeed, dogs in households without a crate often try to create a snug den on their own—by lying under a table or desk or next to a particular piece of furniture, for instance. They have an instinct to seek shelter, even in the house. But why leave it to your pup to anxiously look for a safe spot? Take care of that detail for him.

Choose a crate that will provide a snug fit—only tall enough for your puppy to stand up without hunching over, just wide enough to turn around, and long enough so that his nose and butt don't touch the ends. (You'll have to buy a bigger crate as he grows out of his first one.) Snug is best for housetraining; dogs instinctively prefer not to soil where they stand or sit, but if the crate is large enough, he will soil at one end and relax on the other.

Best is a crate with solid sides and top and a wired front. That affords the most seclusion. If the crate is made entirely of wire, throw a cover over it so that only the door is uncovered. A puppy—as well as an older dog— should also be provided with a soft pad, blanket, or towel to lie down on in the crate. Bumper pads, like the kind you would find in a baby's crib, are a good idea as well. They are more comfortable to lean against than wire and safer, too, eliminating the possibility of trapped paws, dental damage, collar strangulations, and other painful injuries.

A crate with bumpers and a cover makes a pup comfy and cozy.

Of course, there should be familiar toys or objects inside—perhaps something you took with you from the breeder's or pound—along with a couple of new toys.

Keep the crate in an area where there's family activity, perhaps near the pup's food and water in the kitchen or maybe in the family room. It may sound counterintuitive, since the purpose of the crate is to afford a separation from the rest of the household, but many dogs want the safety and comfort of their own space at the same time that they want to be with the family.

Remember, a crate is a place where your pup should feel that he never has to watch his back, even if he is watching others. It should become his haven, his retreat, like a teenager's bedroom. For the most part, the door should be kept open, but you can nonchalantly close it for a few minutes here and there so your pup becomes acclimated to staying inside in preparation for housetraining sessions.

Things Not to Have on Hand

At the same time you want to buy for the puppy everything that will make him comfortable and secure, you also want to puppy-proof the house. That means, first of all, not leaving electric wires festooned around the rooms; make sure they are taut and out of the pup's reach, if possible, so he cannot chew through them and get a serious electric jolt. Throw drapes and tablecloths over railings or the back of a chair so the puppy won't tousle them. Keep cords, including phone cords, well out of harm's way. Secure closet doors and cupboards near the ground. Puppies love getting into things that should be off-limits. (Adult dogs don't have so much of that babyish curiosity that leads them to places and things verboten.) By the same token, elevate above puppy height items that you don't want chewed or broken. (Many people start the new puppy in the kitchen. Get the Ming vase out of there.)

You may want to put up kiddie gates in certain places, for instance, at the bottom of the stairs, if you don't want your new pup wandering around upstairs by himself. And if you don't want him sniffing around the grand piano or the good furniture, create a barrier to the formal living room. Where you do let him wander, make sure the floor is easy to clean in the event of an accident. (Expect accidents at first.)

Of course, keep items toxic to dogs well out of reach. These include the following:

All household cleaners. These do not taste good to dogs, so poisoning from soaps, detergents, and so on is uncommon.

All medicines. Many are coated, which makes them palatable. A dog can eat an entire bottle of ibuprofen in a single sitting. Even one or two pills are potentially dangerous. Many drugs that are okay for humans are toxic for dogs. Don't ever assume, "It works for me, so it's okay for my pup."

Antifreeze. If you drain your car's radiator, clean up afterward. Even a couple of tablespoons can make a dog really sick.

Garbage. It could contain waste that might upset the pup's intestinal tract, leading to vomiting or diarrhea, or both.

Certain household plants. In truth, we don't see a lot of plant toxicity in dogs. It's much more common in cats. That said, consult with your veterinarian, since some plants are poisonous to puppies. Different plants have different names depending on what part of the country you're in; your vet will be able to walk you through any that might pose a problem.

Pennies minted in 1983 or later. They contain zinc, which in dogs can cause hemolytic anemia—a type of anemia caused by the destruction of red blood cells.

THE CAR RIDE HOME

After you've bought all the things your puppy is going to need, and *after* you've made the house safe for him (and for your belongings), you're ready to go get your pal and bring him home.

Driving a new puppy home might seem simple; you plunk him in the car and drive. That's a bad idea. So many clients come to our Animal Behavior Clinic precisely because their dog barks incessantly during car rides or salivates excessively or is simply panic-stricken once the car gets going. The reason is often that the dog's first experiences with car travel were suboptimal, with little thought given to his feelings about being put into motion in a one-and-a-half-ton metal box. Those adverse experiences, imprinted on the dog's psyche during the sensitive learning window between weeks three and twelve, can have lifelong adverse effects.

Think carefully even about how to carry your new charge to the car. We believe that generally speaking, the best way is by holding him close to your warm body, wrapping your coat around him if it's cold outside. We are not absolutely opposed to taking the puppy to the car in a carrier or crate, but keep in mind that he is being separated from his mother and littermates for the first, and probably the last, time. Remember, too, that the last thing you want to do during the sensitive period of learning is teach an eight- to ten-week-old dog who will never see his birth family again that life with you will be a rather cold, impersonal experience. Like a bad car ride, it could have a lasting effect that backfires on you. Better, if you can, to treat your new love almost like a human baby, cooing and cuddling while you carry him.

You may want to swaddle your new "baby" as you carry him to your car to take him home. You want to let him know that he's going to a warm, loving place.

For the drive home, you should have a second person with you so that one of you can stay with the puppy on the back seat, carrier or not. You absolutely don't want him in the front, for a variety of reasons. One is that, still uncoordinated and possibly curious, he could end up in the driver's lap, beneath the pedals, or somewhere else near the steering wheel or gear stick, endangering both his safety and yours. Also, should the airbag deploy, that could be the end of him. Front seats with airbags are the least safe seats in the car for a puppy.

It's not just about safety, however. The puppy should be in the back seat so the nondriver can sit next to him, reassure him, and perhaps distract him with toys through what he might perceive as a traumatic experience. Care, attention, comforting from a human—all of these will help diminish his nervousness. (He *cannot* get the necessary assurances sitting alone in the back of a station wagon or SUV.) Also important is a "transitional" object or two from his first home, a squeaky toy, perhaps, or a stuffed animal, or a blanket that's familiar to him.

A particularly anxious puppy may need to stay right in the human passenger's lap, where he can be constantly coddled. (Don't wear clothes you care about, as there may be an accident. Put an old sheet on the back seat, too, over some nonabsorbable, large trash bags or a piece of plastic.)

A calm puppy who perhaps is already used to a crate or carrier may be able to stay in one for the duration of the ride. (Put a pad on the bottom for his comfort and because, again, there may be an accident.) Just make sure, if you do use a carrier, that it is tied tightly in place for safety. Or, secure it with the rear seatbelt, snaking the belt through one side and then the other. That way, the carrier doesn't have a chance of flying around and endangering the dog's well-being—and yours.

If you put the puppy in a carrier for the ride, keep the door of the carrier open—or make sure the back-seat passenger keeps touching the puppy through the wire and communicating with him. In someone's lap or not, he needs to feel cared about and to know that everything is okay.

Drive smoothly, as though you're trying to balance a glass of water on the dashboard—no lurching or slamming on brakes, if possible. And take the highway rather than the byway, even if it means a somewhat longer trip. The puppy needn't learn on his first excursion to your house about the back-road shortcut with all the bumps and potholes.

Don't keep the air conditioning or heat at full blast. And keep the radio off, or at least play it very softly. Introducing a puppy to too many things at

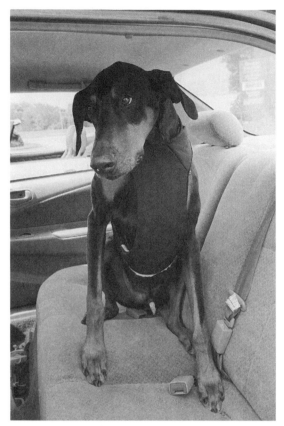

Doberman pinscher belted in for a car ride.

once will add unnecessary stress during his first ride home.

It is best not to give your pup solid food prior to a short car ride. (Most puppies do not suffer motion sickness and its attendant throwing up, but why take a chance?) However, if you have a long trip ahead of you, you may have to bring some food along for the journey. Puppies generally eat every four hours. Even for shorter rides—an hour or two—having water on hand is a good idea. Keep the water in a tightly closed container, and have a bowl on hand to pour it into.

Driving Home the Older Pup

Puppies several months old and dogs who are no longer puppies have usually been in cars before and, anyway, are past the particularly impressionable period of their lives. Thus, the experience for them isn't as critical as for a very young puppy.

Still, much of what applies in taking home a very young puppy applies for older pups, too. You want to be very considerate toward a new dog traveling home with you for the first time, which means there should still be a second person to help the dog feel comfortable. Furthermore, the dog should still not sit in the front seat. Here are the differences from driving with a young puppy.

1. Walk the dog from the pound or shelter—or other kennel—to the car on a leash. (If he's a larger dog, you may not be able to lift him anyway.)

2. Check the dog's reactions once you get to the car to determine the best way to secure him. For instance, if you have a station wagon or SUV, see how the dog reacts when you open the back of the vehicle and signal for him to get in, perhaps by tapping it. If he jumps right in and seems happy, drive him home that way. Some older puppies and adult dogs *like* to sit in the back compartment of the vehicle, which is fine as long as you

have a grill or a gate (see "Resources" for more information) between the back and the passenger seats. You don't want the dog to become a missile and hurt himself—or you—if you have to stop suddenly or there's an accident. (He'll be less apt to get hurt when confined to the back of the vehicle than when riding shotgun—which we do not recommend at all—or in the back passenger seat without being secured by means of a safety harness.)

Some dogs past early puppyhood are okay riding in a crate. If you have a crate behind the passenger section when you bring the dog out from the shelter (or a carrier on the back passenger seat for a smallish dog), see if he wants to go in. If he does, that's a good way for him to travel home. It may be best to try to get small dogs into a carrier/crate *before* leaving the shelter. The dog may feel more secure if he's brought out to the car that way.

If the dog is not going to stay in the back of a large car, crate or not, and if he is not in a secured carrier next to you, *make sure his seatbelt is on.* Pet stores sell body harnesses that click into seatbelts, and they are a must *whenever* the dog rides with you but is not in a carrier or gated off in the back of the vehicle. A forty-five-pound (or heavier) dog hurtling around the car in the event of an accident could cause a lot of damage, both to himself and others. Even a lighter-weight dog can become a dangerous projectile when hurtling forward under his own momentum. Fortunately, safety harnesses are available for dogs as light as ten pounds and under, not just for larger dogs.

THE HOMECOMING ITSELF

The temptation when someone brings home a new puppy is for everyone to come rushing out to the car. That could prove overwhelming for dogs who are shy. Facilitate

> ## Pit Stops
>
> It's a good idea to try to get your new puppy to eliminate before he gets into the car. After that, keep in mind that a puppy can hold his urine for his age in months plus one. For example, a two-month old puppy can hold his urine for three hours. If your ride home is short, that's not an issue. But if you're traveling quite a distance, you'll need to let your puppy relieve himself periodically. Don't stop where there are a lot of other people or dogs; he still hasn't had all his vaccinations. And unless you take him into a field off a country road, it will be necessary to put him on his leash, even if he squirms. You can't risk him running into traffic.
>
> Of course, even if you let your puppy relieve himself at appropriate intervals, that doesn't mean he definitely won't have an accident. Anxiety can play a role here.

If There Is Already a Pet in the House When Puppy Arrives

The decision about which puppy to bring into your home—and even whether to get one—should have as much to do with whether you already have a pet as whether you have young children. The approach differs depending on the animal who's already in the house.

Dog meets dog: If you already have an older dog who is not calm and confident and won't appreciate the boundless energy of a puppy, it will probably work out better for everyone if the new dog is more mature, too.

It's best if the new dog is not too assertive, either. The incumbent dog has a right to maintain his place as "top dog" without having to struggle too hard to establish his supremacy.

The best bet for those who already have a dog is to make sure the second one, puppy or not, is of the opposite sex; that cuts down on aggression from both sides.

Dog meets cat: Age, energy level, and gender of the new pup are less important in houses with cats, although you'll want to

Dogs and cats often get along better than people think.

your pup's homecoming by keeping things happy but low-key and by reminding children that they should not approach running and yelling. Let the pup relieve himself when he gets out of the car, then carry him into the house, keeping him swaddled if it's cold outside. Keep up some sweet talk; the pup will understand your well-meaning tone if not your words.

Once in the house, bring the puppy over to his water bowl and food bowl—and make sure there's water already in the water bowl and that it's always available to him. That will help signal to him that he's "home." In addition, have him stay in a relatively small area for a while so he will feel snug. There'll be plenty of time to let him explore more of his new home later in the day. (Preferably, you'll get the puppy home earlyish, by late morning or mid- to late afternoon, so he'll have plenty of time to start adjusting before bedtime.)

Make sure someone is around to stay with the puppy for the first few hours, at a minimum. Having to start out without any company while experiencing the new sights, sounds, and smells of your home could be scary.

If There Is Already a Pet in the House When Puppy Arrives, continued from page 48

make sure the puppy doesn't have a history, in his first eight to ten weeks of life, of acting aggressively toward felines. Introduce the pup to the resident cat while he is on leash. You don't want the cat to get hurt, and you also want to keep the dog out of harm's way should the cat lunge toward him with teeth and claws extended.

Make them both feel good by arranging pleasant contingencies—fine food treats, petting, and encouraging tones while speaking to them.

And never let the dog chase the cat. Arrange escape routes and high hiding places for the cat so that he always has a chance to get away. Let the *cat* initiate contact if he wants, not the other way around, until the two are quite used to each other.

Keeping the cat and pup in separate rooms for a day or two may be helpful as long as both feel comfortable where they are.

Dog meets hamster, bird, or other small animal: With all dogs, but especially those with predatory tendencies, proceed gingerly. It could take weeks, or even months, for the dog to lose interest in the small mammal or other animal, and even longer for the two to be alone in a room together without you there to supervise. For that reason, keep the bird or hamster's room off-limits to the dog until you feel comfortable letting the two cavort in any way. Alternatively, make sure the bird or other small animal is always out of the new dog's reach. Some dogs will always view birds and pocket pets as lunch, so those creatures will need to be protected.

Feeding Schedule

As we stated earlier, puppies need to be fed roughly every four hours—or four times a day. That means **it's not a good idea to get a puppy if you are going to have to leave him alone for eight to ten hours a day.** Water should be available at all times (for *all* dogs, young and old).

After a few days, you may want to switch to a brand of puppy food different from the one the dog has been getting. That's okay as long as the food has a seal of approval from AAFCO—the Association of American Feed Control Officials. (More on appropriate dog food and feeding practices in chapter 4.)

Taking Puppy to the Bathroom

From the minute you get your puppy home, you're on the clock for housetraining. It's best to take him out every so often, keeping some sort of schedule. Some puppies, even those with fairly untrained bladders, are able to defy the months-plus-one rule and make it through a short night, say, 11 PM to 6 AM. A few will need even more trips outside than the month-plus-one rule dictates.

Do not train the puppy by putting paper on the floor; you'll just be creating a habit you must break later on.

BEDTIME

One school of thought advocates that puppies should learn to be on their own as soon as possible, with the idea that if they're left by themselves for relatively long periods of time, they'll be able to fend for themselves sooner. With that in mind, proponents of this philosophy insist that puppies sleep in a separate room from the first night they're in their new home, even if that room is on another floor of the house.

We feel strongly that such an approach is not a good idea. If the bond between an attachment figure (you, the new owner) and the pup is weak or disrupted, the pup may be more likely to have separation anxiety later on —which is miserable for the dog *and* hard to treat.

The right approach is to rear dog babies with something of the same psychology as you would human babies. The more attention a puppy gets and the more his needs are met early on, the more independent he'll be later.

Translation: Let your new puppy sleep in the bedroom with you. If you had just lost your mother and siblings, you wouldn't want to sleep alone in the kitchen either. You'd want to be comforted by hearing the breathing rhythm of your new caregiver. A night-light also isn't a bad idea, or perhaps some dim illumination from a hallway light if you don't want a direct source of light in the sleeping chamber.

Before settling down, spend a bit of time with the pup in the bedroom (not just in the family room before coming upstairs). Perhaps give him a couple of food treats and roll around on the floor with him. That will let him know you're there for him and that the bedroom is a nice, fun, and safe place to be. (It will also ensure that he's tired at the end of a long day. Puppies have a tendency to crash and burn.)

In the bed or out of the bed? It's the age-old question. The answer, we say, is your call and may depend on how well he's housetrained. Some people make the decision up front to allow the dog in bed for life. That's okay. (We've never heard of anyone rolling onto a puppy while asleep and hurting him.) You can even change your mind later on if you decide once the puppy matures that you don't want to inhale the essence of dog all night, are concerned about fleas and such (see chapter 3 for flea and tick prevention), or just want more privacy.

It takes up to three nights for an older pup to adjust to sleeping in a dog bed or crate after he has gotten used to sleeping right by your side. Just be sure to make the transition cold turkey. Trying to accomplish it on an intermittent schedule—one night in the bed, one night out of the bed—makes it much, much harder for the pup to understand that the aim is to keep him out of the bed every night. He'll keep you awake at night if he knows he gets to come into bed *sometimes*.

This is not to say that you should readjust the older puppy to life off the bed insensitively. You need to go over to him intermittently while he's whining or whimpering and reassure him, without pathos in your voice, that you're nearby and that he should settle down and go to sleep. (If you let the dog know the separation is hurting you, too, or start playing with him or pick him up to comfort him, you'll be sending a clear message that his sleeping off the bed is indeed intolerable.)

If you want to keep the puppy out of the bed from the first night he comes to live with you, you'll probably need to start with a crate—not a crate *or* dog bed. You can use the crate that you keep in the kitchen during the day or have a second one in the bedroom.

Some pups take to a nighttime crate immediately, sleeping like, well, like babies as soon as you guide them in. Others, the minute you put them in and clip the door shut (shutting the door *is* important at first), start whining.

Don't show any annoyance—no yelling, no raised voice, no exasperation. The right reaction is to wait about five minutes, go over to the crate, and speak calmly, kindly, yet assertively, perhaps offering your hand for reassurance. Do *not* pet him or give him any food treats or toys. That's a way of turning night into day; you'll never get any sleep.

The idea here is to be friendly but firm. If you cater to the dog's anxiety, you will be communicating to him that he is going through something horrific. The best route is to be caring but matter-of-fact about it. Rather than "Oh, you poor thing," it should be more like, "Good boy; you're okay. You have a good sleep now."

If the puppy still whines when you get back to bed, wait about ten minutes, then pay him a repeat visit. Same routine. The third time, wait fifteen minutes; the fourth, twenty; then twenty again; twenty more; and so on. Don't worry. The pup will not stay awake all night. In fact, on average, you will have to get out of bed only about three times the first night, two the second. After that, you may be home free.

Only in extremely rare cases will the puppy feel so anxious or so desperate that he cannot fall asleep despite your best efforts. In such cases, let him stay on the bed for the first several nights. It's really important to cut the puppy a lot of slack at the very beginning in order to help him bond with you in an emotionally secure and stable fashion.

That's true for all situations. Allow your puppy to remain too nervous up front and you'll have anxiety and behavior problems down the road. You can truly ruin your relationship with him by disciplining too firmly from the get-go.

DEVELOPING A ROUTINE

It's important for both puppies and older dogs to have a fairly consistent routine. Think of yourself the first few days at a hotel you've never been to. When and where are breakfast and lunch? Where's the pool? It's all a bit disorienting. Same for a pup in his new home, so the sooner you can provide structure to his day, the sooner he'll settle in and the less anxious he'll be.

Maybe the routine is to take the puppy out to relieve himself as soon as you wake up, then feed him, and take him out again fifteen to twenty minutes after the meal. (Pups still have a vestige of the so-called gastro-colic reflex, by which eating stimulates the urge to defecate.) Following the post-meal excursion, engage him in some training exercises if there's time. Then allow a little downtime before another bathroom break midmorning. Depending on the pup's precise age, you may need to factor in a lunchtime trip outside, too, then a mid-afternoon break along with a walk and some more free time before another feeding.

Obviously, such structure is a lot harder to provide if no one is in the house for seven to eight hours a day. It leaves the pooch at a loss — and lonely. Dogs are social animals. **If you feel you must have a dog despite long daily absences, we strongly suggest one that's not a puppy — and that the dog you choose has lots of confidence and is largely free of anxiety. Better yet, get two dogs to keep each other company.** The "home alone" situation still won't be ideal — it's best if the owner can be there for much of the day. But modern life being what it is, we sometimes have to make reasonable compromises. (Another option for the latchkey older pup or adult dog is doggy day care. Lots of pups get a real kick out of the company and fun they find there. Or you might search for a reliable petsitter who can walk your dog in the neighborhood once or twice a day while you're at work.)

SETTING LIMITS

You can, and should, start training your pup right after his homecoming. You shouldn't wait until he's several months along.

Of course, you're already training your puppy by sticking to a routine, keeping his

The Legal Ins and Outs of Bringing Home a Dog

As soon as possible after you bring home a puppy *or* older dog, you need to register him at your town hall, where he will get a tag with a number. A dog *must* have his tag on whenever he leaves the house. If he gets loose, the tag is what allows the police, dogcatcher, or anyone else to make sure he's not a stray and to get him back to you; the number on the tag can be traced to you by town administrators. (Some owners have their dogs tattooed or fitted with a microchip at the veterinarian's office to further ensure proper identification. More about that in chapter 3.)

A town administrator can also let you know your area's leash laws and laws for poop scooping and whether your dog needs to wear a rabies tag once he gets his rabies shot (see chapter 3 for the timing of that shot). Some towns limit the number of dogs any one family can own, and you will learn that, too.

Be certain to have a new tag made if you move, because the address and phone number on file for you will no longer be valid. We cannot tell you how many dogs we have seen at Tufts Cummings School whose owners had dutifully put outdated and therefore useless tags on them!

accouterments in certain parts of the house, and making certain areas off-limits. You can also directly, rather than indirectly, provide structure at mealtime. Have the puppy sit for food. (See chapter 8 for details.) Don't worry —you're not being harsh. In fact, it's not a big deal for a pup to be required to do that, which is why training can start there. You will accomplish a number of things by doing so.

One is that if the pup has a dormant or even a budding streak of dominance (willfulness, if you prefer), it will teach him manners and help keep uppityness from developing. Even if he doesn't want to run the show, say, by lying on furniture you don't want him on or by trying to take control when visitors come, all dogs need to know from whence they meet their needs and derive their pleasures, and since your dog is completely dependent on you for food, mealtime makes a logical starting point for establishing this awareness.

You need to do this for your own sake, too. It's important that you get used to exercising good leadership. Puppies need to respect their owners if they are to grow up to be fine canine companions. If your new pup doesn't learn the lesson that not everything in life comes without strings and that he has to play by certain rules to obtain the things he wants, you may very well have no peace. Even a pup who's middle-of-the-road regarding pushiness may end up co-opting more of the power in the household than he rightfully should if you don't set any rules. Besides, dogs, like children, are happier with structure. They'll structure *your* life if it doesn't happen the other way around, and that won't be good for either of you.

Lead or be led is the message here. But limit setting aside, caring and giving tons of affection at appropriate times remain critical components for the first few days and indeed for the rest of the dog's life with you. The boundaries have to come packaged with lots of good feelings.

Another way of putting it, to borrow from legendary British dog trainer Barbara Woodhouse, is that from the beginning, you have to establish a leadership program composed of the three Fs—fun, fair, and firm. The "firm" part of this trio of Fs is about the structure and discipline, but without the "fun" and "fair," it simply won't work.

3

Puppy's Physical Well-Being: Preventive Medical and Health Care

IT MIGHT SEEM AS THOUGH, FOR THE MOST PART, YOUR PUPPY'S HEALTH is basically in your veterinarian's hands. It's not. It's basically in yours. One reason is that puppy medical care is a rapidly evolving science, and even some excellent health practitioners who administer care to puppies may not necessarily be aware of all the latest medical recommendations. For instance, new vaccines against certain bacterial infections have been developed only within the last couple of years, after literally decades during which the number of vaccines against those bacteria remained unchanged. You need to know what they are so you can partner with your vet to deliver the best preventive care to your puppy. It's also worth being aware that only over the last five years has the basic vaccination schedule gone from once a year to once every three years.

Making basic health care still more involved is that there is no shortage of misinformation on the Internet and elsewhere that provides faulty, even dangerous, information about puppy medical issues. One myth recommends letting your young female dog go through a couple of heat cycles, perhaps even have a litter, before spaying her in order to reduce her chances of developing mammary cancer down the line. But having your puppy go through even one heat cycle significantly increases her chances for developing malignant mammary tumors.

Another owner's tale that won't go away is that *all* vaccinations are dangerous, causing more harm than good. That tale, too, can be deadly. One client of ours lost three Sussex spaniel puppies to a completely preventable yet lethal virus because she "didn't believe in" vaccinations.

Basic health care at home also goes awry. For example, we see many puppies whose owners haven't trimmed their nails, so the nails grow into a circular shape and back into the puppies' paw pads, causing painful infections that turn red and ooze pus—and necessitate costly emergency room visits in the bargain. Then, too, a number of owners purchase over-the-counter deworming medications rather than pay a little more for prescription drugs to do the job. But the over-the-counter products come with more potential side effects than the prescription medicines, including severe vomiting and diarrhea that can lead to serious dehydration and even seizures in some cases. Some of the clients we end up seeing in the emergency room spend far more on medical bills to right the effects of those drugs than the $8 to $10 they saved in their purchase.

The long and the short of it: By adopting a puppy, you have become not just the owner of a delightful pet. You have also become a health care provider, specifically, a veterinary nurse practitioner. That makes you the most crucial partner on your dog's health care team—her first line of defense against illness. You absolutely need to know what you're doing.

Not to worry. You're up to the task. Follow our advice and you'll become the finest health care provider anyone can be. After your puppy's first year, when she officially leaves puppyhood, she'll stay in the best shape possible for the long run.

CHOOSING A VETERINARIAN

The first order of the day is choosing the other crucial member of your puppy's health care team: the right veterinarian. "Right" is different for different people. Of course, as the American Veterinary Medical Association has learned in surveys, the vet's proximity to people's homes is the biggest factor in their decision. But there should be more to it than that.

It's best to get recommendations from friends and family. After all, what's an extra ten- or twenty-minute drive for a doctor who gets glowing referrals from a number of people you know?

Beyond considering people's recommendations, it's important to think about the size of the veterinary practices you're contemplating. Some people prefer a small practice with just one or two vets because there's more assurance that your dog will end up seeing the same doctor on every visit. A bond will develop, both for the puppy and for you. Just as important, the doctor will be intimately acquainted with your dog's baseline health profile and will thus be in a better position to assess the magnitude of changes in health status over time.

On the other hand, you might prefer a larger practice with as many as ten or twelve veterinarians. While you probably won't see the same veterinarian every visit, the practice may have more state-of-the-art equipment and more specialists on board who can be easily consulted in the case of a difficult diagnosis. For instance, a staff oncologist can quickly get to the bottom of whether a lot of swollen lymph glands are cancerous or just enlarged as the result of a severe infection. Granted, that's not a major advantage, because small practices can refer owners to specialists, if necessary. (Many hospitals have specialists whom you can bring your dog to see by referral only.) But it does cut down on the possibility of having to take your dog from office to office. In other words, there are always tradeoffs. You just need to decide which ones you are willing to make.

Along with considering the opinions of friends and the size of the practice, here are eight questions to ask before making a choice. The first five are the most important.

1. *What are your hours?* If nights and weekends are the only times you're going to be able to take your dog for visits, a 9-to-5 practice is not what you're looking for.

2. *How long does it take to get an appointment?* Of course, if a practice is busy, that's a good sign, but you don't want to have to wait months for routine shots and other types of care. A wait of a few days is typical for routine care, especially if you want an evening or weekend appointment.

3. *How long is the standard appointment?* Standard appointments vary from fifteen to thirty minutes. Twenty-plus minutes is optimal.

4. *Do you see dogs on an emergency basis?* If not, what service does the practice use? And how close is the emergency clinic? (It could be an hour or more away—too much time to lose in certain emergencies.)

5. *Do you provide twenty-four-hour care?* Let's say your dog has to stay at the vet's overnight. Will she be left alone? Many clinics have a staff member who stays through the night to make sure the dogs are okay. The staff member may be a technician rather than a veterinarian, but he or she can page the vet on call in case of an emergency. In some practices, dogs who cannot be at home, perhaps because they are recuperating from a procedure, are transported to an emergency clinic each night and then brought back to the vet's office in the morning.

Leave Price out of the Equation

A lot of people factor in the cost of veterinary visits when deciding which practice to go with. But within a geographic locale, cost remains within a pretty narrow range. Maybe there'll be a $10 difference in the price of an exam from practice to practice. Thus, for most people, cost shouldn't be a make-or-break decision. Go for the veterinary practice that you think will keep your puppy in the best health.

By the same token, don't decide on a vet by calling up the office and asking the price of spaying (females) or neutering (males). That's probably the biggest up-front cost of bringing home a new puppy ($150 to $350), and some veterinarians offer relatively low prices for those particular procedures to attract new clients. That doesn't automatically make the vet the right doctor for your dog. On the other hand, if you can't afford the full price of spaying or neutering, your local humane society, shelter, or nonprofit animal care groups can direct you to a veterinarian in your area who offers these procedures at reduced costs.

---

6. Do you provide boarding? Some people, when they go out of town, prefer boarding their dogs at a veterinary practice rather than a kennel, particularly if the dog has a medical condition.

7. Do you offer grooming services? Certain owners prefer that their dogs be groomed at the vet's office rather than at a groomer's.

8. Is there pickup and drop-off? We would prefer that you bring your dog to the veterinarian yourself and pick her up, because she'll be most emotionally comfortable under your watch. But some veterinary practices in large cities, such as New York, do provide a pickup and drop-off option for people whose schedules are that hectic or chaotic.

A number of veterinary practices now have Web sites that not only answer the preceding questions but also provide staff bios and other information. You may want to Google some practices in your area to see if they have Web sites that can assist you in making your decision.

FIRST WELL-PUPPY EXAM

As with a first well-baby exam, the first well-puppy exam will generally last longer than others and will be more about client education than puppy care. Sure, the veterinarian will give the pup a physical examination,

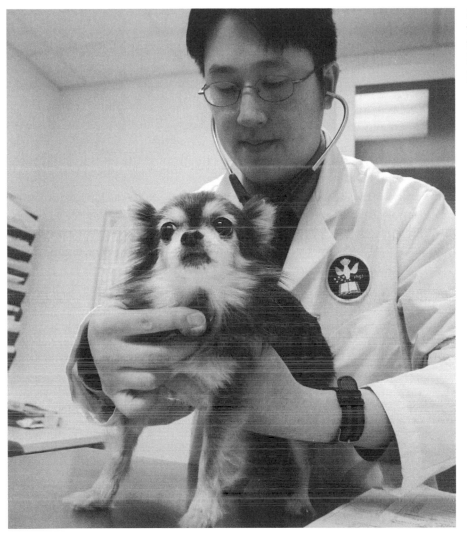

First well visit: The veterinarian listens to a puppy's heart.

checking her mouth, teeth, eyes, and ears to make sure there's no sign of infection. He will also check for heart and respiratory problems and will likely palpate your pup's abdomen to make sure all the internal organs feel normal. But mostly, the long appointment is to set up a plan for future medical care and to answer your questions so that you and your puppy get off on the right foot.

Of course, if your pup has not yet had her first set of vaccinations, the veterinarian will administer those, too.

VACCINATION SCHEDULE

Vaccinations are an essential part of puppy *and* adult dog care. You would be remiss *not* to vaccinate, despite anything you may have heard or read online.

That said, vaccinations *are* capable of causing certain autoimmune diseases in dogs. But the safeguards provided by vaccinations far outweigh the risks. Web sites that insist too many dogs are getting sick from vaccinations are relying on anecdotal testimony rather than reliable and convincing scientific evidence. The vast majority of puppies come through their shots just fine.

Like the American Animal Hospital Association, we recommend that puppies receive their first shots between six and eight weeks of age. In some cases, the puppy will already have had her first set of shots by the time you pick her up from the breeder or other caretaker. In others, whoever is handing your puppy off to you will tell you that her first shots are due.

There will be a series of shots that potentially go through the puppy's twentieth week. If the first shot is given at six weeks of age, most veterinarians will recommend a schedule of six weeks, ten weeks, fourteen weeks, and perhaps eighteen weeks, depending on the breed and other circumstances. If the first shot is given at eight weeks, the schedule should be eight weeks, twelve weeks, sixteen weeks, and perhaps twenty weeks. In other words, there should be four weeks between shots. It's not the best idea to give the puppy one set of shots at six weeks and the next set at twelve weeks. By the same token, don't give the first set of shots at eight weeks and the second set at ten weeks. A variation of more than a few days from the schedule prescribed by your veterinarian could leave your puppy susceptible to a serious infectious disease.

Six to Eight Weeks

The puppy will receive one shot that inoculates her against four different conditions. The combination vaccine prevents:

1. Distemper—a viral infection of the nervous system that may cause anything from gastrointestinal upset to pneumonia to seizures or tremors.

2. Canine hepatitis—liver disease that can cause liver failure (and death) in young pups.

3. Para-influenza—a component of what is known as kennel cough complex, which can cause pneumonia in addition to a hacking cough.

4. Parvo virus—a virus that attacks the gastrointestinal tract and immune system and can cause death from severe vomiting and diarrhea, as well as by causing a secondary bacterial infection that spreads from the GI tract throughout the body. Parvo virus is by far the most common of these four conditions.

Ten to Twelve Weeks

Four weeks after the first shot, the puppy will come back for a booster. It will boost protection against the four conditions just listed, plus provide initial vaccination against leptospirosis. Leptospirosis is a life-threatening bacterial infection that affects the liver and kidneys. It is very common in New England, the West Coast, and in the South. Unfortunately, while there are more than three thousand kinds of leptospirosis bacteria, about fifteen of which spell potential trouble for dogs, only four kinds are routinely vaccinated against: *canicola, grippotyphosa, icterohemorrhagica,* and *pomona.* Thus, just because your puppy gets the vaccine doesn't mean she'll never get a leptospirosis infection.

> # Booster Frequency
>
> Ironically, claims of overvaccination have led to rigorous scientific inquiry about whether dogs require a DHLPP booster every year once they reach adulthood, as has been standard practice. The answer: no. But it has nothing to do with risks from the vaccine. It's simply that researchers have discovered that immunity from the booster remains adequate for three years. That's why the American Animal Hospital Association now recommends giving an adult dog a booster shot every three years instead of annually. We agree.
>
> Of course, it's still important to take your dog to the vet for a well visit once a year so she can have a physical exam. Also, certain boosters do require more frequent updates, including those for kennel cough, leptospirosis, and Lyme disease. Regulations for the frequency of rabies boosters differ from state to state.

Fourteen to Sixteen Weeks

Four weeks after the previous shot, your puppy will again get a booster shot, this one the exact same as the last. It is called the DHLPP, *D* for distemper, *H* for hepatitis, *L* for leptospirosis, *P* for para-influenza, and *P* for parvo virus. The reason for so many booster shots is that young puppies lose their maternal immunity as they're growing, yet their adult immunity hasn't kicked in yet. It's important that they remain protected from those diseases that are most likely to kill them.

Eighteen to Twenty Weeks

Certain breeds' immune systems are slow to mature. These include Great Danes, Labrador retrievers, pit bulls, and rottweilers. We recommend a twenty-week DHLPP for these dogs.

Optional Vaccines

At sixteen or twenty weeks, certain puppies receive anywhere from one to three optional vaccines. The number depends on where you live and, to some degree, the lifestyle the dog leads.

1. *Lyme disease vaccine.* Lyme disease, a bacterial illness spread by ticks, is most prevalent by far in the Northeast, but it has spread to other states, including (but not limited to) Texas, Florida, and several states in the upper Midwest. Vaccination does not guarantee that your puppy won't get the illness, but if she does, it will potentially be less severe than it otherwise would have been.

2. *Kennel cough vaccine.* In a normal, healthy adult dog, kennel cough is simply a hacking cough. It's very unpleasant, but it usually resolves on its own in three to five days. In very young puppies, however, it can lead to life-threatening pneumonia (particularly if the puppies are under physical or emotional stress). The vaccine is not 100 percent effective, in part because it only protects against kennel cough brought about by one of several types of bacteria that can cause it. Furthermore, it doesn't protect from kennel cough caused by viruses. But even so, it may help shorten the course of the illness from any source and will generally lessen the severity of the disease in a dog who gets it.

Note that the type of bacteria the vaccine does protect against, *Bordetella bronchiseptica,* is airborne and therefore highly contagious. That is why many kennels insist you show proof that your dog has been vaccinated against kennel cough before they will board her. The vaccine can be administered via either nose drops or injection. We prefer the nose drops. They provide better immunity in the route through which the offending bacteria travel.

3. *Leptospirosis vaccine.* Not all leptospirosis vaccines provide protection against the four varieties of the illness mentioned on page 61. Some inoculate against only two types: *grippotyphosa* and *pomona.* Vaccination against *L. canicola* and *L. icterohemorrhagica* is new. Speak with

your veterinarian about the leptospirosis vaccine used at your puppy's practice, and discuss whether a separate vaccine that protects against *L. canicola* and *L. icterohemorrhagica* is necessary. These two varieties are not present in all areas of the country, and the lifestyle your puppy leads may not require it. Consider that leptospirosis is transmitted through other animal species' urine and can multiply in standing water. Therefore, the vaccine makes more sense for people whose puppies go swimming or playing in the woods, where squirrels, badgers, and other animals urinate (although lap dogs have been known to get infected, too). If the vaccine is deemed necessary, it should be given at sixteen weeks and then boosted three weeks later.

Vaccinations for a Newly Adopted Older Pup or Adult Dog

If you adopt a dog who is more than a few months old, chances are the pound or shelter will have a vaccination record. Many will vaccinate and deworm older dogs as soon as they arrive. If it's unclear whether an older dog has been vaccinated, don't hedge your bets. Make sure she gets a DHLPP booster and a rabies shot. You don't have to worry: double shots will not present a health risk.

DEWORMING

All puppies get roundworms in their small intestines. They develop from roundworm larvae in mother's milk during nursing and from roundworm larvae that cross the placenta while the pup is still in utero. A worm can grow to be up to eight inches in length in a puppy, and every puppy will have several. (Icky but true.)

Left unchecked, the worms can cause vomiting, diarrhea, and failure to thrive. But most breeders deworm puppies at about four weeks of age with a prescription medicine called pyrantel pamoate (Strongid). It gets squirted

Rabies Shots

The timing of the first vaccination against rabies, a virus that can cause neurological problems leading to death (in both animals and humans), differs from state to state, according to state law. In Massachusetts, for instance, the first shot must be given when the puppy is between twelve weeks and six months of age. Younger than twelve weeks, a puppy will not be able to mount a response to rabies even with the shot. Also, younger than twelve weeks, a puppy is generally not interacting with potentially infected animals such as bats, raccoons, and foxes, so she is relatively safe. But by the time a pup is six months old, she's old enough to contract rabies—and do harm to others.

Check with your vet to see how the law mandates rabies shots in your own state.

Heartworm Infection 2003
© American Heartworm Society

Prevalence of heartworm infection in the continental United States.

in a puppy's mouth with a syringe. (If your puppy does not come from a breeder, make sure to find out whether she has been dewormed.)

There needs to be a booster squirt three to four weeks later, again with a prescription medicine. Over-the-counter deworming medicines are available, but they cause many more side effects than the vet-administered drug.

Your vet may administer the prescription version at the eight-week visit. Your vet may also ask for a fecal sample at the eight-week visit (one-fourth of a single stool is enough) to check for parasites other than those treated by pyrantel pamoate. If necessary, he or she will give medicine to kill off those organisms as well.

Taking Care of Heartworm

In addition to worms in the intestine, parasites can live in the vessels of a puppy's heart. They are transmitted via mosquitoes, can clog up arteries going from the heart to the lungs, and result in severe illness and even death.

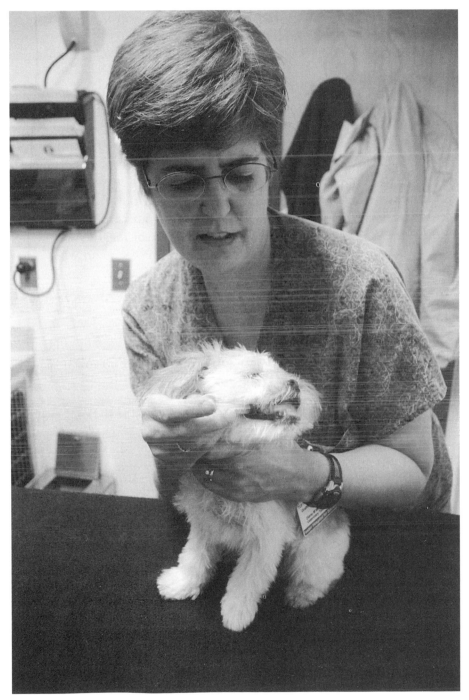

Puppy gets a
syringe worth
of deworming
medication.

Puppies living in areas where mosquitoes carry heartworms (some areas of the country are free of them, as the map shows) should be started on a monthly heartworm pill at the age of sixteen weeks. Unlike the medicine for worms in the intestines, which has to be given only to young puppies, heartworm pills have to be taken for life. Even in an adult dog, heartworm can be life-threatening.

Dogs at the highest risk for heartworm are those taken from a nonheartworm area, such as California, and transported to a high-heartworm area, like Florida, or other parts of the South where mosquitoes live pretty much all year. (Dogs who have had a little bit of exposure to heartworms build up a little immunity—but not enough to go without the pills.)

Most heartworm pills are chewable and can be put right into the dog's food. Those that are not can be rolled up in a piece of meat as a treat and given to the dog to be swallowed whole. Talk to your vet about which kind your dog should take. Also, speak with your vet about whether you need to give the heartworm pills year-round. In areas where winters are particularly severe and mosquitoes don't live in the cold months, heartworm pills can be skipped for several months each year.

Don't make the decision on your own not to give heartworm pills in the winter. Even in New England, they are recommended year-round.

KEEPING FLEAS AND TICKS AT BAY

Depending on what part of the country you live in, and what time of year it is, flea or tick preventatives, or both, may be recommended. Fleas carry tapeworms, and ticks carry Lyme disease bacteria as well as other harmful infectious organisms.

One route owners go to keep those pests off their dogs are flea and tick collars. But it's important that you read the label very carefully to see whether the collar is safe for a dog of your puppy's age. If the pup ends up chewing the collar and eating some of it, the contents can prove toxic, requiring an immediate emergency visit to the veterinarian's office or a hospital.

Then, too, collars don't work as effectively as other medications to keep fleas and ticks off your dog. They're best used as adjuncts to other medications in areas where exposure to the bugs is high.

For fleas alone, you can give your dog an oral medication called lufenuron (Program). It's taken once a month in pill form. Alternatively, you can apply a topical product such as imidacloprid (Advantage). Either way, a prescription from a veterinarian is required.

If you need to take care of fleas and ticks together, most vets will prescribe one of several topical parasiticides. (Do not worry that the parasiticide will poison your pup; that's a myth that floats around on the fringe.) To apply the liquid directly to the skin, you need to part the dog's fur, generally on the neck or between the shoulder blades (where the dog can't lick it before it has a chance to spread out).

Don't let the dog go swimming for twenty-four hours — it takes that long for the liquid to be fully absorbed. But after that it works for about thirty days, after which you need to reapply. (Mark your calendar.)

Do not be alarmed if you see a live flea or tick on your medicated dog. The drug needs about twenty-four hours to kill either one of those parasites, but that's fast enough, since it takes those bugs a full twenty-four to forty-eight hours to transmit disease.

Of course, you do want to remove a tick should you find one. It's easy. You can buy a plastic tick-removal device that's shaped sort of like a spoon with a V cut out of it to scoop up the tick. Or you can simply take a tissue or cotton ball, firmly grip the tick, and pull it out perpendicular to the skin. (This works whether or not the tick is already plumped up.) Tweezers work fine, too.

No need to worry that you're leaving the head in. That's just an old tale. Don't worry about any redness you see on the dog's skin, either. That's simply a little irritation, not a sign that the puppy has been infected.

SPAYING AND NEUTERING

Contrary to popular belief, it is *not* healthier for a female to have a litter and then be spayed. Quite the opposite. A female puppy who is spayed before her first heat has essentially no chance of ending up with mammary cancer, a condition that is often fatal. If you spay between the first and second heat cycle, her chance of getting mammary cancer rises somewhat. Any potential cancer-sparing benefit is lost after the third heat; the risk for a mammary gland malignancy increases dramatically.

Spaying also reduces the risk for a severe uterine infection called pyometra, which often requires an emergency hysterectomy.

Neutering a male puppy also comes with health advantages. It will reduce his risk later on for a perineal hernia, a hernia of the muscles around the anus, and it will lower his risk for certain perianal tumors. It will also cut down on the possibility later in life of contracting various diseases of the prostate gland at the base of the bladder. Certainly, a puppy whose testicles haven't descended by six months of age (the condition is called cryptochidism) should have his testicles removed. Undescended testicles are prone to becoming cancerous.

Simply put, unless you plan to breed your dog, you will want to have your puppy spayed or neutered. These procedures not only reduce the risk for certain diseases but also help with dog population control. The general recommendation is to have the procedure done when the puppy is about six months of age, although you can also safely do it when the puppy is as young as two to three months.

The aim is to catch males before they start lifting their hind leg and marking everything in sight with urine (somewhere between six and nine months) and to catch females before their first heat cycle (generally somewhere between eight and fourteen months, although sometimes as early as six months).

Neutering a Male Puppy

Most male puppies are neutered with surgery. The doctor makes a small incision right in front of the testicles, through which they are both removed. If the operation takes place early in the day, the puppy will probably be able to go home the same day. If the operation occurs in the afternoon, the puppy may have to stay overnight to fully recover from the anesthesia.

Once home, the puppy should be confined to short walks on leash for ten to twelve days. If he licks or chews at his incision, you'll want to talk to the vet about fitting him with one of those plastic Elizabethan collars, which some dogs hate but which keep them from opening up the wound. (The oft-repeated idea that it's good for animals to lick their wounds does not apply to surgical incisions.) Also, watch for swelling, redness, and discharge at the site of the incision; these may be signs of infection and therefore necessitate a trip back to the vet.

A male puppy who has been getting more aggressive than you would like will lose some of his edge after neutering. Male-on-male dog aggression will be most affected, but owner-directed aggression will also be reduced (although not eliminated).

Neutering will not completely eliminate humping in most dogs, either.

And in a third of dogs, it won't help diminish the behavior at all. That's because humping, or mounting, can be more of a dominance issue than a sexual issue and should be corrected with proper training (see chapter 8).

Note that while it will take only about three hours for your pup's testosterone level to fall to zero, behavioral changes sometimes lag behind by a month or more.

Spaying a Female Puppy

Spaying is a more involved, more invasive surgery than neutering and often involves an overnight stay. The vet makes an incision in the belly and enters the dog's abdomen to remove her uterus and ovaries. (The uterus is not always removed in Europe, but to prevent the uterine infection pyometra, which can be life-threatening, removal of the uterus, or hysterectomy, is routine practice in the United States.)

Once you get the puppy home, you may need to give her pain medication, although almost all spayed dogs are ready to walk within a couple of hours. In two to three days, virtually 100 percent of spayed pups appear to be feeling normal, but as with neutered males, they should be walked only on leash for ten to twelve days. And as with males, you should watch for swelling, redness, and discharge at the site of the incision.

Female dogs' personalities change less after spaying than males' do after neutering. Males are more victims of their hormones.

> ## *Female Heat Cycle*
>
> A heat cycle in a female dog lasts about three weeks. It starts with some bloody vaginal discharge. Then, from about the fifth to the fifteenth day, the dog is considered fertile. The actual fertile period lasts only forty-eight to seventy-two hours (twenty-four hours in human females). But male dog semen lives seven to ten days in the vaginal tract (human sperm lives only up to about seventy-two hours).
>
> Male dogs can sense a bitch in heat from several blocks away. Pheromone scents clue them in.
>
> Heat cycles come every six to ten months.

THE NEXT VET VISIT

Once you've had your puppy spayed or neutered, you probably won't need to go back to the vet until he or she is a year old. At that point, the dog will receive booster shots, if necessary, along with an annual wellness exam.

NOTE: While most puppies remain perfectly healthy and don't need to see the veterinarian between well visits, a fair number of puppies do end up with hot spots—bacterial skin infections that can occur when the dog's skin gets wet and then doesn't dry quickly. A hot spot can be very uncomfortable, with the puppy scratching away at it. The solution is for the vet to shave the affected area (often under the collar or in a skin fold) and clean it. She may also apply a topical antibiotic and prescribe an oral antibiotic for you to give the puppy at home.

A second common condition, much more apt to occur in female puppies, is a urinary tract infection (UTI). About one in five female puppies gets UTIs, most commonly between six and eight months of age, but sometimes as early as twelve to sixteen weeks. Don't worry that you won't recognize one. A UTI will make a puppy quite uncomfortable. If housetrained, she will be asking to go out all the time. Or she may do a lot of little dribbles indoors, perhaps with a bit of blood in her urine.

If you suspect a UTI, take your puppy to the vet for proper diagnostic tests and antibiotic therapy.

ROUTINE HEALTH CARE AT HOME

Puppy medical care doesn't take place just at the vet's office. A fair amount of caregiving goes on at home, too. Along with serving as your puppy's veterinary nurse practitioner, you should be running her hair and nail salon, a dental hygienist's office, and a walk-in clinic for eye and ear cleaning. These routines aren't just for looking good. Taking care of your dog's body at home on a regular basis will help keep her free of illness, and in some cases may even help her live longer. It will save on medical bills, too.

Tattooing Fido?

For identification purposes, a vet can tattoo a puppy during spaying or neutering to ensure a positive ID in the event that you and the dog ever become separated. While most dog owners don't feel such a step is necessary, the owners of show dogs often take such a precaution as a matter of course. Unlike a tag on a collar, a tattoo (often a number placed on the inside of the thigh) can't fall off, and you can't ever forget to put it on.

In lieu of a tattoo, the vet can also place a microchip under the puppy's skin, usually in the neck, for roughly $50 to $60. (This can be done at any visit, not just while the dog is under anesthesia.) The information in the chip is kept by the microchipping company and can be read by a scanner for identification—and reunite you and your dog should you ever become unintentionally separated. The drawback here is that there is more than one microchipping company, and the companies don't work together. Thus, a local animal control officer's scanner, for instance, may not pick up the information on your dog's particular chip. And one company cannot necessarily read the information on another company's chip—a potential problem if you move out of the area.

The more conscientious you are about maintaining your puppy's coat and the rest of her body, the less likely you'll be to end up at the veterinarian's office unexpectedly.

Grooming

How and even whether to brush your puppy's hair is going to depend on her breed(s). Dogs with a flat coat (as opposed to curly hair), particularly a long, rather flowing coat, need to be brushed regularly—at least once a week. **Without regular brushing, tangles and mats of hair will form, which not only can be uncomfortable for the puppy but which also make it easier for skin infections to take hold.** And once there, a skin infection can be hard to treat without shaving the affected area.

Introduce your puppy to brushing with lots of short, fun sessions. Most puppies take to brushing very well, but it's better to hedge your bets at first to make certain she enjoys it and doesn't end up needing to be pinned down for every grooming session. Use about as much pressure as you'd use on your own hair. And offer lots of praise and cooing, with some delicious food treats, at least the first few times.

A long-bristled brush, like one used for people, works just fine. The purpose isn't to pull out a lot of hair. It's simply to keep the hairs individual—untangled and free from becoming all stuck together.

Shedding blade (left) and curry comb, both good for dogs with long, thick undercoats.

If your puppy has a long, thick undercoat (think Labrador retriever and German shepherd types), you'll want to brush with what is known as a shedding blade—a wire loop with serrated edges that you pull along the dog's hair with a handle. You can also use a curry comb—a rubber disc with short, teeth-shaped prongs. Brushing these dogs will protect your furniture as well as your pet. The ones with thick undercoats don't shed all the time (changes in season tend to bring it on), but when they do. . . .

Some dogs don't need brushing at all. The curly hair on poodles and Portuguese water dogs, for instance, doesn't shed a lot and doesn't tangle. It separates naturally.

But those dogs do have to go to a groomer every three months or so to have their hair trimmed. So do other dogs whose hair grows long, including Lhasa apsos and Shih Tzus. It will become apparent pretty soon whether your dog is one of those who need regular hair trims.

On Whether to Purchase Pet Health Insurance

Ask yourself the following two questions. First, if something catastrophic happens to my puppy or older dog, can I afford to spend $300 to save her? Second, if something catastrophic happens to my puppy or older dog, will I be able to afford $5,000 to $7,000 to save her?

If your answer to the first question is yes and your answer to the second one is no, seriously consider taking out a health insurance policy for your pet, which will run about $300 a year. Otherwise, you may have to put down your dog because of the cost of taking care of an illness, not because the illness is incurable.

Most pet health insurance policies don't cover routine care, so you'll get no discounts on vaccinations, neutering or spaying, or other planned care that you expect to pay for. But you can't plan for emergencies.

(That's what makes them emergencies.) And if something catastrophic happens to your dog that might take $5,000 or more to fix and you don't have the money to cover it, health insurance will take care of most, if not all, of the cost. You'll be able to make your dog comfortable and perhaps get to spend many more years with her as well.

Look closely at any policies you are considering, just as you would for yourself. While pet insurance companies are reputable, you need to be clear on exactly what different policies do and don't cover, whether there are deductibles, how the premiums vary depending on coverage, whether the premiums rise with the dog's age, and so on. Talk to the staff at your vet's office, too. They'll be able to clarify which procedures and conditions the plans cover.

Some veterinary offices offer grooming services, and going to people you know may make you or your dog feel more comfortable. What we don't recommend is trimming your dog's hair without proper guidance. A lot of people end up at our emergency room with their dogs because they've nipped their dog's skin while clipping. Trimming hair mats behind the ears is a particularly common way to unintentionally cause a dog to start bleeding.

Nail Trimming

If a dog's nails get too long, walking can become uncomfortable. In some cases, the nails grow so long that they curve around in almost a 360-degree loop and grow back into the paw pads. That's not only painful. It can also lead to infections.

So how often should you clip a dog's nails? Some people wait until they hear clicking on the floor. That's not harmful (except to your floor), but we suggest you make a habit of clipping your dog's nails every few weeks. That way, you're just taking off the nail tips, and you will never take off enough to hurt your dog or make her bleed—an all-too-common complication.

Dog nails, like human nails, are composed simply of dead cells, so there's little chance

Don't clip into the darker part of the nail. Called the quick, it has nerves and blood vessels that can cause bleeding—and pain—when cut.

of hurting your dog when you clip the nails properly. One important difference, however, is that a dog's nails have a lot of nerves and blood vessels running partway down the middle—the quick. (The quick in humans ends at the fingertip and doesn't extend into the nail.) Cut into a dog's quick and it won't just bleed. It'll cause the dog a lot of pain, too.

If your dog has clear nails, you can see the pink of the blood vessels in the quick of each nail. If your dog has dark nails, it's much harder to discern where the quick begins. Either way, regular clipping of just the tips will let you avoid any possible mishaps—and trips to the emergency room.

For an eight- to twelve-week-old puppy, baby nail clippers will work fine. Once the puppy is older than that, two kinds of clippers do the job, both available at pet stores. One type has a metal ring with a handle. You put the ring over the nail and then a blade shoots out of it guillotine-style and shaves off the end of the nail. We find this kind of clipper relatively hard to control.

Bathing Puppy?

Contrary to popular notion, dogs do not need routine baths. That said, *you* may need for the dog to be bathed on the order of every month or two if her doggy smell offends you. Should that be the case, use only veterinary bathing products; human shampoos are too harsh for a dog's skin and can cause irritation. And *really* make sure you get out all the soap; leftover suds can be irritating and can cause skin infections. Be superthorough, because even with lots of rinsing, it's not always clear whether all the soap has been removed. Direct a jet of water right against the hair and make sure that what's running off is clear, not sudsy.

Bath time.

The other type is closer to a regular nail clipper (even though it looks sort of like a pair of pliers) and easier to use. It's really a nail *snipper,* not a clipper—all to the good for taking off just the tips of the nails with little snips. Throw out either type of clipper when it starts to become dull. Dull clippers prolong the session and squeeze the nail instead of slicing cleanly, causing more pain. The replacement cost of a clipper is about $8 or $9.

Groomers sometimes use nail *grinders,* which take down nail tips with a little rotary sander. Not all dogs like the feel—or sound—of a grinder.

Make sure to keep styptic powder in the house in case you do accidentally cut into the quick of your dog's nail. If the cut is shallow enough, the powder will keep you from having to take the bleeding dog to the vet.

Styptic powder is available at pet stores. Sprinkle some into the cap provided, then push the cap onto the nail. This works better than trying to pick up the powder with your fingers. Also, styptic powder can stain flesh, and it's virtually impossible to wash off the black marks. You have to wait for your skin to slough off. Styptic powder stings, too.

Be aware that a lot of dogs aren't thrilled about having their feet or nails handled. Before you clip your puppy's nails for the first time, play with her feet. Get her used to that. Then clip one nail a day at the start. They don't all have to be done at once. Later on, as the pup matures, she'll come around and lazily let you do a foot, or maybe even both feet, in one sitting.

Ear Cleaning

If you've got a dog with tall, erect ears, she's probably not going to have a lot of ear problems. Air will reach into her ear canals and keep them dry. It's moisture that promotes ear infections and other complications.

Cocker spaniels have the worst ears of all dogs, as far as health is concerned. But any dog with long droopy ears—basset hounds and the like—and any dog who goes into the water a lot will be prone from puppyhood to ear infections, usually caused by a mixture of bacteria and yeast. Note that even though German shepherds have erect ears, they, too, are somewhat prone to ear infections.

If your dog's ears are infection strongholds waiting to happen, clean them once a week and after every swimming session. Ear-cleaning solutions available at pet stores are a combination of alcohol, a cleaning agent, and a drawing, or desiccating, agent (to keep the area dry).

Secondhand Smoke Is Bad for Dogs, Too

Practicing good health care for your pup includes not letting people smoke around her. Although there has not yet been definitive research on the risk that secondhand smoke poses for dogs, research at Tufts has already shown that cats living in households with cigarette smokers are at increased risk for oral and other cancers. In other words, it seems likely that certain known risk factors for cancer in people are also risk factors for companion animals.

If you smoke yourself, perhaps bringing home a puppy could be your motivation to quit. You'll be enhancing the quality—and, possibly, the length—of two lives: yours and your dog's.

To start, lift up an ear. Pull it up gently so the ear canal is open and easily viewable. Then squirt enough of the liquid solution in to fill the canal—not to overflowing, but not just a drop or two, either. Now, massage not the ear itself but the area under the ear and down toward the dog's neck. You will probably be able to feel the ear canal going in that direction beneath the dog's hair.

Work the massage gently but firmly for fifteen to twenty seconds. This will disperse the fluid all through the canal and break up wax and other gunk in there (most dogs love the massaging part). When you're done, pick up a cotton ball (never a Q-tip, which can damage the ear drum) and wipe only as far into the ear as you can comfortably go (many dogs don't love this part). There will usually be a lot of crud and moisture to wipe out.

This weekly procedure should help keep your dog's ears infection-free, but if your dog starts shaking her head a lot and scratching at it, there's a chance she's infected. Look into the canal. If it looks very red or inflamed, or if there's some puslike discharge, take the dog to the vet. He will probably prescribe a medicine for you to apply once or twice a day for a couple of weeks. It contains a mixture of a topical antibiotic, an antifungal agent, and a steroid. The steroid will take down the extreme discomfort that dogs experience with ear infections.

Eye Care

Most dogs don't require special treatment for their eyes, although some with short noses, such as pugs and Shih Tzus, tend to build up a lot of eye gunk. It's not a sign of anything serious. Just take your finger or a tissue and lightly wipe off the buildup. If the gunk gets crusty, use a warm washcloth to remove it. You just don't want to touch the eye. The goal is to clean off the gunk, not clean the eye itself.

Note that if there's *a lot* of discharge and the eyes are runny, red, or inflamed, the dog could have an infection, allergies, or an ulcer on the cornea (which happens a fair amount to puppies who get scratched on the eye by the family cat or who have an eyelash that grows inward toward the cornea). Get to the vet's office immediately. Particularly in the case of a severely scratched eye, there may only be a certain window of opportunity, as little as a few hours, to save the dog's sight—not enough time to wait until a vet appointment is convenient.

Oral Hygiene

New research suggests there may be a relation between oral health and heart health (not just for dogs but also for humans). Therefore, it's in your best interest to keep your puppy's teeth clean. At the very least, regular brushing will mean she has to go under anesthesia less often as she grows older. Adult dogs need periodic teeth cleanings at the vet's office, for which they have to be anesthetized so they will not move during the procedure and risk being harmed by the cleaning instruments. (We haven't yet met a dog who will open wide for a cleaning and polishing!) The more assiduous you are about cleaning at home, the longer it will be before the first professional cleaning, and the more time between cleanings.

Puppies start getting their adult teeth between three and six months of age. They start coming in at the front, then work back to the molars. By the time they are a year old, virtually all dogs have all their adult teeth.

You won't always find the baby teeth. Puppies frequently swallow them, which is perfectly harmless. (In some cases, a baby tooth has not fallen out by the time the corresponding adult tooth comes in. The vet can remove it during spaying or neutering.)

As the new teeth are coming in and cutting through the puppy's gums, she will teethe—on everything she can get her mouth around. (She may bleed a little from her mouth, too, which is perfectly normal.) Teething is uncomfortable, even painful, for many puppies, just as it is for human babies. To dull the pain, run a washcloth under water, wring it out, put it in the freezer until it's hard, then give it to the puppy to chew on. They really seem to enjoy chewing on a nice, icy washcloth. There are also fluid-filled chew rings made specifically for teething that can be frozen and then given to the pup.

Don't let teething interfere with starting routine dental care. It's so much

Dogs don't get cavities, but you have to brush their teeth every single day to prevent gum disease, which can make their teeth fall out.

easier to get a dog used to regular teeth brushing if you start early in the game—as young as eight to ten weeks—than if you wait until the pup grows into an adult.

Every single day of her life, brush puppy's teeth—either with a soft human toothbrush that fits easily into her mouth, or one made for dogs that has a longer handle, or one that fits over the fingertip like a flexible thimble with bristles on the end. Use veterinary toothpaste only, because dogs don't spit out the paste and the ingredients in human toothpaste can be upsetting to their stomach. Also, brush at the gum line both on the inside and outside of all the teeth, just as you would brush your own teeth.

You're not preventing cavities; dogs don't generally get cavities. You're preventing periodontal, or gum, disease, which can cause teeth to loosen and eventually fall out—not fun in old age.

Forbidden Foods

Your dog's teeth will certainly do better with dog food than human food. But there are other, more serious reasons to keep certain human foods out of dogs' mouths. For instance, as intuitive logic would suggest, neither puppies nor older dogs should ever be able to get at a coffee cup or alcoholic beverage. But there are other foods dogs should not eat: onions, garlic, grapes, raisins, and chocolate.

Onions and garlic can cause hemolytic anemia, a form of the disease in which red blood cells fall apart. It's uncommon—a dog would have to eat a large amount of either of these foods. But better safe than sorry.

Grapes and raisins have been associated with kidney failure. Even a few may be enough to make your dog sick.

Chocolate is bad for dogs because a caffeine-like chemical it contains called theobromine affects their systems. It can cause signs like those of a major caffeine overdose, replete with agitation, hyper-excitation, and even seizures if the dose is high enough.

A single chocolate chip cookie left out on a plate is not going to be a problem for a larger, adult dog who scarfs it down while you're not looking. But puppies can get sick even from rather small amounts of chocolate. Dark chocolate is worse than milk chocolate. Here is a chart of chocolate doses that can prove toxic to dogs, depending on the size of the dog and the type of chocolate.

Dog's Weight	Toxic Amount of Milk Chocolate	Toxic Amount of Dark Chocolate
5 pounds	4 ounces	0.5 ounces
10 pounds	8 ounces	1.0 ounces
20 pounds	1 pound	2.5 ounces
30 pounds	2 pounds	3.25 ounces
40 pounds	2.5 pounds	4.5 ounces
50 pounds	3.0 pounds	5.5 ounces
60 pounds	4.0 pounds	7.0 ounces
70 pounds	5.0 pounds	8.5 ounces
80 pounds	6.0 pounds	10.0 ounces
100 pounds	8.0 pounds	13.0 ounces
120 pounds	10.0 pounds	16.0 ounces (1 pound)

A MATTER OF HABIT

Brushing, clipping, cleaning every day, or even every week, sounds like it takes a lot of time. It doesn't. Many people brush their dog's hair or clean her ears as they watch television; nail clipping and teeth brushing take two minutes when you get the hang of it; and so on.

More important, basic health maintenance is even more worthwhile when you consider what you get in return: a healthy, comfortable puppy who grows into a healthy adult dog who can use her body well into old age. Who wouldn't trade off a very small amount of time every day for all that?

4

The Best Puppy Diet Ever

"*Sensitive systems*"; "*Antioxidant-rich nutrition*"; "*strong, firm Muscles*"; "*Supports Brain Development*"; "*Omega-3s*"; "*Premium*"; "*Gourmet*"; "*Human-Grade*"; "*Holistic*"; "*Organic.*"

Pet food is a $15-billion-a-year industry in the United States, and companies spend no small amount of money deciding what words to put in large, bold letters on the front and back of their packages to entice you to buy their brands.

Skip those marketing ploys—terms like "organic" and "premium" don't even have legal definitions when it comes to dog food, and there's scant to no scientific proof that puppies or adult dogs in general benefit from extra antioxidants or other supplements. Skip, too, the feeding advice from fellow puppy owners, pet store brochures, and Web sites and other Internet venues.

There's going to be plenty to skip. *Everyone* seems to have an opinion on canine nutrition in general and puppy nutrition in particular—whether or not they're trained in the field. Moreover, many are *convinced* that their approach is completely right. We've had clients proudly tell us that they feed their pups steak tips in the belief that their young pets deserve "only the best." We've had others who spend hours over the stove preparing Rover's meals because nothing in a bag or a can compares to home-cooked. Still others insist that raw food is the only way to go. Yet being convinced of one's correctness does not make one correct.

Puppy nutrition is a *science,* not a school of thought. And it's an exact science at that. Feeding a puppy appropriately is extremely important, because when a dog is in his developmental stages, he needs to get just the right combinations of nutrients in just the right concentrations. That's what will keep him healthy over the long term.

We learned this by studying canine nutrition closely. Large, well-respected pet food companies come to us, in fact, for consults on their offerings.

One of the things we know for sure is that prime-grade beef doesn't come close to approximating a pup's complete nutrition needs. A raw food diet is not nutritionally balanced either. And preparing your pet's meals over the stove is risky business at best and a setup for serious nutrient deficiencies at worst.

Puppy owners also make lots of other well-meaning feeding mistakes. Fortunately, avoiding them is easy—much easier, in fact, than going what is often a nutritionally inadequate route. Getting on the right track starts at a dog food label's fine print, one sentence in particular.

THE STATEMENT OF NUTRITIONAL ADEQUACY

When you're standing in the pet food aisle of the supermarket or in the food aisle of the pet store, faced with dozens of choices, go straight for something on the label called the Statement of Nutritional Adequacy. It will tell you the bulk of what you need to know once the puppy has been in your house a few days and it's time to start switching him from the food he knows to the food you choose.

Specifically, the Statement of Nutritional Adequacy, a legal requirement on packages of dog food rather than simply a form of advertising, will apprise you of the following three critical points for making a decision about which dog food to buy:

1. Whether the food is complete and balanced.
2. Whether the food is appropriate for *puppies.*
3. Whether the food was actually tested on dogs or simply formulated to meet a certain standard for various nutrients without any feeding trials to see how it works inside dogs' bodies.

Unfortunately, the Statement of Nutritional Adequacy on bags and cans of dog food does not have a heading that says "Statement of Nutritional Ad-

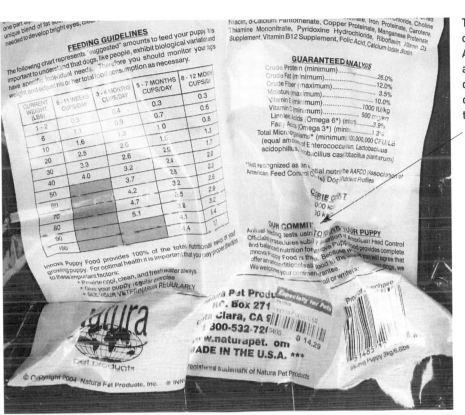

The Statement of Nutritional Adequacy on a package of dog food is often not easy to find.

equacy." And it doesn't stand out in any way from a lot of the less relevant fine print on dog food packages, such as where the food was manufactured and who owns the brand trademark. It's usually not even in a prominent spot. For instance, you can buy a fifty-pound bag of dog food and won't find it on either the large front or back panel but on one of the skinny side panels, mushed up in the way that occurs when the sides of large bags fold in on themselves.

The way to find the statement is to look for a single sentence that contains the words "Association of American Feed Control Officials (AAFCO)." AAFCO regulates the production, labeling, distribution, and sale of animal feeds, promotes uniform pet regulation, and establishes nutrient profiles — sort of like the canine equivalent of the Dietary Reference Intakes set for people.

Once you find the statement, you have to decipher it, which is easy to do if you know what to look for.

The first part is simple. Ninety-nine percent of the time, if not more, the statement will say that the food provides "complete and balanced nutrition." That's not mumbo jumbo. It means the food is designed to meet all of your puppy's nutrient requirements.

Second, you have to look for the word "growth" or the phrase "for all life stages." Either one of these in the Statement of Nutritional Adequacy signifies that the food is adequate for puppies until they are full grown (twelve months of age for most dogs). The reason a food *for all life stages* is okay is that it not only will support an adult dog's health but also is rich enough in nutrients to support a puppy's. Puppies need more nutrient-dense food to support their rapid growth.

What you should *not* get for your puppy is a food for which the nutritional statement includes only the word "maintenance." That's strictly for adult dogs, who need less than puppies in the way of vitamins, minerals, and other nutrients. Maintenance chow will leave your puppy with serious nutrient deficiencies.

You should also not choose a food based on pictures of dogs that might appear on the front of the package. A photo of a cute puppy doesn't automatically mean the food is appropriate for your young charge. And a picture of an adult dog does not automatically mean the food is *in*appropriate for puppies. A lot of products show an adult dog even though the chow inside is appropriate for all life stages.

Last but not least, the Statement of Nutritional Adequacy will tell you whether the food was fed to puppies to see whether they thrived on it. If the wording includes something about "animal feeding tests using AAFCO procedures," the food not only meets AAFCO nutrient profiles but also went through a feeding trial. On the other hand, if the statement says something about how the food is "formulated to meet the nutritional levels established by the AAFCO Dog Food Nutrient Profiles," it was produced perfectly legally and is also legal to sell—but was never actually put to the test.

Go with a food that has been subjected to an animal feeding test. The tests, which last at least six months, can detect problems with bioavailability of vitamins and minerals and also any problematic interactions between nutrients. They are not a guarantee that the food will be right for your puppy, but they are at least a minimum standard. That's very different from standardizing a food according to an AAFCO nutrient "recipe" but never checking to make sure it works right inside the puppy's body. A food that looks fine on paper can still present problems in the GI tract.

Don't assume that if one dog food from a particular brand has been through animal feeding tests, then all foods from that brand have been. Even within a brand, whether a feeding test was used differs from food to food. Always check the Statement of Nutritional Adequacy.

Make Sure It's a Reputable, Well-Known Company

The Statement of Nutritional Adequacy will tell you much, but not all, you need to know about choosing the right food for your dog. The brand is just as critical. It is extremely important that you buy dog food made by a reputable, well-known company that has been in the business of making dog food for many years. New dog food manufacturers come on the scene literally every single month, and no matter how earnest they are in trying to get it right when it comes to producing a quality dog food, they simply don't have the money for testing and the years and years of research on puppies that a well-known firm has. Remember, your puppy is a dog, not a guinea pig. You want a product that was fed to thousands and thousands of dogs before you give it to yours.

Puppy Food for Large Breeds

If your dog's adult weight will be less than fifty pounds, the Statement of Nutritional Adequacy on a food package, in conjunction with an established brand name, truly will tell you everything you need to know about whether it's an appropriate choice. But if your puppy will eventually mature at more than fifty pounds, in addition to checking the statement and brand, you should buy a large-breed puppy food, a relatively new entry to the dog food market. It will say "large-breed puppy food" on the front of the label in big letters.

Testing, Testing . . . Would You Be Able to Choose the Right Puppy Food?

Which of the following two statements on a bag or can of dog food would lead you to buy the food for your puppy?

1. "This puppy dog food is formulated to meet the nutritional levels established by the AAFCO Dog Food Nutrient Profiles for Gestation, Lactation, and Growth."

2. "Animal feeding tests using AAFCO procedures substantiate that this food for dogs provides complete and balanced nutrition for all life stages."

If you chose the second one, you're on the mark. The food has been tested in puppies (and adult dogs—as well as in pregnant/lactating dogs—as signified by "all life stages") rather than simply formulated according to an AAFCO nutrition profile.

Large-breed puppy foods have the same high concentration of nutrients as other puppy foods, but they are different in two important ways.

1. They have lower calorie density.
2. They have carefully controlled calcium levels.

These departures from other puppy foods are crucial for dogs who will mature to a weight of fifty pounds or greater. Fewer calories means the puppy will reach adult size more gradually, which is desirable. When puppies who will eventually be large or fairly large adult dogs grow too quickly, it can lead to all kinds of orthopedic diseases, including the all-too-common hip dysplasia. Consuming fewer calories also reduces the risk of obesity, itself a risk factor for adult orthopedic problems, for all the obvious reasons. (Don't worry. You will not stunt your large-breed dog's growth by letting him reach his mature size a little more slowly. That notion is a myth.)

As far as calcium is concerned, too much in the diet increases the risk for orthopedic complications, too. It's counterintuitive but true. Rather than protecting dogs from bone problems later in life, extra calcium predisposes them to various orthopedic ills.

Unfortunately, there's a widely circulated myth that large dogs do need more calcium than others. The thinking is that if more calcium is good for

What Must Appear on the Label Versus What May Appear

The label on a bag or can of dog food is both a legal document and a form of marketing. The marketing consists of much of what jumps out at you as you're looking over the rows and rows of dog food choices either at the supermarket or the pet food store—the big, bold statements about how wonderful the food is for your puppy. Here's what must legally appear somewhere on a bag or can of dog food:

- Product name (and a brand name, if any)
- Net weight
- The fact that it's intended for a dog (animal species intended for)
- Guaranteed analysis (more on that on page 87).
- Ingredients statement
- Statement of Nutritional Adequacy
- Feeding directions
- Name and address of manufacturer or distributor

humans, it must be good for canines. You can even find calcium supplements marketed for larger dogs. Indeed, one of our own veterinary students adopted a Labrador retriever puppy from a breeder who insisted the student sign a contract to continue feeding the pup calcium supplements at home. (He did not.)

While a breeder may mistakenly think calcium supplements are a good idea for a large dog, some breeders, and even some veterinarians, err in advising owners to switch their large-breed puppies to adult dog food at around six months of age rather than wait till they have stopped growing (usually at the end of the first year). Their reasoning is that because adult "maintenance" dog food has less protein than puppy "growth" food, it will spare the dog orthopedic problems later on. But this, too, is just a myth.

The only thing less protein will do in a large-breed puppy is create a protein deficiency, which is why large-breed pups, just like all others, need puppy food. If your puppy is a very large breed, like a Newfoundland or a Greater Swiss mountain dog, he should be fed large-breed puppy food for the first eighteen months rather than twelve. Such big dogs need to mature even more slowly to avoid hip and other orthopedic problems later on.

NOTE: Certain large-breed pups are so energetic, burning so many calories in their day-to-day activities, that feeding them relatively low calorie large-breed puppy food could leave them too skinny. If, for instance, your high-energy Irish setter or German shorthaired pointer pup is not maintaining good body condition on a large-breed puppy food, speak with your vet about whether to switch to regular puppy provisions.

Dry versus Canned

Many people wonder whether they should feed their dog dry or canned food. The answer: It doesn't matter. The nutritional quality of the two is not inherently different.

That might not seem so at first glance. There is a part of the label, often near the Statement of Nutritional Adequacy, called the Guaranteed Analysis, which always shows a much higher percentage of protein, fat, and fiber in dry dog food than in canned. But that's only because canned food contains more moisture, or water. The actual amounts of nutrients the dog eats are adequate whether the food is dry or wet; they're just more concentrated when the food is dry.

Nutrient profiles aside, dry food is cheaper and better for dogs' teeth (although you still have to brush). But by the same token, wet food makes urine more dilute—something you want if your dog is predisposed to bladder stones.

The bottom line is that you should go with what works for you and your pet. A lot of owners feed dry food with just a little canned mixed in to moisten it. That's fine, too.

DIET DON'TS

If you've read the chapter to this point, you know everything you need to know about how to choose the right food for your puppy. Given the colossal mass of misinformation out there on what to feed your dog, however, we feel that before we discuss *how much* food to feed, it is imperative to discuss in some detail what *not* to feed.

Is "Natural" Better?

Terms on dog food packages like "holistic," "premium," and "human grade" do not have legal definitions. They mean whatever the manufacturer wants them to mean. But the word "natural" is governed by law. It means the product does not contain any ingredients synthesized in a laboratory—except, perhaps, for added nutrients.

In the case of a "natural" dog food with added nutrients, the package must say "natural, with added vitamins, minerals, and other trace nutrients." Synthetically produced nutrients will often appear on ingredients statements as terms like pyridoxine hydrochloride, which is simply a form of vitamin B_6, and ferrous sulfate, which is iron. Don't let the multisyllabic words scare you. They're just a chemist's way of describing ingredients that are essential for your

puppy. Such lab-produced nutrients are perfectly safe for your dog and perfectly effective forms of the vitamins and minerals your pup needs for growth and health.

Truth be told, concerns about nutrients are not why a lot of people want "natural" dog food, anyway. They are much more concerned about preservatives and want natural rather than synthetic ones. Lab-produced preservatives have been blamed for everything from canine cancer, kidney disease, and pancreatic disease to arthritis, hair loss, and blindness. No proof of such harm has ever been scientifically documented. Even a synthetic preservative called ethoxyquin, which appears to cause the most concern for some dog owners who believe it's not good for their pets, has never been found to be responsible for adverse health effects,

Raw Food Diet

Proliferating on the Internet and in brochures and other print media are calls to feed your puppy, and later your adult dog, a diet with raw meat as its centerpiece. The claims for a raw food diet are myriad. It will supposedly improve the dog's coat and skin; eliminate breath, body, and feces odor; improve your pet's energy and behavior; add to the dog's overall health and immune function; and reduce the dog's incidence of allergies, arthritis, pancreatitis (inflammation of the pancreas), and cancer.

The argument for raw food grew largely out of the belief that dogs are carnivores who evolved in the wild eating raw meat only and that the heat processing of commercial foods destroys nutrients and essential enzymes.

All of that is untrue. Dogs are not carnivores; they are omnivores, like humans, eating both animal foods and plant foods. In addition, while heat does degrade certain nutrients, like the B vitamin thiamin, nutrient deficien-

---

Is "Natural" Better?, continued from page 88

even in well-conducted studies in which high doses were fed to dogs.

On the contrary, preservatives, synthetic or natural, are an absolute must for dry dog food (the airtight storage that results from canning protects canned dog food). Consider that dog food is high in fat, and that fat is the ingredient in food most susceptible to spoilage and therefore very much in need of preserving. Fat that does spoil (oxidizes) decreases the nutritional quality of food (certain vitamins need fat to remain stable); makes it taste less palatable to the dog; and can even make the food unsafe to eat. After all, spoiled fat is rancid fat.

Commonly used synthetic preservatives are BHT and BHA, also used in food for people. Natural preservatives include vitamin E (often listed on the ingredients statement as tocopherols), vitamin C (which may

be listed as ascorbic acid), and rosemary. By all means, look for natural preservatives If feeding those to your puppy makes you feel more comfortable. Note, however, that they are not as potent as the synthetic ones, so the duration of their protection isn't as long. If your dog food contains natural preservatives (the package may or may not say on the front that the product is "naturally preserved"), buy smaller quantities than you would otherwise. Also, go through it quickly. Don't let it linger in your kitchen or mudroom. And make sure the store you buy it from has good product turnover.

In the next five to ten years, all dog owners may need to be following these guidelines. Despite a lack of problems with synthetic preservatives, consumer demand is pressuring just about all major dog food companies to switch to the natural kind.

Canned vs. Dry Food

Here are the guaranteed analyses for the dry and canned versions of a particular brand of dog food. The canned version *looks* as though it has much less protein, fat, and fiber, but it doesn't. Its nutrients are simply less concentrated because it has a higher moisture (water) content, as the chart below shows. Serving for serving, your puppy is getting the same amount of nutrients whether he eats the canned or dry version.

	Dry Food	Canned Food
Crude Protein	21%	8%
Crude Fat	9%	3%
Crude Fiber	5.5%	1.5%
Moisture	12%	82%

cies do not abound. Pet food companies compensate so that the end product still has sufficient vitamin and mineral levels.

Then, too, even if dogs evolved eating raw meat only (as opposed to meat and plant foods), we should not take our feeding cues from that. Dogs taking care of themselves in the wild, as opposed to dogs who safely inhabit human homes, live only a few years. Their "natural" diets don't promote the long, healthy lives we wish for our pet dogs.

Of all the benefits cited for raw food diets given to dogs, the only one that may be true is a better-looking coat, because raw food regimens are typically very high in fat. The rest are, in a word, unproven.

What *is* proven are the many downsides to raw food diets. Consider that consuming raw bones can lead to esophageal obstructions, fractured teeth, and an inflammation of the GI tract called gastroenteritis. We've had no shortage of dogs appearing in our emergency room who needed costly surgery to have bones removed from their throat or esophagus; had broken their teeth on raw feed; or ended up spending days in the intensive care unit because of damage done to their GI tract.

There is also a very real risk of bacterial contamination, just as there is for humans who eat meat uncooked and therefore don't kill offending bacteria via heating. In some cases, as many people know firsthand, the bacterial infection causes vomiting and diarrhea and sometimes other complications.

Not only are the dogs at risk. So are the people in the household, because harmful bacteria may not be cleaned thoroughly enough off utensils, dishes, counters, and hands that are used to feed the dog. The very young, the elderly, and anyone who is sick are especially at risk because the immune systems in those groups don't work as well as in other people.

Just what kind of bacteria are we talking about? When researchers at Tufts analyzed five different raw food diets, three homemade and two commercial, one of them tested positive for *E. coli* 0157:H7, the leading cause of kidney failure in children. Two other studies found rampant contamination of commercially available raw meat diets tested for various *E. coli,* salmonella, *Campylobacter,* and clostridium bacteria.

Along with the threat of bacterial contamination (freezing the food does *not* kill the bacteria), raw food diets come with the threat of nutritional inadequacy. When Tufts researchers examined the three homemade and two commercial raw food diets, they found shortfalls in sodium, iron, zinc, potassium, manganese, calcium, and phosphorus. Some of them contained *too much* of vitamins D and E and the mineral magnesium, among other nutrients. Such nutrient imbalances can lead to a host of health problems, including (but not limited to) skin conditions, anemia, and orthopedic complications. Especially in growing puppies, out-of-whack nutrient profiles can result in serious compromises to health.

Our advice: Skip raw food diets for your dog, as a puppy and when he's older. One study presented at an American Academy of Veterinary Research symposium even found blood abnormalities in dogs to which they were fed.

Vegetarian Diet

A person may choose to be a vegetarian for a number of reasons: an antipathy for eating other animals; a wish to avoid diseases commonly associated with diets high in animal foods, including coronary artery disease and hypertension; and a desire to eat in a way that's more compatible with sustainable agriculture. Growing plants is much easier on the land than growing cattle, chickens, and hogs.

While all of these are fine, even noble, arguments for eschewing meat, they are not good reasons for keeping meat from dogs. Dogs, much more than humans, need some

Water, Water, Always There

Having water always available to your puppy is very important, not just for making him feel at home but also so that he can quench his thirst when necessary. Adult dogs need roughly an ounce of water per pound of body weight each day to meet their water losses in urine and elsewhere, largely the lungs during breathing. Puppies need considerably more—up to an ounce and a half of water per pound of body weight, a difference of about 50 percent.

The exact amount of water any dog needs depends, of course, on such things as whether he is eating wet or dry food and how much he is panting, say, on hot days or when he feels stressed. But all things being equal, puppies can become dehydrated more quickly if they do not have water at their disposal.

meat on a regular basis to remain healthy; it is extremely difficult to keep a dog in good shape on a plant-food-only diet. Furthermore, dogs are not prone to most of the diseases that drive some people to become vegetarians. Their arteries do not clog the way human arteries do, and they rarely get high blood pressure. That is, the heart disease that kills more Americans than any other condition hardly ever befalls our canine friends. *Their* heart disease comes in the form of heart valve or heart muscle problems, which have nothing to do with high-fat diets.

Health Claims: Which to Trust and Which Not To

The only allowable health claims on dog food have to do with oral hygiene. If a dog food's shape and consistency allow your puppy's teeth to sink into it in a way that lets the food act as an abrasive, there can be wording on the label to the effect that the contents will "cleanse, freshen, or whiten teeth." (Claims for control of breath odor are bogus.)

There are also dog foods with a seal from the Veterinary Oral Health Council (VOHC), which means the product either contains an active ingredient that will reduce plaque or tartar or allows for a scraping action upon chewing that reduces those substances.

Beyond claims for improved oral hygiene, health claims on packages of dog food are simply illegal. Saying that a dog food might fight cancer or help prevent heart disease or stave off high blood pressure is prohibited.

That doesn't mean manufacturers can't make claims that sound an awful lot like health claims. A label can state "Supports Brain Development," for instance, or "Helps Muscle Function," and it's perfectly legal. Why? These are not health claims but structure/function claims.

How can you tell the difference? A health claim implies that if you eat the food, you will avoid a problem down the line—osteoporosis, stroke, what have you. But a structure/function claim merely makes a statement that any food can make. *Of course* food supports brain development. A puppy needs calories for his brain to develop. And of course food helps muscle function. A pup's muscles can't function if he doesn't eat, right?

Take structure/functions claims with a grain of salt. That's about what they're worth. (They're permissible on food for people, too, by the way.)

Take phrases like "Antioxidant-Rich Nutrition" and "Omega-3s" with a grain of salt, too. They are just saying what's in a food. They're not proof that the substance that has been added does anything for a pup's health.

The bottom line here: While health and moral concerns are valid for vegetarian humans, they do not make a vegetarian diet healthy for a dog.

Homemade Diets

"Homemade" goes hand in hand with loving and caring, so some people assume that their puppy will eat better if they make the dog's food themselves—say, a stew with beef chunks, barley, and carrots—than if they buy puppy chow at the store. The sentiment is right; the thinking is not.

Puppies are highly sensitive even to minute nutrient deficiencies. What might be a subclinical deficiency in an adult dog could be a frank nutrient deficiency in a puppy, which in turn could cause serious health problems. We've seen puppies fed homemade diets brought to our hospital who were so severely malnourished that not only were they small for their age, but they also had crooked and deformed bones. If caught early enough, the nutrient insufficiencies can be corrected and the puppy can pretty much catch up. But if too much time elapses, bouncing back becomes difficult to impossible. That's why we strongly advise you to purchase your puppy food rather than prepare it, even if you prepare it from recipes presented in a book or on the Internet. Just because it's printed doesn't ensure that it's nutritionally adequate.

That said, if you feel your dog simply *must* be fed a homemade diet, make an appointment with a board-certified veterinary nutritionist; don't wing it on your own. He or she can tell you exactly what foods you need to mix, in which proportions, to keep your growing puppy in the best health possible. Some veterinary nutritionists will also provide phone consults, which are particularly helpful when your dog grows old and you may need a consult for, say, a diet to slow the rate of kidney disease (see "Resources" for more information).

On Byproducts

A number of dog owners want to make their own puppy food because they are turned off by the idea of byproducts in dog food. They have a negative connotation, translating roughly to "the junk that's not fit for humans to eat and therefore goes into pet food."

It's not true. In fact, ingredients used as byproducts in the United States are often considered delicacies elsewhere. Tripe (cattle stomach), sweetbreads (thymus gland), tongue, and other organs that make up byproducts here are prized for their taste in many countries and even by some in our own country.

Simply put, byproducts are the nonmuscle meat of an animal, largely the organs, including the liver and spleen. And they are rich in nutrients. If your dog's food has byproducts, you don't have to worry that your pup is not eating well.

Dietary Supplements

Many dietary supplements are available over-the-counter for puppies — and for dogs in general. Antioxidants such as vitamin E are among the more popular ones. But don't buy any supplements unless your dog has a specific condition and your veterinarian has prescribed a particular supplement. Puppy food that has undergone AAFCO feeding trials contains *everything* your growing dog needs. Besides, certain supplements can *create* problems. As we said before, calcium supplements given to puppies increase the risk for hip dysplasia rather than decrease it, as is commonly thought. The story is similar for vitamin C. Despite a myth based on one old, poorly designed study that excess vitamin C will help prevent hip dysplasia, it will not. All a vitamin C supplement will do is increase the risk for urinary stones — and unnecessarily thin your wallet.

Supplements can also interact with medicines a dog is taking to create adverse effects on the body. Gastrointestinal problems like vomiting and nausea are among them, but there can be even more serious outcomes. For instance, if a dog is undergoing chemotherapy for cancer, some supplements may actually make the treatment less effective.

Also important to consider is that unlike foods and drugs, supplements require no review prior to marketing in order to test for product efficacy, safety, or quality, meaning that a supplement may not do what its manufacturer says it does; may not be safe; and may not even contain the ingredients it is purported to contain. In fact, while drug manufacturers must prove their products safe and effective before putting them on the market, the Food and Drug Administration must prove a supplement *un*safe in order to remove it from the marketplace. With limited government funds allocated to such endeavors and thousands upon thousands of supplements on the market today, that is an unrealistic expectation.

AVOIDING OVERWEIGHT

Until now we have focused on what and what not to feed your puppy. But an equally important part of feeding is *how much,* now more than ever. As more and more people are going from healthy weight to overweight or out-and-out obese, so go their dogs. An estimated 30 to 40 percent of our canine friends are now overweight or obese, an unprecedented number.

Part of the explanation is that dog food is much more palatable than it was even twenty years ago. Back in the 1980s, if you put out too much food for your dog, he was reasonably likely to eat until he was satiated and then stop. Today, it's too hard to stop. Dog food tastes *really good* to dogs.

Another issue is that dogs, to some degree, mimic our lifestyle. We are eating more and getting less physical activity, and so are our dogs.

It's a problem, because just as excess pounds are unhealthy for humans, they're unhealthy for humans' best friends. It's not that the extra weight contributes to the development of cardiovascular disease, as it does in people (although excess poundage in a dog can *exacerbate* preexisting heart, lung, and other diseases). It's that it greatly predisposes a dog to back, joint, and endocrine (hormone-related) problems like diabetes.

We had one patient—a dachshund named Herman—who was so overweight that he had already had one back surgery for a ruptured disk and was soon going to rupture another one. At twenty pounds instead of the ten pounds that would have been right for him, he was 100 percent over ideal body weight and could hardly get around. Granted, dachshunds are predisposed to back problems, but all of this little dog's weight was complicating matters greatly. For larger dogs, excess weight greatly increases the risk for hip dysplasia and other orthopedic conditions.

A premature death is also quite possible for an overweight dog, large or small. In a long-term (fifteen-year) study, investigators fed two groups of dogs from puppyhood on. One group was given enough food to keep them in trim body condition. The other group was fed 25 percent more food— enough that they were just a little bit overweight throughout their lives. The upshot: The trimmer dogs were less likely to develop hip dysplasia and osteoarthritis—and they lived, on average, nearly two years longer.

Just how much should you feed your puppy to keep him trim? The answer differs from puppy to puppy and is based on activity level and the dog's own rate of metabolism, even his build. Some Labs might be just right at seventy pounds; some might be overweight.

One place that offers advice on amounts is the food label, since it is required by law to provide feeding directions. But taking that advice can often prove dicey. In many cases, the suggested serving sizes are overestimates of how much a dog should be eating.

A case in point: The owner of one overweight black Lab who came to Tufts Cummings School veterinarian Lisa Freeman, DVM, PhD, a diplomate of the American College of Veterinary Nutrition, was thoroughly confused because he was giving his pet exactly the portion suggested on the bag of dog food and no treats whatsoever. After taking a careful diet history, Dr.

Freeman advised the owner to cut back on the food somewhat and even "made room" in the dog's diet for occasional treats—a strategy that was appreciated by both the pup and his owner and strengthened the already good bond between them.

Most brands of dog food give a *range* of portions, so *start on the low end.* For instance, if the label says to feed a twenty-one- to thirty-five-pound puppy 1⅓ to 2 cups of the food per day (not per feeding, but per day), give 1⅓ cups. With two cups, your pup could very well end up fat.

Since after the age of three to four months, puppies generally get fed twice a day, that means, in this instance, two thirds of a cup per meal for a day's total of 1⅓ cups. Use a true measuring cup (level, not heaping) rather than, say, a mug. You want to get it just right so you can adjust accurately, if necessary.

Then see how it goes. You don't need to weigh your dog at home or count your pup's calories, which are not required to be listed on the label (although if you're a calorie-oriented person, you can contact the dog food company to find out how many calories are in a serving). It's perfectly reasonable to go by how your dog *looks* and take it from there, adjusting accordingly if necessary. Looking down at the pup from above, you should easily be able to see his waist behind his ribs. And you should be able to see a clear-cut abdominal tuck, at least when looking at the pooch from the side. Also, when you touch your pet, the ribs should be easily felt, without too much fat covering.

By making these assessments, you're checking the puppy's body condition, which is probably the single most important thing you can do to make sure his growth is optimal.

You can also judge your puppy's body condition using a scale developed at the Nestlé Purina Pet Care Center that rates dogs from 1 to 9. Referred to in several veterinary journals, it is called the Body Condition System. "Ideal" is a score of 4 to 5. Higher than that and your dog is too heavy for his size. (See page 97 for the complete scale, with illustrations.)

You should give the pup a visual check for body score every two weeks, along with feeling his ribs. A dog, like a person, can start packing on a lot of excess fat pretty fast. That's true even if you're feeding him puppy food for large-breed dogs, which is less calorie dense than other puppy food. Too much is too much. You want to adjust food amounts as often as is necessary to keep the dog from becoming overweight.

There is a fair amount of adjusting. Sometimes the pup will be in a

Nestlé Purina Condition System

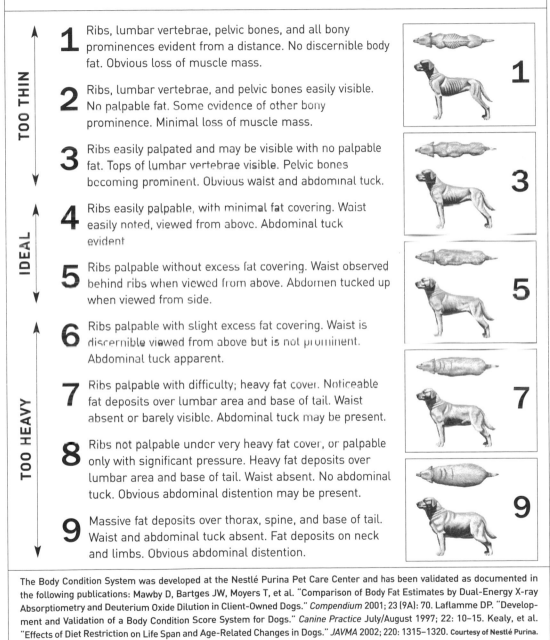

TOO THIN

1 Ribs, lumbar vertebrae, pelvic bones, and all bony prominences evident from a distance. No discernible body fat. Obvious loss of muscle mass.

2 Ribs, lumbar vertebrae, and pelvic bones easily visible. No palpable fat. Some evidence of other bony prominence. Minimal loss of muscle mass.

3 Ribs easily palpated and may be visible with no palpable fat. Tops of lumbar vertebrae visible. Pelvic bones becoming prominent. Obvious waist and abdominal tuck.

IDEAL

4 Ribs easily palpable, with minimal fat covering. Waist easily noted, viewed from above. Abdominal tuck evident

5 Ribs palpable without excess fat covering. Waist observed behind ribs when viewed from above. Abdomen tucked up when viewed from side.

TOO HEAVY

6 Ribs palpable with slight excess fat covering. Waist is discernible viewed from above but is not prominent. Abdominal tuck apparent.

7 Ribs palpable with difficulty; heavy fat cover. Noticeable fat deposits over lumbar area and base of tail. Waist absent or barely visible. Abdominal tuck may be present.

8 Ribs not palpable under very heavy fat cover, or palpable only with significant pressure. Heavy fat deposits over lumbar area and base of tail. Waist absent. No abdominal tuck. Obvious abdominal distention may be present.

9 Massive fat deposits over thorax, spine, and base of tail. Waist and abdominal tuck absent. Fat deposits on neck and limbs. Obvious abdominal distention.

The Body Condition System was developed at the Nestlé Purina Pet Care Center and has been validated as documented in the following publications: Mawby D, Bartges JW, Moyers T, et al. "Comparison of Body Fat Estimates by Dual-Energy X-ray Absorptiometry and Deuterium Oxide Dilution in Client-Owned Dogs." *Compendium* 2001; 23 (9A): 70. Laflamme DP. "Development and Validation of a Body Condition Score System for Dogs." *Canine Practice* July/August 1997; 22: 10–15. Kealy, et al. "Effects of Diet Restriction on Life Span and Age-Related Changes in Dogs." *JAVMA* 2002; 220: 1315–1320. **Courtesy of Nestlé Purina.**

growth spurt—you'll see him growing pretty rapidly—and will need to be fed a little more than usual. Sometimes he'll plateau and you'll need to cut back his food intake. You may also want to cut back a little during kenneling, when the puppy is less active than usual. Otherwise, he can really lay on the excess pounds.

Remember, too, that once your puppy is spayed or neutered, you won't be going back to the vet for many months, so it's up to *you* to keep a close eye. If you don't, a dog can go from healthy weight to grossly overweight by the time of his one-year checkup.

If Your Puppy Does Become Overweight

Prevention is better than cure, of course. But if your puppy does become overweight (more than 20 percent above ideal weight), there are solutions. One of the solutions people tend to assume is right for their pup is doggie diet food; there are a number of diet foods on the market for canine pets. But while many of those foods serve a useful purpose in helping dogs who are overweight get back to ideal body size, do not decide on your own to start your pup on diet food if you see him starting to get pudgy.

One reason is that the diet food may be appropriate for adult health maintenance but not for puppies. But also, the problem may not even be the meals you've been serving in the first place. Maybe you're giving exactly the right amount of food but too many treats. (We met one large mixed breed who was getting the right amount of dog food but also two big biscuits every day with almost 300 calories each, and some owners unwittingly give 1,000 calories' worth of treats a day.) Maybe you're feeding just the right amount of food and treats, but your significant other or your children are giving treats of their own.

In other words, the problem could be behavioral—yours or your family's —rather than nutritional. So diet dog food may not be the answer. Start by having a thorough discussion with your veterinarian to work out where the problem lies—and *then* work out a successful program to correct it.

That's what Molly's owners did. Molly was a lovely golden retriever who tipped the scales at 102 pounds when she should have weighed 85 pounds, tops. When she came to our offices, we determined, based on discussions with her caretakers, that she was actually eating a light diet (700 calories a day, when a dog her size should have been getting closer to 1,000 calories to lose weight). But her treats and table scraps amounted to more than 800 calories daily! She began eating fewer between-meal goodies and *more,* not less, dog food, for a lower calorie level overall. (We also recommended increased exercise.) Molly's weight-loss program is still in progress, but if her people stick to the game plan, she should slim down nicely.

DO TREATS EVEN HAVE A PLACE?

Combine the focus on obesity prevention with the fact that doggie treats can be extremely high in calories (extra-large Milk-Bones have 225 calories apiece and jumbo-size Greenies each have 270!), and it's a wonder treats are recommended for puppies at all. But they are.

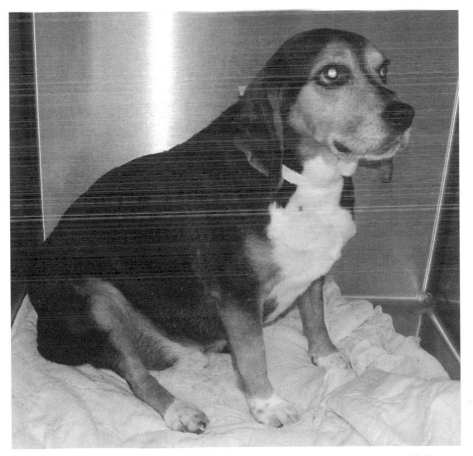

Bandit has already lost twelve pounds on a weight-loss program overseen by Tufts veterinarians.

True, a dog doesn't *have* to have treats. But they strengthen the bond between owner and pet. And they're used to reward puppies during training to reinforce the lessons they learn. Besides, what kind of an owner would you feel like if you never gave your pup a treat?

So how can you dole out treats without making your puppy look like a sausage?

Follow the 10 percent rule. Treats and table scraps should make up less than 10 percent of the dog's calories. Not only do more treats mean more calories. It's also that the more treats you give, the less balanced the diet is.

The Calories in Commercially Available Treats

A forty-pound dog should average roughly 1,000 calories a day for weight maintenance (although calorie needs will vary, depending on the forty-pound dog in question). Given that treats should add up to no more than 10 percent of a dog's calories, some treats are difficult, if not impossible, to fit into a healthful diet without breaking them up. Here are some popular examples. A number of them have more than 100 calories per treat.*

Treat	Calories	Treat	Calories
Alpo Liv-A-Snaps	13	Milk-Bone Puppy Biscuits	10
Beggin' Littles (Bacon Flavor)	7	Old Mother Hubbard Couch Potato (Small)	47
Beggin' Strips (Bacon and Cheese)	30	Old Mother Hubbard Couch Potato (Large)	211
Greenies (Petite)	54**	Old Mother Hubbard P-Nuttier (Mini)	12
Greenies (Large)	144**	Old Mother Hubbard P-Nuttier (Small)	51
Greenies (Jumbo)	270**	Old Mother Hubbard P-Nuttier (Large)	225
Eukanuba Healthy Extras Puppy Growth Biscuits	13	Old Mother Hubbard P-Nuttier (Jumbo)	596
Science Diet Puppy Treats	20	Old Mother Hubbard Puppy	12
Science Diet Jerky Plus Adult Treats (Chicken and Vegetables)	45	Pedigree Trainer	5
		Pedigree Jumbone (Medium)	270
		Pedigree Jumbone (Large)	567
Iams Puppy Formula Biscuits	18	Snausages (Beef & Cheese Flavor)	25

*These were the calorie counts as we went to press. Manufacturers may change product formulations from time to time. Check with manufacturers for the most up-to-date calorie information.
**Not recommended for dogs younger than six months.

Treats are usually not "complete and balanced," and neither are the table scraps that fall from your hands during dinner.

One way to keep treats to less than 10 percent of calories is to use vegetables. Nonstarchy vegetables—carrots, green beans, green peppers, cucumber—all make great treats for dogs, who generally love them. (Don't use fruits if your dog gains weight easily. They are higher in calories than vegetables.)

You can also break up treats into small pieces, especially for obedience training, which may require lots and lots of rewards. For dogs, it's receiving the treat from you that counts, not how much they receive.

A third option is to turn some of the puppy's regular food into treats. That is, give him only half his food at mealtime and save the rest for training or just good times during the day.

Once you know the approach to take, preventing obesity is not hard. Nor is feeding in general. First, pick a food made by a well-known, reputable company. Then check the Statement of Nutritional Adequacy to make sure the food has undergone AAFCO feeding trials. Finally, check your pup every two weeks to make sure his body condition is ideal, and you're 95 percent of the way there.

What often gets in the way of proper feeding are people's own issues around food, combined with beliefs or opinions about the food industry or our food supply in general. Keep feeding a health issue rather than an emotional one, and all will turn out well.

Table Scraps

A puppy's nutritional world won't come to an end if you occasionally throw him scraps from your meal. But dinner as you know it might. It takes no time at all to unwittingly train a pup to *expect* table scraps, but lots of fortitude is required to untrain him. Unless you're okay with your dog hounding you for some of your food at every single meal, don't get him started by sharing with him at dinnertime. Even if you start holding off on giving table scraps until the end of the meal, you may spend your entire dinner with pleading eyes on you.

By the same token, don't create a finicky eater by consistently garnishing his rations with some people food—bits of ham or ground beef, for instance. That will teach him very quickly that his own food without any "topping" is not acceptable. (The owners of toy dogs often end up creating finicky eaters because the very small amount of food dogs that size need to thrive frightens some people, which in turn leads them to feed their pets every imaginable delicacy in the hope of getting them to eat more.)

Whatever you do, don't feed any dish with onions or garlic, which can cause serious harm to your dog's health, as we explained in chapter 3.

5

The Socialization Period

"BEHAVIOR, THAT'S WHAT IT'S ALL ABOUT REALLY," SAID MARGARET THATCHER, Britain's former prime minister, when she was introduced by the president of Tufts University to animal behaviorist Dr. Dodman.

She couldn't have been more right. If dogs didn't behave appropriately, *endearingly,* toward people and other living creatures via proper socialization, you simply wouldn't have one. This is not the Heartland a hundred years ago, where someone came to the door once every three months so it didn't matter whether the family pup got on well with others. It's a social life in the here and now. We live in cities, in suburbia. Your dog will have to go into congested areas. People will come to your home. There are dogs, cats, birds, everywhere. If your puppy doesn't learn to get along with all these live creatures, including other humans, it can literally be a matter of life and death.

Consider that almost half the dogs in the United States never see their second birthday largely because their owners are unhappy with how they have turned out and thus surrender them to shelters and pounds, where two out of three are put to sleep. For that reason, you could argue that while proper health care and feeding are crucial for keeping puppies healthy and alive, as we discussed in the last two chapters, proper socialization is at least as important for your dog's well-being.

We say this not to scare you but so that you'll put as much into socializing your pup for proper behavior as you do into choosing her food and making sure you get her to the vet for her vaccinations. Too many people give lip service to proper socialization but don't really understand how to follow through. Even a number of breeders we have spoken with *say* they socialize their puppies but don't spend nearly enough time acclimating them to the world around them—or spend the time too late, when the pup is already a few months old. Knowing the word "socialization" and acting on it are two different things.

What, exactly, goes wrong in a dog's deportment if she is not socialized properly as a puppy? Most often, she develops fears in her early weeks and months that make her seem like a shrinking violet (it could even look cute if a sweet little pup manifests her cowardice by trying to hide under the bed). But the fear may transform into aggression later on, when she's bigger and more confident about being able to scare off what she perceives as a threat. Consider that if a growing pup sees that a loud, guttural bark or growl makes people she's afraid of jump back, she'll learn that threatening behavior serves her well.

We illustrated the point in a recent study conducted at our Center for Animals and Public Policy. It was found that puppies who had dysfunctional backgrounds with inadequate socialization were 580 times more likely to end up with fear aggression toward strangers.

You don't need to be a statistician to get the drift. Socialize your puppy properly and she'll be much less likely to end up with behavior problems down the line—and much less likely to end up in a shelter or pound.

This is particularly important if your pup is a breed that's genetically hard-wired for aggression in the first place. Take the case of Roxanne, a pit bull–boxer mix whose owners brought her to see us at our Animal Behavior Clinic when she had already reached full maturity. She had not been raised by a family that was properly mindful of socializing her in a gradual, gentle way but, rather, had been obtained from a shelter when she was already five months old, after a rough start in life. The upshot: She growled, lunged, and generally tried to attack all who came into her sphere other than the people in her household, whom she knew and trusted. Her fear aggression was pretty well cemented in place, and it was going to be tricky, though not impossible, to take the edge off it.

Fear aggression is also more of an issue for relatively large dogs, whether or not they are genetically predisposed to aggression, simply because a larger dog who learns to act out aggressively is more dangerous to have around.

SHARING THE RESPONSIBILITY OF SOCIALIZING WITH THE BREEDER

For better or worse, you're not alone in the endeavor of appropriately socializing your dog. As we intimated in chapter 1, proper socialization begins at the breeder's, or wherever the puppy starts her life. That's why we said that pups should be raised not off in the garage or an outdoor kennel but right by the human family so they can start adjusting from the get-go to the social life they are going to lead. (It was pups *not* raised right alongside human families in domestic situations who were hundreds of times more likely to develop fear aggression in the Cummings School study.)

It's also why we said a puppy should not be taken from her mother and littermates earlier than eight weeks of age. That's especially important for a puppy's education on how to interact with other dogs. From the third through sixth week in particular, a pup is learning canine etiquette through the look, sound, feel, and *behavior* of the other pups around her. She is learning how to diffuse an attack ("I give in") as well as how to fight fair — when to check herself when another pup has tired of her playful aggression ("I see you've thrown in the towel"). Call it learning to live by the Marquis of Queensbury rules, if those rules were for pups instead of for keeping boxing a "gentlemanly" sport. It's all about recognizing signals of dominance and deference.

A puppy who is removed from her mother and littermates too early (or born a singleton rather than with siblings) may attack and not know to stop when another dog signals deference. Likewise, she may not be able to signal deference to get another dog to halt aggressive action toward her. Think about the fact that weeks three, four, five, and six are a total of only twenty-eight days. If a pup misses just one of those weeks with her birth family, she loses out on a quarter of her early dog-on-dog socialization classes. Imagine if you missed a quarter of any class. You probably wouldn't pass the final, and you wouldn't have all the correct information to take out into life with you, either.

Dog-Human Interactions

Let a puppy live long enough with her brothers and sisters and mother, and dog-on-dog socialization will in large part take care of itself. But what about dog-human interactions? Many breeders fall short here. They have a lot of semantic knowledge of the socialization process, but they don't always follow through as well as a puppy deserves — and needs. One breeder blithely told us that of course she socialized her pups: she and her husband went into the dogs' room for five or ten minutes each day and played with them. That just won't cut it.

Inadequate socialization is particularly unfortunate in light of the ratio of puppy years to human years. By the time a pup is eight weeks old and near ready to be taken from her mother and littermates and handed over to her new owner, she is the equivalent of about three or four years old in human age. You'd have a hard time living with an improperly socialized pre-schooler, and so it goes with an eight-week-old puppy whose social requirements with humans have not been tended to.

Not only should people outside the breeder's family have been coming and going; the breeder—or whoever else is raising a newborn puppy—should have been throwing parties on her behalf to introduce her to all sorts of other people.

Certainly from the age of six weeks, the puppy's guardian should have been making a concerted effort to regularly have visitors to the house who have held the puppy, petted her, cooed over her, and generally let her know that humans are okay and can be trusted. It's when a puppy is about six weeks old that she begins to start exploring outside the immediate environment of her whelping area without being picked up and brought back by her mother. And **it's soon after the age of six weeks that a sense of fear of the unknown really begins to creep in, which is why it's very important at that time to preempt fear with positive interactions.** In other words, much of what you're aiming to do by properly socializing a puppy is teach her not to be afraid of people. You're preventing unreasonable fears from forming in the first place.

If the breeder has been throwing puppy parties and having frequent comings and goings in general, great. But you're certainly on the clock for throwing puppy parties and otherwise desensitizing your young pup to whatever living creatures she might come across in life from the time you get her home.

This is not a casual, come-what-may part of puppy rearing, where, say, you bring your young charge to the park and let anyone and everyone pet her and other dogs carouse with her as they will. That kind of immersion is called flooding and, to continue the metaphor, may very well drown the dog in negative emotions. Having unselected people and animals coming at a young pup too fast and perhaps too roughly can and often does back-fire. It sends a message that the world is a chaotic place where everything happens too fast and the human in charge does not offer protection. The result is a dog who doesn't get along well with anyone or anything.

Instead, puppy socializing should be a planned and structured process. You have to *make* it happen, rather than let it happen, in a tightly controlled environment. Don't give this short shrift, no matter how cautious it seems on the face of it.

For instance, let's say a couple of days after you get the puppy home, you decide to throw a puppy party. You don't just call over a few neighbors without any forethought. Maybe the guy next door is loud and obnoxious and will not understand that your new charge needs to be treated with kid gloves. Maybe the person living on the other side of you wants to bring a toddler who is too young to understand that a puppy is a living creature with feelings, not some battery-operated toy put there for her pleasure.

The Sensitive Period of Learning

As we explained on page 25 in chapter 1, weeks three through twelve in a puppy's life (some say through week fourteen) constitute the "sensitive period of learning." It used to be known as the "critical" period when it was first identified by psychologists John P. Scott and John L. Fuller some fifty years ago, at a point in their careers when they studied dogs to shed light on the genetic underpinnings of behavior. But the term morphed to the less definitive "sensitive" period, since a puppy who misses the right cues for socialization from weeks three through twelve can make up for some lost ground later on.

Still, we feel it's more instructive to consider the period as critical rather than sensitive. Think of the way children learn a foreign language. When a child is young, she is a veritable sponge for language learning, which is why European children growing up exposed to different tongues are often multilingual. But her ability to acquire a new language falls precipitously with advancing years. An older learner may be able to get the words, and even the grammar, but chances are that her accent, intonation, and use of idiomatic expression will never be as nimble as that of an early learner. The brain loses its early flexibility over time.

It's the same with dogs. You can make up for lost ground when a puppy is six months of age, but it will take much more effort and become harder and harder as time goes by.

That's why it's so important that a puppy be socialized correctly through her first twelve weeks of life, the equivalent, in many ways, of the early years for a child. Habituate the dog to the basics at the right time, and they'll stay with her forever.

Those individuals would not make good invitees. You may graduate your puppy to such types two to three weeks later, after she has developed a sense that humans in general are not bad and will be able to tolerate the occasional lout or loudmouth. But start your puppy with *gentle* people who really love dogs and will be happy to come over and give yours lots of happy attention, perhaps with little bits of food treats here and there. You can literally have four to six people sit in a circle and hand the puppy one to the other after they have each fussed over her for a while. What she will be learning, imbibing with all of her senses, is that with people around, nothing bad happens, and sometimes really good things happen. (Wouldn't you trust another species if every creature you met from that species treated you so wonderfully?) Then, when the dog does run into someone who isn't friendly or who is too rough in his friendliness, she can say to herself, "Hmm, I love people, but this particular one is a bit of a problem. I don't have to rush at him or away from him, however. This doesn't happen often enough that I feel threatened by it."

Ideally, you'd want to throw a puppy party every day until the dog reaches at least twelve weeks of age. After all, the sensitive period of learning, when your pup's mind is a sponge, lasts only until she is twelve weeks old. And you will not have her before she is eight to ten weeks, so you won't be getting much of an opportunity to habituate her to various types of people before her attitude toward the human race is pretty much set.

But few people can invite several friends and relatives to their house every single day for two to four weeks straight, despite the puppy's fast development. For that reason, we feel that having puppy parties three times a week is a reasonable compromise between doing nothing at all and what you should be doing in the best of all possible worlds. (Even once a week is better than nothing.) Make the time. If you commit to bringing a puppy into your life for the entire length of *her* life, you can certainly make room for an hourlong puppy party every other day for the first few weeks that she's in your care.

You can even have puppy parties until the dog is fourteen weeks old. The sensitive period of learning is generally considered over at twelve weeks of age, but it doesn't come to a full stop on the last day of the twelfth week. Learning goes on after that; it just comes more slowly and gets ingrained less easily.

Mix it up as the parties progress. While you may want to start out with avowed puppy lovers who couldn't raise their voices or sound sharp if their lives depended on it, you should also include, here and there, men with deep voices, grade school children who move a little more quickly than adults (but who listen to your instructions), women with loud voices—more or less any prototypes for people your puppy might meet down the road.

By the same token, you should also arrange for people to come to the house "out of the blue." That is, you'll arrange it, but it'll be out of the blue for the pup. For instance, have somebody come to the back door to deliver a parcel—a box or an envelope. Have someone come to the front door. Arrange for a "surprise" visit from someone wearing a hat. Many dogs are afraid of hats; therefore, hats are good things to desensitize and habituate them to. Boots, too, make a lot of dogs nervous, so have an especially nice person come to the door in his or her Wellies or work boots. In each scenario, make the experience memorably pleasant—with praise, petting, or treats.

You can take your puppy to other people's houses, too, as long as any dog that might be there is healthy and fully vaccinated. She needs to learn that humans are okay not just within the four walls of your family room.

The more people, and the more kinds of people, to whom you expose your puppy, the less likely she'll be to overreact in a meeting with a type of person she *hasn't* met before. She'll be able to generalize her positive experiences to the world at large rather than assume everyone is going to be a problem from which she needs to guard herself.

GET-TOGETHERS WITH OTHER ANIMALS

Social occasions for your new pup shouldn't just be with people. Every kind of animal your dog will come in contact with should be introduced to her in a fashion orchestrated and controlled by you in order to habituate her without trauma.

Often, owners heed the advice to go slowly when it comes to people but not when introducing other dogs. That is, you shouldn't just let your puppy off the leash when you're outside together and see how she does with the dogs who happen to be around. Would you take a young child who had never played with anyone other than his brothers and sisters and let her loose in a park filled with loud, sometimes obnoxious children while you sat on a bench and watched passively?

Instead, just as you would arrange play dates for your preschooler based on careful screening, arrange formal introductions to other dogs. That is,

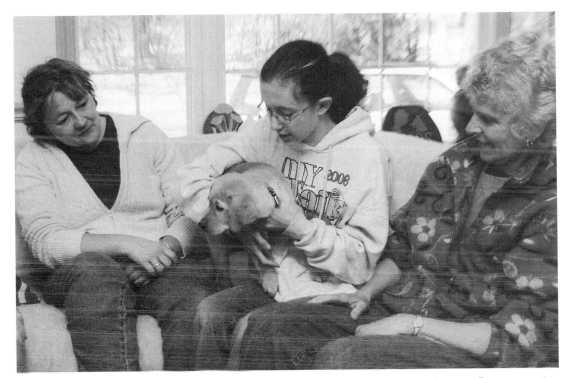

Puppy party in progress.

when outside, keep your puppy on leash and work it very gingerly when it comes to interactions with other dogs. Let the pup acclimate gradually; protect her rather than throw her "into the deep end of the pool."

You should also throw adult dog/puppy parties at your house. Imagine having two or three gentle dogs over—a calm golden retriever, perhaps, and another couple of low-key dogs. With the visiting dogs properly controlled and on leash, praise them all, give them all biscuits, pet them all, and perhaps introduce a toy. Your puppy will soon be saying to herself, "Hmm, even though these dogs aren't my littermates, they're pretty cool. We have so much fun when they're around." It won't be a big stretch from those formal occasions to romps in the park where your pup can interact with other dogs without fear or untoward aggression.

Just as your puppy needs to be introduced to other dogs in a friendly, nonthreatening manner, she also needs to meet whatever other animals are going to be in her life in a calm, orchestrated way. Arrange all puppy-animal introductions in a tightly controlled fashion. If you have a cat in the house who is hissing and spitting at the pup, keep the two at a safe distance until they gradually get used to each other and finally make peace. Whatever animal you need the dog not to be afraid of, one controlled experience at a time is the way to go.

The Wrong Kind of Dog-on-Dog Socialization

Many dog trainers suggest bringing an already fearful pup to a dog training class to "desensitize it." You now know that's flooding, and we had direct experience of how that tactic can backfire when a visiting trainer had a fearful dog sit on the sidelines at one of our puppy training sessions. One of the pups approached the fearful dog to investigate. She was bitten in the face. Thus, instead of desensitizing the fearful dog, the trainer had reinforced the fear, and created an additional fearful dog in the bargain—a two-fer deal, if you will, but not a good one. We have never allowed that to happen since. Once bitten, twice shy.

ACCLIMATIZING PUPPY TO WHAT'S *NOT* ALIVE

Socialization is about getting along with other creatures—humans, other dogs, cats, hamsters, and anything else that's alive. But the third through twelfth weeks of a puppy's life that make up her socialization period are also the best time for habituating her to nonliving things that she's going to encounter and that could cause her to feel afraid. What are these things? Some are general to life in and around most homes: thunder, lightning, and cars, for instance. Others may be particular to *your* home: a bicycle, a wheelchair, a lawnmower, a doorbell with a distinct ring . . .

How do you acclimate your puppy to potentially fear-inducing phenomena in her life that are not alive? Gradually and mindfully. For instance, you might sometimes want to play a tape of low, rumbling thunder. If you're home and cheerfully going about your business with that noise in the background, your puppy might get the idea that thunder is nothing to be worried about. After she's used to that sound, you can move on to a tape with louder thunder, still happily going about your business—perhaps reading or watching television or doing chores—while it's playing.

If there's an *object* you want your puppy to grow up feeling comfortable around, perhaps a machine that's loud when turned on, bring her over to it when it's not on and play with her there. If, like a vacuum cleaner or lawnmower, it moves, perhaps walk with it, pup by your side, so she'll see it's safe. Try it first without the noise. Later, turn it on at a distance so she can get used to it. She may never love the sound of a vacuum cleaner (just as you don't), and she may walk away when you turn it on, but at least it will be much less likely to strike terror in her.

That's good not only because the terror is undesirable in itself. It also gets imprinted on the puppy's brain in a way that doesn't really let her recover from it, so she goes through life with a kind of mini–posttraumatic stress disorder that makes it hard for her to cope. In fact, the phobias she develops are specific, long-lasting, may be multiple, and will always generate stress and possibly avoidance behavior or aggression. They will not get better over time. If anything, they will accelerate.

Socializing Before Vaccinating?

When your puppy comes home with you somewhere between eight and ten weeks of age, some people, including perhaps your breeder and maybe even your veterinarian, will tell you not to let other dogs near her until she has been fully vaccinated.

But by that point, of course, your pup will be between sixteen and twenty weeks of age —well past the socialization period and well past the ideal opportunity for her to become habituated to other dogs and animals. In other words, without socialization with other animals until she is four or five months old, she may *never* come to fully accept other dogs, as well as cats, birds, and so on.

So you're left with something of a catch-22. Wait until the dog is fully vaccinated and she'll be disease-free but a social misfit. Introduce your pup to other animals before she is twelve weeks old and she'll get along with various doggie friends but run the risk of succumbing to some infectious disease.

How do you deal with the dilemma? By dealing safely. First, recognize that there's only a small zone of time during which your new puppy may be at risk for conditions she has not been vaccinated against. That's because until she is eight weeks old, she's largely protected by maternal antibodies, as we explained in chapter 1. And near the end of the socialization period, when she's twelve weeks old, she will have had her second set of shots, and the protection they afford will have to a great extent kicked in.

Between times, when she is about ten weeks and she is new to your household, *don't* take her to public places—parks or woods where other dogs and various animal species roam and where illness-causing organisms can travel from one animal to another. But *do* arrange parties with dogs who are completely vaccinated and in A-1 health. (Don't worry about puppy parties with people, whether on your turf or someone else's— bacteria and viruses that affect humans are generally not a problem for pets.) Follow these simple, commonsense guidelines and your puppy will stay perfectly healthy.

LOOKING AHEAD

You couldn't possibly expose your puppy to everything she's going to come across in her life in that short period between the time from bringing her home and the end of the twelfth, or even fourteenth, week. So don't look to cover everything and don't aim for perfection. You'll just drive yourself crazy.

Instead, do the best you can, which is a lot. You'll end up with a dog who, in general, likes people — big ones, small ones, deep-voiced ones, squeaky-voiced ones, hat-wearing ones, and so on. Your dog will like other dogs, too, which will allow her to enjoy the pack socializing that dogs really get a charge out of.

Bringing people and other dogs into your puppy's circle of trust is a lot by itself. And if you play it right, your dog will even like your cat and other crea-

Adjust your puppy to objects that make loud noises by letting her play near them *before* they are turned on.

tures in your home. That old tale about dogs and cats hating each other—it's not true. It's true only if they're not acclimated to each other and taught respect and tolerance.

Your dog, socialized properly, will end up being okay around animals and machinery she's never come across before, too. Why? It's about a learning process known as generalization. The more you expose your puppy in the right way, the less likely she'll be to overreact to whatever you *haven't* previously exposed her to. Her take on the world will be a curious, not fearful, one.

PART 3

Puppy Insights

6

How Puppy Perceives the World Around Him

SPOCK, A MIXED BREED WITH GIANT EARS REMINISCENT OF *STAR TREK*'S Mr. Spock, was brought to our Behavior Clinic by his owner because he was having panic attacks at least a few times a day. Seemingly out of nowhere, the poor dog would start running around, panting, pawing, and drooling. He was in a terrible state, and his caretaker did not know what was wrong —or how to fix the problem.

With each episode, the dog would eventually calm down on his own, but not because of any reassurance the owner provided. The panic would dissolve as mysteriously as it had appeared.

Spock's house was near the Massachusetts Turnpike, a six-lane (sometimes eight-lane) highway traversing the state, so we wondered at first whether the traffic might be bothering him at rush hour, or the wheels turning on certain large trucks. But it wasn't the Mass. Pike. Spock had one of his panic attacks right in our facility, and we are situated on a 585-acre oasis. The loudest noise around is generally no more jarring than the sound of cows and sheep grazing in nearby fields.

Little by little, it came together. The panic attack in our office, we deduced, was caused by a sound source we had not been picking up with our human ears—high-speed drills used for dogs undergoing orthopedic surgery several doors down.

From there, the pieces fell into place. Spock's owner's neighbor was a power tool guy, and several times a day he fired up his drill, circular saw, and other equipment. Spock's owner couldn't hear the high-pitched sounds but to Spock, they were like fingernails being drawn across a blackboard—and were literally driving him crazy.

With the source of the panic attacks detected, solutions amenable to both households were worked out, and Spock stopped suffering on a daily basis.

Spock's experience points to a basic truth about humans and dogs. The two species live in overlapping but not identical sensory worlds; we don't share all perceptions. To a pup, we are sort of like the Brobdingnagians of Jonathan Swift's *Gulliver's Travels,* extra-large beings whose ways don't all make perfect sense. The *dog* knows there's an intolerable sound that needs to be responded to, but his humans are oblivious.

That's a hard position to be in, because a dog's world is controlled by yours. Even for a willful dog, pretty much what you say goes.

Making matters more difficult still, a dog can't explain to you with language what you're failing to understand about him. While humans live in a world of language, dogs communicate in a variety of other ways.

Thus, it's important that you learn to *understand* your puppy, and understand what he's "saying" to you, as you call the shots. The better you understand how he experiences his world, the less likely you'll be to become frustrated or angry (and perhaps treat your charge unfairly). In addition, the more your pup will appreciate your efforts to consider where he's coming from. And, ultimately, the better and stronger the bond between the two of you will be.

One of the best ways to get inside a dog's head is to understand the differences in the five senses between dogs and humans: sight, hearing, smell, touch, and taste. Knowing where the senses don't overlap is key to a respectful relationship.

SIGHT

It is often assumed that dogs see everything in black and white. This is not true. Granted, they don't see as many colors as people do. Their color vision is similar to red-green colorblindness. Dogs can distinguish yellows and blues fairly well, but they see red (and orange) as yellow, and green appears to them as white. In other words, their world consists pretty much of yellows, blues, and grays. Thus, a red ball in green grass wouldn't stand out to a dog the way it would to you.

Dogs are also not able to see detail as well as humans. If perfect human vision is 20/20, a dog's is somewhere between 20/50 and 20/100.

Don't worry. Your puppy is not at a disadvantage. Dogs' visual systems adapted evolutionarily over many thousands of years to suit their needs. Consider that humans are diurnal: we need to see best during the day and therefore rely on color and detail. Dogs, on the other hand, are naturally crepuscular creatures—they are biologically set up to be most active at dawn and dusk, when they can hunt rodents and other varmints for food and engage in other canine activities. So being able to distinguish colors and details is less important to them than seeing shades of gray in low light and discerning movement in those gray shades. And that's exactly what dogs' eyes are set up to do.

Here's the crux: The canine eye has two types of cones—receptors in the retina for color vision—while the human retina has three types. But dogs have many more rods in their retina than humans do, and rods are great for distinguishing the many gray shades between black and white. They're also sensitive to motion detection and are at an advantage in dim light—both helpful for hunting.

Dogs can also see things much better at night than we can. When humans look at an object in relative darkness, they may see only shadows cast by, say, moonlight or a faraway streetlight. But dogs' eyes can use any available light much more efficiently. That's partly because of the large number of rods. But the back of the canine eye also has a reflecting layer called the *tapetum lucidum*, which, to oversimplify for a moment, acts sort of like a mirror. Whatever light goes in is reflected back out, jingling sensor cells in the eye a second time and, in essence, doubling the effect of whatever light is available. (The presence of the *tapetum lucidum* is the reason that if you look at a dog in headlights, you'll often see a green flash in his eyes.)

Think of those antique candle holders with a mirror behind the candle. The light from the candle that goes back into the mirror also comes forward because the mirror reflects it outward. Light entering the human eye, by contrast, lands at the back with a thud. It doesn't come back out through the eye again.

There's yet another reason your puppy can see better than you in dim light. His pupils, the black circles in the middle of the colored irises (usually brown in dogs), can open up so wide that the irises are practically obliterated. That lets in much more light than the human pupil, which does become bigger in darkness than in bright light but never so big that you can't tell whether a person has brown, blue, or green eyes.

The point here: You shouldn't let your puppy drive the car—he won't be able to distinguish well enough between the red and green lights. But when it's late at night and he's staring intensely out the window, won't budge, and perhaps is making a beeline for the back door, he may well be seeing something invisible to you. He's not being ridiculous or trying to interrupt your television program. Perhaps he's spotting a squirrel off in the distance when all you see are tree branches. The rods that enable him to see shades of gray allow him to detect camouflaged movement where you wouldn't be able to.

HEARING

Dogs are sometimes said to have superhuman hearing. It's true. It's just not as "super" as is often assumed. In fact, canine and human hearing is pretty similar, with one notable difference. Dogs can hear in the ultrasound range, meaning they can hear sound waves with ultra-high frequency—around 65,000 cycles per second as opposed to the human maximum of 20,000 cycles per second. In practical terms, that means a dog can hear sounds approximately two octaves higher than a person—a range that includes the sound made by a dog whistle. (No wonder poor Spock was so miserable. He could hear not just the loud sounds of power tools that we hear but screechy noises in the higher range.)

The reason for dogs' hearing in those upper, upper octaves is that rodents communicate with each other in that range. If a dog in the wild needed to dine on a rodent, one way to track it was to listen for it.

Not only can dogs hear sounds that humans can't, they detect and localize sound with superb accuracy and discriminate better than humans do between noises occurring at the same time. Their brains simply decode and translate sound signals better than ours can. (Adult hearing patterns are in place in puppies by the time they are seven weeks old—pretty amazing when you consider that they can't hear much for the first two weeks after birth because their ear canals are still closed.)

Then, too, a dog's ears are relatively bigger and much more mobile than a human's. Dogs' ears have many more muscles than people's ears, some thirty muscles per ear as opposed to nine in ours. All that muscle power allows dogs to move their ears in the direction of sound in a way that lets them zero in on sounds more acutely (unless they have flop ears like cocker spaniels, which are too heavy to move easily even with a lot of muscles).

Thus, just as with sight, if your pup is agitated and you can't tell why, it may be the boiler in the basement starting up every so often or a passing truck (again, a dog may hear more screeching than we do, since he hears in the ultrasound range). He's probably not acting out or "refusing" to calm down for no reason.

SMELL

If a dog can hear two octaves higher than we can and can see better in the dark, his sense of smell leaves us absolutely in the dust. The differences in the sense of smell between dogs and humans can be quantified in several ways.

1. Dogs have nearly twenty times more primary smell receptor cells in their noses than people have.

2. Dogs can detect smells at concentrations at least a hundred times less than a human can. In some cases, they can detect smells at concentrations a *million* times less. (A dog can detect a human scent on a glass slide that has been lightly fingerprinted and left *outside* for two weeks. You touch something, they know you've been there.)

3. After accounting for differences in size between dogs and humans, the olfactory lobes—which reside in the brain and decode signals of scent arriving from the nose via the olfactory nerve—are dramatically larger in a dog than in a person.

4. If you ironed out the scent-detecting membranes covering the scrolled-up, coral-like bones in a human nose, their surface area would be roughly the size of a thumbnail. If you ironed out the same membranes in a dog's nose, they would be the size of a pocket handkerchief.

Not only can dogs smell better than we do, their olfactory lobes can distinguish between scents much better than ours; they are able to mentally filter out confusing smells to get a more accurate sniff. For instance, a dog can sniff two to five footprints on a trail scented with all kinds of smells—animal urine, garbage, plant, and tree odors—and know what direction the person walked in *three hours earlier*. (Bloodhounds and basset hounds are especially good at this. It's the stars among *them* who are used for detective work; one can only imagine how keenly they are able to pick up scents.)

There's more. Dogs have a nose within the nose. Called the vomeronasal organ, or VNO, it is especially useful for detecting pheromones—chemical communication signals coming from other dogs.

The VNO is reached through the hard palate in the roof of a dog's mouth. Let's say a puppy sniffs a lamppost. In a very subtle move that people generally miss, he touches his tongue against the lamppost and deposits some material from it onto the roof of his mouth. From there the material enters two ducts that lead to the VNO sensory nerve endings, and the dog might learn, for example, that he has come upon parahydroxybenzoic acid, a pheromone present in both vaginal secretions and in urine. Once the scent has registered in the dog's brain, the substance is automatically flushed out through his palate.

Smelling, whether from the VNO or otherwise, can tell a dog *a lot* about who has been around and what they might be up to, at least as much as you would get from walking down the street and seeing the parked car of some-

Can Dogs Smell Cancer?

Not long ago, research showed that by sniffing, laboratory-trained dogs could detect lung cancer with 99 percent accuracy and breast cancer with 88 percent accuracy. Previous work had shown that patterns of various biochemical markers could be found in the exhaled breath of patients with lung and breast tumors that differ from the patterns of people without those malignancies. So investigators trained dogs to sit or lie in front of people on whom they "smelled cancer" and to ignore people on whom they did not smell it. What was particularly remarkable about the study was that the dogs used were ordinary household dogs with only basic puppy training; they were not extraordinarily sophisticated in their ability to learn new "tricks."

We should point out that cancer is not the first disease dogs have been believed to be able to sniff out in humans. Blood sugar problems that can precede seizures in people with diabetes are also thought to be detectable by some dogs.

In the old days of veterinary medicine, it was the vet who used his nose to diagnose various conditions in dogs. A dog's ear might smell "yeasty," for instance, or his diabetic breath tellingly fruity. Now it might be dogs' turn to return the favor, if scientists can identify and isolate the chemical odors dogs appear to be picking up.

one you know in a neighbor's driveway. ("I wasn't aware that so-and-so and so-and-so got together. Hmm. I'll have to think about this.") It may even be why some puppies get jittery the minute they step into a veterinarian's waiting room for the first time, even though they don't know what to expect. They could be smelling accumulated chemical signals from a large assortment of dogs who have already been there and have experienced being injected with needles, handling by strangers, and so on.

Consider that when a dog is scared, his anal glands deposit a stinky, skunklike odor. Some scientists believe the odor is a fear pheromone that reminds the dog and other dogs later on—that something horrible happened at that location a while ago, so the place should be avoided. (It certainly makes sense from an evolutionary point of view.)

If all of these extraordinary abilities to pick up odors aren't enough, a dog's nose can pick up smells, like those in bombs and other explosives, with greater accuracy than a mass spectrometer, which is built to detect chemicals.

Clearly, dogs live in an olfactory world about which we have very little perception. It pays to keep that in mind when you're taking your puppy for a walk or letting him go for a romp in the woods (once he has had all his vaccinations). That is, your pet is not trying to annoy you by sniffing around the same spot for a lengthy period of time. Granted, you may have a limited time before you have to move on, but imagine if you were reading a newspaper headline that declared "Income Tax Abolished for All" or "Your Next-Door Neighbor Had a Barbecue and You Weren't Invited." You would not want to have your head and neck yanked away with a leash just as you were picking up the important details—who, exactly, was there; whether any of the participants were feeling, shall we say, frisky; and whether any of them were sorts you had only recently run into.

That's what a dog feels like if you don't let him "read" various communications with his nose as he takes his daily constitutionals. (He may even want to leave pee-mail messages of his own along the way. That's his method of responding to recent "events.")

TOUCH

While human beings have a pretty good sense of touch on the lips and around the face, most of our touch is felt on our fingers. It's exquisitely acute at the tips of our fingers. A dog, on the other hand, could never use his paws to learn to read Braille. The pressure receptors in his paws just wouldn't be sensitive enough to distinguish all those little dots and other shapes. He's got a really thick skin there. The pain and temperature receptors in his paws aren't powerhouses of sensitivity, either—a good thing for an animal who doesn't wear shoes. How else would a dog be able to walk over gravel and sidewalks without feeling pain?

Instead, a dog's touch receptors are most numerous around his muzzle, that part of the face comprising the nose and mouth and the areas between and around them. That doesn't mean touch receptors are absent from other areas of his body. A dog will retract his paw when you touch it, and he usually does like the feel of being stroked and brushed on his trunk. It's just that the touch sensations in those areas are not as big a deal as on the face. That's because a dog's face is almost like a hand in terms of all the things he uses it for. He goes about so much of his business—eating, sniffing, and so on—with his head.

Interestingly, one of the areas *least* sensitive to touch on a dog is around the base of the neck—which is why your pet won't respond well when you tug on the leash to get him to do something or to keep him from doing something. It's like trying to control a horse with a piece of twine. The tugging motion is just not having much effect or even annoying him all that much.

Some owners take that as a sign that they must graduate an unruly pup

Where a human has lots of nerve endings (plus in the lips).

from a flat collar to a choke collar and then to a collar with prongs in order to get their young charge to obey. That's about the worst thing a person can do. Choke and prong collars really *can* hurt a dog, and won't teach him anything in the bargain. They'll just make your puppy distrust you. Better to use instead a head halter in training. When you apply gentle traction to it, it transmits a pressure signal to the dog's snout and nape similar to the signals his mother sent when she was admonishing him. It doesn't hurt. It just means no. It gently keeps him from doing what you don't want him to do. (More on head halters in chapter 8.)

The muzzle, which includes the mouth, nose, and jaws, is where a dog's nerve endings are concentrated.

TASTE

Here's where humans have it over dogs. Just think about the fact that dogs don't really try to taste their food. They just gulp it down.

That's not to say dogs can't detect sweet, sour, bitter, and salt, just as we do. But they don't even have a genuine sweet tooth, like humans (or rabbits or horses). And their taste detection abilities are relatively poor. While a person has about nine thousand taste buds on his tongue, a dog has approximately two thousand.

Note, however, that even within their relatively taste-less world, dogs' phenomenal smell does enhance their tasting ability. Just think about how well you were able to taste the last time your nose was blocked with a cold.

Note, too, that dogs have a strong aversion to bitter. They will not eat a food sweetened with saccharin because they can detect that chemical's bitter undertones.

Another difference between us and them is that they are neophilic, which means they like to try new foods. Humans, on the other hand, are neo*phobic,* at least when they are young. While a puppy will pretty much try anything you put in front of him, a human toddler may need ten to twenty exposures to a particular food before he will try eating it.

TRANSLATING FROM ENGLISH TO PUPPY: UNDERSTANDING THIRTY-FIVE THINGS THEY DO

Understanding the differences between the human and canine senses doesn't explain all of a puppy's behavior. Pups (and older dogs) engage in some activities that you can't figure out solely by thinking them through sensewise. Here are thirty-five of them, with explanations, so you'll be able to trust that your dog's not strange; he's simply dog.

1. *Moves away when you pet his head.* How are you doing the petting? A lot of people are taught that the way to pet a dog is to keep patting the top of his head. But a dog perceives that action as a signal of dominance, not affection. It also just plain doesn't feel good. Dogs prefer to be *stroked,* particularly on the side of the face, under the chin, or on the front of the chest. They also like having their rump scratched.

2. *Circles the mat before going to sleep.* This is an ethologic vestige. Dogs in the wild flattened the grass by circling around it a few times before settling down. They were creating a safe and comfortable nest. Today, dogs are acting out a primordial sequence that was genetically encoded and began to be passed down from generation to generation many thousands of years ago.

> The more you pick up a young puppy and hold him, **the faster his brain will develop** and the sooner he'll reach mental and emotional maturity. His mother's presence may be a factor here. When the mother picks up your odor on the pup's skin, she will lick him to get him back to a neutral odor. It's the licking that is believed to help mature him. Your own physical interactions with the puppy will bring him along, of course. But they probably won't have quite the same effect as his mother's touch.

3. *Barks at the mailman no matter how well acquainted the two are.* Your pup probably thinks he's exerting some power by getting the mail carrier to leave. He does leave soon after the dog starts barking, doesn't he?

4. *Grunts.* A grunt from a puppy is a communication of pleasure. Sought-after warmth or communion has been attained.

5. *Whines.* A puppy whines if he is cold, hungry, or separated from those he feels he needs near him. Put a warm towel over him, feed him, or pay him attention, and the whining will probably stop.

6. *Blinks.* That's what a dog does when he is thinking hard. If you say "Down" to get him to lie down and he blinks before doing so, he is thinking, "Do I have to?"

7. *Yawns.* A dog may yawn if he's tired, but more generally, it indicates stress. With yawning, the dog is trying to displace the stress, or inner conflict, with a safe, neutral behavior. Humans do the same thing when they find themselves in a situation of conflict that causes stress—not yawn necessarily, but do something to cope until the unpleasant situation passes. Let's say you're in a hurry and you reach a red light. You want to be *there,* but you have to be *here,* both because that's the safe thing to do and because someone else, the police, will enforce the behavior that causes the stress: staying still until the light turns green. So what do you do? You groom yourself in the rearview mirror, or you look at the driver in the car next to you. Neither of these actions is directly related to what's pressing on your mind, but engaging in them is better than doing nothing while you're stuck in a state of conflict between what you want to do and what you must do despite your desires. That's pretty much akin to a dog's yawning when he's not tired.

8. *Licks his lips.* This is a sign of nervousness, anxiety, and submission. People do it, too.

9. *Licks* you. This is not really a kiss. Rather, it's a deferent, attention-seeking gesture, similar to what a pup is expressing when he licks his mother's lips to get her to regurgitate food. (Young puppies will sometimes feed off their mother's regurgitations.) Why, then, do dogs often lick people in moments of affection? Most likely it's because they get good feedback for it. For instance, puppy happens to lick baby, baby squeals with delight, Mom and Dad are overjoyed and pet puppy while racing for the camcorder. The puppy learns, "Ah, when I lick the kid, everyone gets in a good mood and treats me well." Inadvertent conditioning has taken place.

NOTE: In some instances a dog will lick to establish dominance. It has happened in our own offices. One owner brought in a rottweiler puppy who needed to have his overly dominant and aggressive behavior curbed. The pup immediately put his two front paws on the treating veterinarian's desk and slobbered him up and down with his big, pink sandpapery tongue. It was clearly not a deferent gesture but rather a gesture in which the dog was exercising control and showing he could get away with it. You've got to read the situation a little (which is not hard to do).

10. *Keeps climbing up onto the couch even when you've told him no.* A puppy who tries to get as high as or higher up than you may be vying for dominance. But puppies also prefer soft surfaces to hard ones. Sometimes a cushion is just a cushion.

11. *Paws and scrapes the ground after eliminating.* A lot of people mistakenly think that a dog, like a cat, is scratching and scraping to cover his "deposit," or at least the scent of his deposit. Nothing could be further from the truth. A dog who scratches the ground after eliminating is engaging in a kind of marking behavior to advertise his presence—the opposite of trying to cover up the evidence. By pawing the dirt, he is leaving both a visual cue—unearthed soil—and an olfactory one coming from, we surmise, sweat glands on his paws. It's for emphasis. If the urine doesn't say clearly enough, "Kilroy was here," the other scents will.

12. *Eats feces.* Called coprophagia, this behavior is commonly displayed by puppies. It is species-typical behavior. Bitches keep the whelping area clean after they give birth by eating their young's feces. There is nothing harmful about this behavior to a pup, who will probably outgrow it by the time he's one year old. But if you find it too objectionable, simply deny access. Always walk the pup on a leash and pick up after dogs—and other species of animals—who have relieved themselves in your yard. (Some say that adding meat tenderizers or breath fresheners to the dog's diet helps curb the habit, but it does not work.)

> The **"dog days of summer"** have nothing to do with dogs. They have to do with astronomy, specifically with the dog star, Sirius. In the swelter of August, Sirius is very high in the sky, so hot days are dog days.

13. *Rolls around in disgusting stuff, including muddy messes, feces, and carcasses.* Remember, dogs "see" largely through their sense of smell. When they roll around in something and stink to high heaven, they're not trying to be disgusting. They're saying, "Look what I found. What a day I had in the cow pasture," and so on. It could also be a holdover from the times when dogs ran wild. Rolling in the excrement of another animal or in rotting material masks the dog's own odor, thereby making him less easily detectable by potential predators—or by prey that he is staking out.

14. *Eats grass.* Some people believe dogs eat grass to make themselves throw up when they have stomach upset; that is, the dogs are thought to self-medicate. Some believe dogs simply like to eat grass and then throw up when they eat too much of it. Who's right? Both. Different dogs have different grass-eating patterns. None of them is harmful, so don't fret if your dog throws up after nibbling on the green stuff.

15. *Sniffs around forever before urinating.* To a human, urination is urination. To a dog, it's an elimination process *and* a way of communicating. So a dog has to take in the various olfactory notices left by other dogs before leaving a message of his own. He may even want to make sure that no other pup has previously urinated in the spot he's considering. An "all-clear" sign takes some time. Be patient. He's not trying to drive you crazy.

16. *Sniffs other dogs' behinds.* If smelling were seeing, humans would be considered legally blind by those in the canine world. Dogs would feel more's the pity for us humans for *not* getting anything out of sniffing the behinds of others. Pheromones generated from the glands around a dog's anus proclaim his identity to another dog. They're as crucial to learning about another dog as the pheromones contained in canine vaginal secretions and urine.

17. *Pants.* Unlike humans, dogs don't have sweat glands on most of their skin. There are only a few on their paws and around the anus. Thus, they don't cool their bodies by losing body heat through the evaporation of sweat. Rather, they regulate body temperature when it starts to rise by panting. The faster a dog pants, the more water-saturated air he is breathing out (evaporating) from his lungs to produce a cooling effect. That said, dogs don't pant only when they're hot. Sometimes they pant when they're anxious. For instance, you might see a dog panting when he's suffering from separation anxiety or thunderstorm phobia, in addition to pacing and looking nervous.

18. *Acts happier around dogs of his own breed.* It is believed that dogs do not have a sense of self-image and do not even necessarily recognize themselves in a mirror, so it's not vanity that is attracting your pet to others of his kind. It may simply be that your pup had good experiences with his siblings, so he seeks out others who look like them. It can work the other way, too. If, say, your pet is a Border collie who has had unfortunate experiences with cocker spaniels, he may spend his whole life acting aggressively or fearfully toward that breed.

19. *Lays his head and front paws splayed out close to the ground while sticking his rump in the air.* That's what's known as the play bow. It's a dog's way of saying that he wants to play—or keep on playing. When a dog does that, he's in a very good mood. All dogs (and coyotes and wolves) are genetically hard-wired for this position. When another dog sees it, he knows that the lowered head is an invitation to come forward, while the

A dog in a play bow is ready for fun.

rump in the air is a signal of playful, frisky readiness. Often the lips of a dog doing the play bow will be retracted in a kind of teeth-showing grin. The oncoming dog will make note of that signal of friendliness, too.

20. *Chases his own tail.* Is your dog a bull terrier or German shepherd? These are the breeds most likely to go after their own tail. But it is not normal doggie behavior, for them or any other breed. It is believed that tail chasing starts in dogs who have a high predatory drive and no natural outlets for their predatory instinct. One day, out of boredom, the dog spies his tail from the corner of his eye and tries to pounce on it. The result is that circular tail-chasing motion, which is perfect, in a way, because the tail moves away just as fast as the dog moves to catch it. Unfortunately, for some dogs, the behavior becomes so intense that they do get hold of and bite their tails, causing bleeding. Other dogs spin themselves into extreme dizziness for hours on end, barely even taking time to eat or sleep. That means the anxiety arising from the inability to stake out real prey has resulted in a compulsive behavior that can be corrected only with a major lifestyle change (allowing the dog a lot more free rein in the woods, for instance) or anti-obsessional drugs.

21. *Nurses on things like blankets or stuffed animals.* If a puppy lives with his mother until he is at least six to eight weeks of age, he will probably not suck on various nonliving items. He will have had the opportunity to nurse to his heart's content as a newborn, and even to suckle from his mother once he moves on to solid food in those instances when he needs comfort after an unnerving event. It's the puppies whose biological drive to nurse from their mother has been denied who end up nursing on things they shouldn't be nursing on. Note that some puppy breeds have a greater propensity to nurse on blankets and such (even on themselves) than other breeds when denied access to their mother. These include Doberman pinschers and dachshunds. The reason is not known. It may be that these breeds have a particularly high nursing drive that is more likely to become displaced when not offered the right outlet.

22. *Sticks his head out the car window during drives.* It's fun! Dogs, like many humans, enjoy the feel of the wind on their faces. In addition, with those noses out the window, they can smell the various neighborhoods they're passing through, which is their best way of "seeing" them. Be aware, however, that a pup or older dog can get hurt by flying pebbles thrown up by other cars, particularly if their eyes are hit. For that reason, one company makes doggie goggles, although, admittedly, not all dogs willingly emulate Snoopy's Red Baron (see "Resources" for more information).

23. *Barks at another dog with his head held high.* When one dog barks at another with his head held high, his eyes directed at the other dog, his ears pricked forward (if they're not floppy), and his body tense with his tail erect, he is signaling confidence and dominance. He is not only calling attention to his presence but announcing his control over the territory.

> There is no difference between hair and fur, other than the one people have in their heads. Biologically, the two are the same. Hair just looks different on different species, and on different breeds within the canine species.

24. *Barks at another dog with his ears pressed to his head, his tail tucked, and his eyes darting from side to side.* Such a dog is afraid. He might actually be barking more ferociously than a confident one, but it's all bluff. Watch how he may charge forward a couple of paces and then step backward. He doesn't *really* want to get into a tussle.

25. *Digs fast and furiously in the dirt, or even in the bed linens.* This action is often derived from aspects of the so-called appetitive phase of predatory behavior. Consider that terriers, for instance, were bred to chase small varmints. The varmint, after running some, would burrow into the ground, and the dog's job was to dig in the dirt and pursue it. When there aren't any true predatory outlets, he might displace these aspects of a hard-wired behavior with seemingly pointless behavior—digging in some leaves in the garden, perhaps, or in some heaped-up bedclothes. Not all dogs dig for predatory reasons. A northern breed, such as a Siberian husky, might dig to simulate what he does in the harsh terrain of some polar region. Wandering around in ice-cold wind blowing seventy miles an hour, he'll dig a little depression into the snow to shield himself from the elements. Likewise, on a very hot day, a dog might dig in the ground and lie in the cool soil to shield himself from the sun. In other words, digging could be a vestige of thermoregulatory behavior rather than predatory.

> Three Dog Night is not just a '70s rock band. It was a phrase used by aborigines in the Australian outback to describe a very cold night. On a one-dog night, the temperature wasn't too frigid and you'd need to snuggle up against only one dog. But on a three-dog night, you'd need to huddle with three dogs to keep warm.

26. *Takes food out of his bowl and then goes into another room to eat it.* Many dogs engage in bizarre behaviors around the food bowl. Some will lift one or more pieces of kibble out of it and position them "strategically" before going back to eat them. Others snatch the food and go to a different area before eating it. It is thought that a dog who sees himself as relatively low in the pack order may be more inclined to move his food around out of fear that some alpha dog might come and take away his meal. Perhaps in the wild, he would have waited his turn in line to grab his share of the kill, then run away to protect his allotment from any potential usurpers. Call it a little paranoia, if you will.

27. *Hides treats rather than eating or chewing on them.* A typical instance of this behavior is a dog burying bones. Going back to nature, if you're a dog and you're currently replete but you don't know where your next meal is coming from, you might stash some food as rations to be consumed at a later time. You'll always be able to locate the food with your keen sense of smell.

28. *"Runs" in his sleep.* With that slight paddling of limbs some dogs experience while sleeping, it is believed they are dreaming about precisely what you might think they're dreaming about—chasing a squirrel or some other creature. Your pup could even be revisiting some great memory of the previous day, when he ran a rodent up a tree.

29. *Wags his tail.* Many people think a wagging tail is a friendly sign, and it can be—but it isn't always. The best way to think of a dog's tail and its side-to-side motion is as an energy indicator. When a dog's energy level is up or when he's excited, his tail will wag fast. When he's interested but not fully engaged, it may wag slowly. Then, as he becomes progressively more riveted or excited, his tail will wag progressively faster. Think of the tail as you would a car's tachometer. It indicates how fast the animal is revving internally. Now, that can be happy revving or frightened revving or conflicted revving. In other words, fast and furious tail wagging could mean the dog is "locked and loaded" and ready to charge. The wagging has to be interpreted circumstantially.

30. *Puts his tail between his legs.* This means submission and is an effort at appeasement. The dog is not at all sure of himself in a particular situation.

31. *Sets his tail bolt upright.* A dog who stiffens his tail into an upright position is showing confidence, even dominance. It's a very forward, confident position. Some dogs, such as chows, were bred to *always* have their tails up in order to always look masterful and in charge

A pup with an upright tail (or as upright as it can be) is a confident pup.

32. *Chews socks or slippers.* A dog's gotta chew what a dog's gotta chew. If you haven't supplied him with appropriate chew toys, he will turn something else into his chewing gum. (Don't run around all agitated trying to get the item of clothing back. The dog will think the two of you are having a game of Keep Away.)

NOTE: Some dogs don't just chew. They swallow—dirty socks, wash rags, pantyhose, and other personal effects. That can cause intestinal obstructions, symptoms of which include vomiting, loss of electrolytes, or shock; it can even cause death. If you see that your dog might be a swallower of such items, eliminate access to them. Otherwise, you'll end up with expensive surgery bills to remove the swallowed fare. And we mean bill*s*, not one bill. Dogs who swallow small articles of clothing do not learn from experience that their actions lead to unpleasant and sometimes dangerous ends.

33. *Sniffs people in the groin area.* A dog can tell an awful lot about a person from one hit of the odor of pheromones coming from that part of the body. Even if you've just bathed, a dog can "read" you, to the point of being able to detect differences between identical twins. He might even be able to tell whether you're afraid or whether you're a super-alpha with a lot of testosterone—a force to be reckoned with.

34. *Shakes toys back and forth in his mouth.* Like digging, this harks back to the appetitive phase of predatory behavior. A dog will shake the neck of his prey in order to kill it.

35. *Keeps the hair on his back standing on end.* Called piloerection, this is sort of like goose bumps. It's not something a dog can control. Consider that a dog's hairs have little piloerectile muscles attached to them. When his sympathetic nervous system, involved in fight-or-flight reactions, releases epinephrine, these muscles contract, in turn raising the hairs. It is assumed that nature programmed dogs to raise their hackles when faced with danger in order to make them look bigger and fiercer. A dog's hair will also stand on end when he is very, very cold. Again, the sympathetic nervous system kicks in, this time to help the dog burn fuel faster, but the muscle-contracting action in the hair takes place, too. When the hair stands up, an insulating layer of air gets trapped between hair shafts, so the cold air cannot get so close to the skin. It works like a down jacket.

7

Young Dogs and Young Children Under the Same Roof

NOTHING MAKES A BETTER KODAK MOMENT THAN A CHILD AND A PUPPY engaged in a high-spirited round of giggles and licks. And often, youngsters of the two species get on just that splendidly. But for such a wonderful relationship to develop and be sustained, the puppy's space must be respected at the same time that a child is given leeway to explore his or her world.

The child cannot create that balance on her own. Neither can the dog. It's *your* role to make it happen. This chapter will focus on how you should broker diplomatic relations between your young human charges and your young canine charge. Get it right and your dog will be thrilled to greet your child when he comes home from school, stay by his side when he's feeling sad, and miss him when he goes off to college. Likewise, your child will be there for your dog by stroking or playing with her when she needs attention or reassurance.

Of course, by facilitating mutual respect, you'll also keep the two of them from ever causing each other harm, accidentally or otherwise. For better or worse, puppies become adult dogs who can nip or bite if they feel threatened, and smaller children become bigger children who can harm a dog in myriad ways, often inadvertently. You want to develop an abundance of trust and good feelings in both directions from the beginning; this is a relationship that is meant to last a long time.

CHILDREN UP TO AGE SIX: THINK TWICE

Many families like the idea of their children growing up with a dog. So when the children are very young, they bring home a puppy. There's nothing inherently wrong with that. But it adds greatly to the responsibility of the adults in the household, especially if the youngest child is an infant or toddler. Not only do very small children require a lot of attention, but puppies also need a considerable amount of care for proper development. Since the parents of infants and toddlers are often sleep deprived, that makes caring for the new puppy all the more difficult. You need to decide whether you're up to raising two "babies" at the same time.

It's not just about walking the dog and feeding her. Someone has to make time to socialize her, coddle her, train her, and housetrain her, all while remaining patient.

Compounding the effort is that a child younger than six and a dog should **never** be left alone together, no matter how gentle the dog and no matter how sweet the child. We cannot stress this enough. Even the most wonderful, well-behaved baby or preschooler in the world, as yours most certainly is, can end up causing a puppy or an older dog harm, no matter how much you instruct him to treat the dog right.

An infant who's crawling around will probably think nothing of startling a sleeping dog by bumping right into her. When the baby is a little older, he may want to press the dog's eyeballs to see if they're squidgy, like his teddy bear's. Once he starts running around, he may think it's fun to turn the hose on the dog, because he thinks it's fun when the hose is turned on *him*. He may want to play with one of the dog's toys. What's the difference, he might surmise. They're all toys, aren't they?

Vulnerable puppies younger than five months sometimes even die at the hands of children—normal, loved children, not just cruel children who are treated cruelly themselves. Small children don't understand the concept of death and don't understand that, say, forcing a pup into a box without any air can cause her demise and that death is irreversible.

Once a puppy reaches nine or ten months of age, it's the children who are in danger—of consequences resulting from their unintentionally threat-

A six-year-old boy and his newborn springer spaniel.

ening behavior. A young pup only five months old doesn't normally pose much of a threat. But by the time a pup is ten months old, particularly if she's a dominant sort, she can deliver her first serious bite—perhaps even necessitating a trip to the hospital emergency room.

A pup—or older dog—of bossy, dominant persuasion will not hurt a child out of left field. Only under provocation will she stand her ground— and sometimes use the language of aggression, if necessary. The difficulty is that what a dog finds provoking may not be meant as an affront. The child simply doesn't have the ability to distinguish between appropriate and provocative, triggering behavior. It's up to you to "translate" for puppy and child so neither ends up assaulted.

It's not always an obvious translation, like explaining that trapping a puppy in a box or trying to poke her eyes can harm her. For instance, young children often like to hug dogs around the neck, as they would hug a person. But a dog may see that as threatening and could respond accordingly. That doesn't make the dog bad. It makes her a dog.

The Golden Retriever from Connecticut

A lovely-looking golden retriever was adopted by a family in Connecticut with two children, ages ten and eight. Every morning, as the children readied themselves for school, the dog was tied up in the hallway.

One day, one of the children went over to hug the dog and kiss him on the nose, which a dog is more likely to perceive as a threat or challenge than affection. The dog bit him on the forehead, hard enough to draw blood.

The entire state of Connecticut became involved. The authorities were called in, the story appeared on the news, and even the governor and state attorney general weighed in.

It was decided that the dog's owners — and the children — should be taught a leadership program that involved not only training the dog to respect them but also showing respect for the dog. In addition, a gate was put between the dog and the children each

morning as they hurried to leave for school.

But one morning, one of the children's friends was over. While the parents were otherwise occupied, he bent over the barrier and, trying to be friendly, leaned right into the dog's face. The dog, seeing the move as an invasion of his personal space, bit the boy so hard on the face that he needed plastic surgery. The dog was then put down.

Whose fault was it? Not the dog's, even though he paid with his life, and not the children's, but the parents'. A dog who has already shown some serious aggression cannot be left unsupervised for *any* length of time with a child of grade school age, especially a child who has not been taught appropriate behavior around canines. Moreover, a dog who shows dominant, aggressive tendencies and a lack of tolerance (gleaned from temperament testing or history) is probably not the best dog to bring into a home with children in the first place.

It's your responsibility to make sure such untoward interactions don't occur. Unfortunately, when they do, it's the dog who too often ends up paying the price for aggression that comes as a result of a child's unwanted advances. We heard tell of one Saint Bernard who was euthanized because he bit a child, but on postmortem it was found that a pencil had been driven through the dog's eardrum into his middle ear.

The message here: Even a very tolerant, docile dog who has never shown any aggressive behavior in the past cannot be counted on to let a child's transgressions go 100 percent of the time. You just never know. That's why, if the doorbell rings or someone comes to the back door, you can't walk out of the room and leave your young child and your dog alone together for a minute. What if you have a baby and he crawls over to the dog to try to kiss her on the muzzle? Or ride her like a horse? Think of it the way you would think of a pot of boiling water on the stove or an unprotected outlet. You wouldn't leave your infant, toddler, or nursery schooler alone for even a second with either of those, and you should think of a small child and a dog together as the same kind of recipe for disaster. If you must be out of the room, take your child with you or secure your dog in her crate (or an exercise pen).

Rules Regarding Infants and Young Toddlers

While you should never leave a child under six and a pup or older dog alone together, there's much you can do to bring them together in a good relationship right from the start—or at least from the time your child is about eight months old and crawling, which is when order in the dog's world is first threatened.

For the infant, older baby, or young toddler who doesn't yet have the ability to act on what you say, the object when the child and the dog are sharing space under your supervision is simply to reduce the potential for conflict. That means:

1. Don't let your son or daughter eat on the run. Small children are very much at a dog's eye level, and a cookie or a small piece of chicken or hamburger meat flying by could prove too tempting to your canine friend and might promote a confrontation that results in injury to your child.

2. Don't let your small child near the dog when the dog is eating.

3. Keep child toys and dog toys separate. How? Bring out the puppy's toys only if you are certain you can keep the child from being able to get to them. It's too hard—and useless—to keep telling a small child, especially one who is preverbal, that the colorful, squeaky, fuzzy toys are not his but someone else's. And you certainly don't want the dog telling him. To keep the pup from thinking the child's toys are hers, dab each of them periodically with some clean-smelling antiseptic. To a dog, with his supersense of smell, the odor will be as pungent as the odor of peeling onions is to a human. Large plastic toys can periodically be put into a bathtub with diluted antiseptic (which, besides making the dog go "Yuck," will help make the toys germ-free).

4. Be certain the pup can always retreat to her own personal space—her crate or dog bed (in an out-of-the-way spot that is off-limits to children). That gives her time to collect herself calmly and take a breather should she wish to temporarily escape the child's squeaky ways and quick, unnerving movements.

5. Don't let the dog on high places, such as the couch or bed. Being up high increases the dog's confidence—and likelihood of aggression—should the child frighten her or get on her nerves.

Training Your Older Toddler or Preschooler

If you bring a puppy to a home with an older toddler or a three-, four-, or five-year-old, you can take some very carefully controlled steps beyond the conflict avoidance steps intended for babies. These steps will help pave the way to a positive relationship between the child and the dog that eventually flourishes. First, explain to the child that the puppy is a *baby* and needs to be dealt with very gently. Children who are not far from babyhood themselves will get that.

Second, teach preschoolers to address the puppy calmly, billing and cooing and petting her in the same direction that her hair grows. If you feel your child can handle holding the puppy (which most children will probably want to do), have your youngster sit down to steady himself; young dogs can really wiggle around. As you're putting the puppy into the child's arms, explain that the pup has to be cradled from underneath. "Don't drop her," you'll want to say. "Handle her like crystal."

You should also explain to your child not to hug the pup around her neck, surprise her from behind, wag a finger at her, stare directly at her (even young pups see that as threatening), or bother her when she's sleeping or eating. And, if you're allowing your child to give the pup a treat, make sure your

Growl, Snap, or Bite?

Starting at about the age of five months, a puppy shows whether she's feeling aggressive, and just how aggressive, through various signals. A growl is the least aggressive signal, but it does mean "Knock it off" and that things will get worse if the warning is ignored. As soon as your child is old enough to understand that, teach it to her.

At the next level is a growl combined with a vertical lift of the lip. Beyond that, if the dog feels put upon enough, she will snap, and finally may bite. An easygoing, tolerant dog may never advance to even a snap. A dominant one may skip over the growl. Having a dominant, or willful, dog in the house with a child under six is tricky to manage.

"Handle her like crystal."

little one keeps it in an open palm from which the dog can easily scoop it up. When dogs go to take a treat from children's fingers, the children often get nervous and back away, which can cause a dog to think there's play involved and then run or jump at the child.

Of course, treat giving, holding, and everything else is *always* happening in your presence when your child is younger than six. Should things start to go awry, you need to be there to correct the problem or separate the two.

You can tell your older preschooler, too, that "when Lucy goes into her crate, that's her own room. Leave her alone." (Then make sure the dog *is* left alone.) You can also keep your young child from acting like too much of a whirling dervish in front of the pup, at least to some degree. The quick, jerky moves that small children make, and the way they run rather than walk, is somewhat similar to the behavior of dogs' natural prey. Your dog may even respond playfully to such behavior, chasing and jumping, but that could still end up in a child's unfortunate spill, perhaps even in a nip.

All of this controlling of the child on your part will let the puppy realize that when children are around, nothing bad happens, and sometimes even good things happen, like petting and treats. That will make the dog less disposed to react negatively to your child should he frighten or bother her without meaning to.

CHILDREN SIX OR OLDER

Once they start school, many children have a way of charging into the house with a pack of similar-age kids. They act boisterously, dart around, speak loudly—in short, they act like children. Your dog will range from not being thrilled about all the racket to taking it as a personal challenge that she has to do something about, particularly if a group of second-graders all come clamoring in together because Bobby or Susie wants to show them the new puppy or older dog.

Don't let a bunch of young friends descend on the dog all at once. You must be there to supervise, even if your child brings home only one other friend. If you feel it's okay for the friend (or small group of friends) to pet

Kids can learn to give a treat, too. (Better if the child offers it from an open palm so the pup can easily scoop it up.)

Which Dog Is Right for Your Family?

There is no surefire formula for making certain that the dog you choose for a household with children will turn out to be a perfect fit. But you can take steps to greatly increase the odds that things will work out well.

If you have a child younger than six who is bent on having a canine companion, you may want to give serious consideration to getting a dog who is no longer a puppy. There are two advantages. First, while an adult dog will need time and attention to acclimate to your home and your way of doing things, she will need a lot less training and supervision than a pup. After all, she is already housetrained and is probably familiar with mealtimes, car rides, and most of life's other everyday events.

The other advantage to getting an adult dog, or at least an older pup, is that temperament testing—along with her prior history—will tell you a lot about her personality. With a young pup, it will only let you hazard a guess about how her personality might turn out. The older the dog, the more it's true that what you see is what you get. Thus, by having your child interact with an older dog you've set your sights on, you can make sure to choose a dog who gets on well with children.

Let's say you're at a pound or shelter. As your child passes the various dogs, keep your eye out for one who comes to the front of the cage eagerly as you approach. See how the dog reacts when you instruct your child to walk toward the cage. If it goes well —the dog seems happy and friendly—you may have a keeper. If not—the dog tenses and raises her tail stiffly, backs away, or seems uninterested—you can move on before engaging in further temperament testing. Some dogs are simply much more sanguine than others about children's quick, in-your-face movements and high squeals.

Beyond the dog's age, consider breed. No single dog, no matter what the breed, is a sure bet for anything. There are cranky golden retrievers from the usually family-loving sporting group and loving, nurturing Akitas. But Akitas, rottweilers, and other breeds from the working group (see page 13) are not immediately what come to mind when you think of family-minded pets whose fondest wish is to treat the children in your home solicitously. Neither are dogs from the nonsporting group: bulldogs, Shar-Peis, chow chows, American Eskimos, and the like.

Coming at it from the other direction, a child, even a small one, can do great harm to a toy dog, as we said in chapter 1. A toddle that turns into a fall could easily lead to serious injury in a dog like a Maltese terrier, and very small dogs may have a hard time coping with the rough-and-tumble play that is part and parcel of childhood, especially when the children in the house bring other children home.

Dogs with a high predatory drive can be a mixed bag when mixed with young children.

continued on page 145

your pup or older dog, keep it all gentle, soft, and on the quiet side. Perhaps have the child sit cross-legged on the floor. Give the child a treat to drop at the dog's feet without looking at her. Remember, while children will almost never experience an unprecedented advance from a dog, dogs experience unprecedented advances from children all the time. They deserve to be protected from the onslaughts.

Once children reach an age at which they can truly be reasoned with and take direction, they are ready to begin developing a relationship with the family dog that doesn't always include you as chaperone. (For some children, that age is six; for others it's seven or older. Know your child.) That doesn't mean your work is done. You have to *teach* children appropriate ways of interacting with a dog. You have to teach them how to be the dog's leader.

Yes, you read that correctly. When a child is about six years old, he or she is ready to begin engaging in the kind of leadership that adults do. That doesn't mean you should ever buy a dog "for the kids." Dogs are *family* pets, and *you* will always be the primary caretaker. Children, until their early teens, don't have the full capacity to take care of all of a dog's needs, especially a puppy's, and older teenagers often don't want to. They're off socializing. But once children are in grade school, they can be taught a lot of the leadership responsibilities we discussed in previous chapters.

For instance, children in grade school can gradually be included in chores that involve meeting the dog's needs, which is very much a part of leadership. They can feed her at mealtime and periodically replenish her water bowl. Nothing suggests "leader" to a dog more than the say-so about when and what she gets fed.

A young child can also help make sure the dog gets enough exercise, engage in some simple grooming by brushing the dog, and perhaps help you pick up the dog's toys or scoop up poop. A dog may not recognize all of these things as leadership, but a child will most certainly begin to get the sense that he is in charge of the situation.

Another way to reinforce a child's leadership status is to have her teach the dog to respond to one-word commands, such as "Sit." (A perfect time for that particular command is mealtime, when a dog must be respectful. This will make the child's leadership role that much clearer.)

It may take a little doing. The child has to be taught to command in a clear, confident voice while standing. And you have to be right there to make sure things go right but not make eye contact with the dog or otherwise deal

Which Dog Is Right for Your Family?, continued from page 143

A dog with a high predatory or herding drive may chase children in the yard or try to corral them.

On one hand, their own high energy level will be right in line with that of the children. But when the little ones are running around playing cops and robbers, or riding their bikes, these dogs with a drive to catch prey may chase after them and nip them, sometimes even bite them. Movement is the essential ingredient for trouble. Children's high-pitched squeals don't help, either.

Thus, when children are running or jumping around and screeching, you may have to engage in some serious obedience work. Stay calm, keep the dog at a distance from the kids, and make sure she does not chase after them. If after a few sessions she's able to stay put on her own, great. If not, keep such a high-predatory-drive dog in the house or in her crate while the children are moving about or on their bicycles or scooters.

Once you've set your sights on a particular dog (if you choose a puppy, maybe her first eight weeks were spent at a house with children who have been trained to respect pets), temperament testing really is important, no matter what the breed. Dogs who exhibit will-

continued on page 147

When children reach the age of six, you can begin engaging them in a leadership program with the family dog, which entails handing over some responsibility. That creates an opportunity for stronger bonding.

with her directly, so that the interaction really is between child and puppy. The child also has to be taught to praise the pup when she follows through, just as you would.

Having the child teach the dog tricks is a great idea, too. One, if it doesn't conflict with your sensibilities, is "Bang." The child says "Bang" while pointing at the dog, and the dog rolls over and sticks her feet in the air. That's also a submissive behavior and one that lends itself to belly rubbing. If the child follows through with underside petting, it will strengthen the child-puppy bond that much more. (More on the ins and outs of training in the next chapter.)

Which Dog Is Right for Your Family?, *continued from page 145*

fulness are the ones most likely to bite a child later on—yours or one who comes over to play—if they perceive themselves to be threatened or under attack. A calm dog who tolerates your turning her over on her back and doesn't startle easily is a better bet. (If you're adopting an older dog, ask the staff at the shelter or pound whether the dog has a nipping, mouthing tendency or has displayed any other aggressive behavior.)

A dog of a timid or fearful nature will probably grant your own child diplomatic immunity. That is, a fearful dog, almost always, will not act aggressively toward anyone in the family. She will simply move to another spot if bothered. But that doesn't protect your children's *friends*. Fearful dogs, in their anxiety, can act aggressively toward strangers who scare them or invade their space, so you must *always* be there to supervise when your child brings friends home, even if the children are older than six. Don't make the incorrect assumption that because your fearful pet is gentle with her own young family member, she will be able to remain gentle with other youngsters—especially if they have not been taught, like yours has, to treat the dog respectfully and give her her space when she wants it.

Note: Dogs with testicles and children do not go together, period. No matter what the dog's general proclivities and no matter what the breed, unneutered male dogs as a group are responsible for the most bites. If there are children in the house, most definitely get your male dog fixed before he's six months old and his hormones have fueled his more aggressive side.

Tricks serve a crucial purpose. They teach a dog to listen, respond, and respect a child rather than simply tolerate one. Even a dog who has been there since she and the child were both babies will think to herself, "I thought you were below me or equal to me in the pack order. But I have to work for you, too. I have to sit when you say to, come when you command it, and eat when you are satisfied with my sitting performance." That alteration in the dog's thinking, coupled with the child's increasing ability to take charge in matters concerning the dog and to understand that the dog must be treated respectfully, will make it safer and safer over time for the two to be together without your being there to police the situation. What started out as giggles and licks can become walks in the woods, quiet time at home together, play time together with a Frisbee or other toy, and, thrown into the bargain, the child's opportunity to learn a lot about loyalty, responsibility, love, and follow-through.

WHEN THE DOG IS THERE FIRST

Frequently, it's not the puppy being brought to a household with a child but a newborn coming to a home that already has an older puppy or adult dog. That's fine, particularly before the baby starts to crawl. The natural instinct of a dog toward a pack member—certainly a *new* pack member—is to protect. It's true of both puppies and adult dogs.

Granted, a dominant dog, after she satisfies her initial curiosity by sniffing the baby and seeing that he just lies there, probably won't care less and will just ignore the new child. She's not going to take a particularly active role. A more family-oriented dog, on the other hand, might hang out with you as you feed and cuddle your infant.

We were acquainted with one older dog, a mixed breed, who was there to welcome a new baby the day he came home from the hospital—and then kept him out of harm's way when he was an eighteen-month-old toddler. His mother was on the second floor of their home folding laundry when the dog, on the first floor, ran to the bottom of the staircase and let out several insistent, high-pitched barks that she had never sounded before. The mother ran down the stairs to find that her toddler had been able to get past her, make his way down the stairs, and, for the first time, push open the sliders leading from the kitchen to the backyard. Because of the dog's quick thinking, the mother caught up to her son while he was running down the driveway toward the street, which was busy enough to have two solid yellow lines running down the middle of it.

Not all dogs will develop that kind of a relationship with your child as he grows from infancy into toddlerhood, but most won't cause problems for a new addition to your family, either. Pretty much the only kind of dog you have to worry about when bringing home a newborn is one who is at least six months old and has a very high prey drive. You can tell whether that's the case if your pet goes crazy chasing squirrels or was bred to hunt or herd other animals or can chase a ball practically nonstop. If all three are true of your dog, her prey drive is probably *very* high. And in very, very rare instances, such dogs fail to recognize the newborn as a member of the pack in its first month of life, mistakenly identifying the crying baby as wounded prey. The high-pitched sound and flailing arms and legs cause the confusion.

The result can be fatal to the child, which is why it's crucial, just as with any other dog, that a very predatory one never be left alone with a newly arrived infant, for the first month at least. That's when just about all the un-

The dog here kept this boy out of a busy road when the lad was a toddler. Now of school age, the boy can return the affection.

fortunate attacks occur (most occur within the first week of the first month). The dog is not acting aggressively or angrily. She's just acting on a primordial urge, the way dogs do when going after prey.

Along with never leaving the baby and the dog alone, including at night, you must have supervised interaction between the two so your pet will see that the newcomer is very much part of the pack. *All* dogs benefit from supervised interaction with a newborn, not just predatory ones. It lets them know they're not being pushed aside.

Allow the dog to sniff the baby; it's her way of identifying the child. Pet the dog, too, while the baby is around and speak gently to her, perhaps offering a food treat as well. Your warm treatment will cue the dog in that having the baby nearby means things will go well for her. She'll be *glad* for you to take care of the baby, because she'll associate it with attention directed toward herself as well. (The parents of the toddler who ran down the driveway always took care to make their dog feel special around their child and treat her kindly from the time the baby first came home.)

TOP: Let your dog sniff your newborn. They'll become better friends that way.
BOTTOM: Don't wait to put the baby in the crib before you pay attention to your dog. You don't want her thinking good things happen only when the baby is out of the way. That'll make her start to resent the little one.

Biting Statistics

An estimated 4.7 million dog bites occur each year in the United States, affecting almost 2 percent of Americans. Medical attention is sought for half a million to a million dog bites annually. Most bites are sustained by children younger than fifteen, and children are at least three times more likely to experience a medically attended bite than adults. One reason, presumably, is that while most adults are bitten on their arms or legs, 70 percent of dog bite injuries to children involve the head, neck, or face. Children's heads are much closer to dogs' faces.

Boys in all age groups are more likely to be bitten than girls, but boys ages five through nine have the highest incidence of all (occurrences increase as boys progress in age from five through nine). The average for the five-to-nine age range is sixty-one bites for every ten thousand boys.

Just as boys are most likely to be bitten, male dogs are the most likely to bite. Breeds currently high on the list for bites (the list fluctuates some) include German shepherds, pit bulls, and chow chows. Others include rottweilers, Husky types, malamutes, Doberman pinschers, Saint Bernards, Great Danes, and Akitas.

In 25 to 33 percent of cases, a sizable fraction, a dog bites someone in the family. But the majority of bites come from dogs belonging to other households (not from strays). Children should be taught as young as possible how to avoid conflict with any non-family-member canine. What to tell them?

1. Stay away from strange dogs.

2. Dogs locked in a yard or chained up are more inclined to bite.

3. If a dog backs away from you, leave her alone. She is afraid and could turn aggressive to protect herself.

4. If you ask someone whether you may pet his or her dog and the answer is yes, make sure the dog sees you before you pet her, and don't stare directly at her.

5. *Stroke* the side of a dog's head; *don't pat* her on the top of her head.

6. Never disturb a sleeping or eating dog or one caring for her puppies.

7. If an unfamiliar dog comes up to you, stand still, with your arms down at your sides. Slowly turn sideways. Do not run.

8. If a dog does attack you, give her your bike, backpack, baseball mitt, jacket, or anything else to chew on. Slowly back away until there is a tree, bench, car, or other large object between the two of you.

9. If a dog knocks you down, roll up into a ball, put your arms in front of your face, and lie perfectly still. Chances are that she will finally just walk away.

What you should never do, although it can be easy to fall into this pattern, is ignore the dog all day and then try to make it up to her at night, when the baby might sleep for a few hours at a time. That only sets the stage for "sibling" rivalry, making the dog feel she gets short shrift whenever the baby's around and is treated well only when that "squirmy thing" is out of sight.

Finally, try as much as you possibly can not to depart from the dog's routine. You'll be tired and certainly will have your hands full with a new baby, but the more you can stick to the dog's usual time of being walked and fed, the less resentment you'll breed in your canine companion, and the more disposed she will be to take the baby's infractions lightly once he starts crawling.

The boy and his springer spaniel from the beginning of the chapter — four years later.

ALWAYS KEEP SOCIALIZATION FRONT AND CENTER

The backdrop against all of your good intentions and all of your efforts to make things work between your dog and your children is a combination of proper socialization and training. We have devoted entire chapters to each of those, but they become all the more important once a child is involved.

If, from the very beginning, you socialize a pup with all kinds of people of all shapes, sizes, and ages, she will be more inclined to tolerate an active or screaming child. She'll be calm and confident that people, even young ones, are good and that you will protect her from harm.

Training, discussed at length in the next chapter, is crucial, too, because in the event of a standoff, you want to be able to successfully command your dog to immediately stop whatever aggressive behavior she appears to be getting ready to engage in. In addition, by being firm and consistent with your commands rather than slacking off, you will keep your pet from developing unwanted pushiness or dominance.

The dog needs to be occupied as well as properly trained. Make sure she gets plenty of exercise and time for play and other interactions. A bored dog who hasn't spent her energy is a dog who is more likely to get into mischief, including mischief involving children. (More on doggie boredom and how to alleviate it in chapter 11.)

Finally, whether children are already in the house or will be at some point in the future, be relatively gentle with the dog. Don't teach her aggressive rough-housing behaviors through such games as tug of war with a stuffed toy. Instead, get her super-comfortable with submissive moves. Teach a long Down-Stay. Have her roll on cue for a belly-scratching session.

Admittedly, it doesn't always work out. Some dogs are just never going to get on well with children. But in the vast majority of cases, by teaching your child and puppy all we've recommended in this chapter, you are ensuring that they will be the best, most enduring of friends—just the way you meant them to be when you decided to bring them together.

PART 4

Sit! and Other Tricks

8

Training Your Pup

YOUR TWO-MONTH-OLD PUPPY HAS BEEN IN YOUR HOUSE JUST A DAY OR two. You're both very excited about the new circumstances, and your motivation to bond with him is high, while his is high to interact with you. That makes it a perfect time to start training him. Successful training leaves both human and dog with a great sense of accomplishment, which in turn strengthens the bond between them. Training is, after all, a way of communicating with your pup; you want him to do something, and he learns to do it. And just as two people feel closer when they are able to "get through" to each other, so do a person and a pup.

Training also keeps your puppy safe. Imagine, for instance, that you and your pup are walking to the parking lot at the edge of the park after he has had a romp off leash. Just as you reach the car-park asphalt, another dog starts barking at him from the window of his own car. Your pup starts tearing toward him, too excited to realize that a vehicle is backing up into his path. But if he's properly trained, he will be able to follow your training cue —"Leave it" or "Come"—to stay out of harm's way.

Training works wonders for keeping your puppy well behaved, too. Let's say your puppy barks like a coyote on a moonlit night every time someone knocks or the doorbell rings. It not only scares people. It's also driving you crazy. With proper training, you can get him to knock off the racket. Likewise for taking walks with your puppy. He may want to pull and tug on the leash to the point that outdoor romps are not fun for either of you, and you find yourself taking him less and less. But training your pup allows you to work out a walking routine that you can both enjoy.

Of course, training is also just plain fun. The average dog is capable of learning fifty to a hundred words. Thus, you can break the language barrier between the two of you, allowing for remarkably effective communication. In research in Germany a couple of years ago, scientists found that a Border collie they were studying had learned two hundred words, including the names of dozens of play toys—and was able to find and bring from another room the one his owner told him to. He was also able to learn the name of a new toy within a single training session, exhibiting a vocabulary about the same size as that of apes, dolphins, and parrots.

Another benefit of training: It helps establish you as the leader. When the puppy does what you want, he is rewarded with food, one of his toys, or your loving praise or petting. When he doesn't, there is no reward. In other words, he knows which side his bread is buttered on. It's one of the

You won't be afraid to let a well-trained pup off leash sometimes.

three Fs of puppy training. It should all be *Fun* and *Fair*, but you also have to add the other component: *Firm*. That is, you hold the line, not wavering, so that your pup understands you mean what you say (*without* being mean).

Training does even more than make clear that you are the leader and strengthen the bond between you and your puppy. It also ensures that your pup will have a better life. Why? When you train, you're insisting that your puppy show good manners. That, in turn, ensures that you'll like having him around. You won't be nervous when people come over that he will scare them or otherwise make them uncomfortable, say, by sniffing where he shouldn't. You'll also enjoy taking him out. You'll know he won't run off when you don't want him to or act inappropriately toward people or other dogs. Thus, you'll be more likely to let him hang around when company comes over, take him on trips, visit friends' houses with him, let him run free on the beach, hike with you in the woods, and so on. He'll end up living much more socially engaged than if you felt you had to leave him at home all the time because he was a law unto himself.

Of course, it will work out better for you, too. After all, you wanted a dog in the first place so that you could enjoy the companionship, not so that you would constantly have to leave him out of the action for fear he'd scare or harm someone or something.

The amazing part is that you can reap all the benefits of training by engaging in training sessions with your new pup for just ten to fifteen minutes each day. Moreover, training sessions can—and should—be broken into quick, two- to five-minute intervals. Puppies have short attention spans. They can't even follow their own instincts for long, chasing a squirrel or some other small animal for only about two minutes.

But just how do you get through to a young puppy, teaching him not to chew through electric cords, to refrain from jumping on visitors, and to keep him from dragging *you* around on the leash?

ALWAYS POSITIVE, ALWAYS GENTLE

The trick of training, in large part, is to keep it full of mirth, making it a good time that the two of you share rather than like onerous homework that neither of you wants to attend to. We can't stress this point enough.

Training sessions should consistently be fun-filled occasions, with the object to keep puppy's self-esteem and confidence high as he learns. Think of teaching a small child to ride a bicycle. You would never try to make him feel bad if he had difficulty getting the hang of it. That would only render him less inclined to keep trying. Instead, you would let him know by your tone that having a little trouble up front is just part of the process, and you'd praise him as warmly and enthusiastically as possible when he began to pedal without your holding the back of the bicycle seat. Similarly, you'd take him out for a lesson only when both of you were up to it. You wouldn't push him too hard, and you wouldn't expect yourself to conduct a bike-riding lesson immediately after you yourself had had a bad day or had run into some vexing snafu.

It's the same with you and your young canine charge. You should engage your pup in training sessions only when you are in a good mood. If you're feeling like it's going to be drudgery, say, because you're very tired or pre-occupied, your lessons are not going to come across well. Wait until you can bring positive energy to a session that will prove infectious for puppy rather than go through the motions simply because you know the dog should have

The Unfortunate Popularity of Punishment-Based Training

There are a lot of misconceptions about proper training, in no small part because of currently popular television shows that preach and illustrate inappropriate and cruel techniques involving large doses of physical punishment—dragging and popping dogs with choke chains and such.

These harsh training methods for pet dogs emerged after World War II. Military dog trainers during the war employed all kinds of aversive techniques—chain jerking, prong collars, and so on. The aim wasn't to keep the dogs happy while teaching them to be obedient. It was to get them to perform various maneuvers to help win the war. The emotional impact was secondary; the animals were not pets.

After the war, people who had been star military trainers and were now out of work trained other trainers for a living, and so a hard line was promulgated in the pet dog training arena. It circulates even to this day, purveyed by some who train dogs on television as well as at commercial dog training centers. Euphemistic names abound, like Canine University, Canine Academy, and Canine Learning Center. Don't let the authoritative-sounding names fool you.

Trainers who believe in physical, or corporal, punishment and other aspects of harsh training say it's the only way you can get a dog to respond reliably. Their general philosophy is that you can train a dog to do tricks with respectful training but if you want a dog

x minutes of training per day. Your best teachers in junior high and high school, you will recall, were fully engaged and excited to be there, and you learned better because of their enthusiasm and the fact that they *entertained* you as they taught. The ones who were just biding their time probably left you uninterested and disinclined to pay much attention.

It's not just you who has to be up for training. The puppy has to be in the right mood, too. If he's bursting with energy because he hasn't gotten to go out all day, it's going to be much harder to get him to obey commands like "Sit," which requires a sedentary response. Likewise, if he's very tired after hours of running around, he simply may not have the energy left to learn. He may need to rest now and learn later.

Also crucial to the training process is rewarding your puppy for complying with your commands — with delectable food treats, warm praise, petting, and sometimes all of these at the same time. That way, you're reinforcing his correct responses.

The Unfortunate Popularity of Punishment-Based Training, continued from page 160

continued from page 160

to obey you all of the time, you must be the "alpha" and punishment must be part of the process.

They are dead wrong, no matter how confident they may appear about their misguided and mishandled methods. More than half the people who end up bringing their dogs to our Behavior Clinic tell us the professional training their pets received was harsh. They are at our clinic because something has gone awry — their pets have become scared, nervous, and often aggressive and unable to listen, and they need to fix the problem.

Why? Jerking a collar or otherwise punishing a dog, with choke or prong collars, for instance, or hitting under the chin, is like physically abusing a child. Such an unenlightened, anti-intellectual approach might be able to get the young charge not to do something, but it has other effects, too. Are those effects — increased anxiety and potentially more aggression, not to mention abject misery — what you want for your dog? Watching a dog comply in fear may make for good television ratings, but it doesn't teach anything about how you should treat him or about how he can learn to go along with your wishes over the long run.

Turn your back on such outmoded training behaviors, decried not only by us but by qualified behaviorists everywhere. Scientific evidence shows that physical punishment creates, not resolves, problems. Thus, we believe you should train your puppy in a way that shows respect and love through the teaching. *That's* the kind of training that will stick with him rather than lose momentum whenever you're not punishing.

Never punish your dog for not following through. That teaches him nothing. It will only make him less trusting of you and distract from whatever you're trying to teach. If, for instance, a pup is punished for not sitting, the training session is no longer about learning to sit when you tell him to. It's about the consequences of *not* sitting. The emphasis shifts from where you want it to be. In short, far better to teach a pup what *to* do (which is the basis of positive training) than punish him for *not* doing something, with all of its negative connotations.

Worse still, punishment undermines a puppy's confidence. Most pups do want to please their owners and reap the rewards of their successful efforts. But who can learn how to do things properly when he's being yelled at during the learning process—or worse, hit, or jerked around by a chain?

One way to make sure that you will never punish, even with harsh words, is by continually reminding yourself not to expect too much too fast. Patience is key. This is not to say that you aren't going to get results quickly. You will. As you will see, your pup is going to learn the command "Sit" within the first couple of minutes of your first training session (although repetition and reward are what will make it stick). Likewise for "Down" and some other simple commands. But keep in mind that even though a puppy can learn from the time you bring him home at eight to ten weeks of age because his brain is like a sponge at that stage, he's still a baby. Training sessions, especially as they involve more complicated cues and as they move to situations outside the house where there are more distractions, are not going to happen without setbacks, plateaus, and so on.

If you do find yourself ready to lose patience, it's time to stop the training session. One reason is that if you're feeling exasperated, you're focused on your frustration, not the goal—getting the puppy to sit, lie down, come to you, or whatever. Furthermore, it's not easy to regain a puppy's trust if you lose your cool. With a person, you can often regain trust by sitting down and apologizing. A dog can't understand your apology—it takes a lot of time, days maybe, to make up ground you lost by yelling, showing annoyance, or otherwise acting in a bullying way.

Luckily, the chances of your losing patience are going to remain low if you keep training sessions properly short. In fact, if you train for too long, your efforts will backfire. Your puppy will become indifferent to them as his ability to focus on a task wanes. A puppy will also be harder to train if *you* get bored and, rather than stop, continue the lesson. He will have an uncanny instinct for whether you're just going through the motions.

BASIC TRAINING TOOLS

Watch Your Language

Dogs don't understand language per se. Humans have a genetic capacity for that which our canine companions lack. What puppies are learning when you teach them particular commands are specific sounds rather than actual words. In fact, they're picking up sound cues, like a dinner gong cueing people to come to the table or a doorbell cueing them that someone is at the door.

The best way to help a pup distinguish one cue from another is to use, as far as possible, single-syllable words that you can almost spit out — chunky little sounds, all of which have a distinct ring of their own. Long or lilting words that end in vowels are harder to pick out of a group of words. That's why "Down" works better than "Lie"; "Quit" works better than "Stop barking"; and so on. "No" is not a good choice at all — first, because it ends in a vowel (No-o-o-o-o . . .), and second, because it is overused. Most of the dogs in this country think their first name is *No.*

When you give a command, give it once and once only. After all, your pup has perfectly good hearing, better than yours, we're willing to wager. Multiple commands only (1) teach the puppy that you don't want him to follow a command until you repeat it several times or (2) cause the command to lose its impact, making it easier for the pup to tune you out as you keep uttering a sound that he obviously doesn't have to do anything about.

Food Treats

For many training lessons, especially at the beginning, you're going to need lots of food treats. Each should be no bigger than your smallest fingernail, but they should be delectable. You want to keep your puppy's motivation super-high. (In fact, if food is going to be the reward for following commands, train before a meal, not right after.) Tiny pieces of frankfurter, very small bits of cheese, or freeze-dried chicken liver are some good examples.

What you should not use for rewards are crumbly treats. Your pup will end up putting his energies into vacuuming them off the floor, which will distract him from the lesson. And big treats are the wrong way to go not only because of concerns about weight but because, again, the time it takes to eat them will distract your pup from the task at hand.

Be aware that your puppy will also be unable to make a proper association between cause and effect if too much time elapses between his successful completion of a required task and your offering the reward. The food has to come within half a second of a successful completion, that is, almost immediately. Spend ten or twenty seconds fumbling in a plastic bag or making the treat just the right size and he will begin to lose the sense of cause and effect you're trying to get across. Both his earnest efforts and yours will falter.

Training Lead

Training leads, typically about ten feet long and usually made of lightweight nylon, are meant for indoors only. You may never need to use one. Your puppy may be wonderfully compliant and prone to sticking right by you when you're trying to interact with him. But many young pups are so naturally inquisitive and wiggly that it would be impossible to guide them through training sessions without making sure they remained within a certain radius. That doesn't mean you should jerk a training lead or snap on it —ever. That's punishment, which is ultimately counterproductive. It's just that if you're holding the end of a training lead (which is like a very long boot lace attached to the dog's collar), your pup will know when he has reached the end of his tether and will have to come back toward you—at which point you can continue the training session. (We will discuss outdoor leads later in the chapter.)

THE BASIC COMMANDS: "SIT," "DOWN," "LEAVE IT," AND "COME"

Okay, you've got your food treats, you've got an understanding about using short, clipped words, you've got your training lead in case you need it. With patience in your head, love in your heart, and tiny scraps of food in your hand, you begin. You're buoyed by the knowledge that once you teach your puppy "Sit," "Down," "Leave It," and "Come," you'll fall even more in love with him than you already are and develop an even better relationship than you might have thought possible. With those four words, you'll be able to keep your dog from running into traffic (or other trouble), from chewing through an electric cord that could harm him, from chasing a squirrel when it's time to come back to you and go home, and from engaging in all kinds of other dangerous or frustrating behavior.

Sit

One way to train your dog to sit is via the clicker method, with a clicker bought at a pet supply shop or a party goods store. It goes in three stages. You start by priming the clicker—clicking it just once to make a sound—and giving your puppy a food treat (for "free"). Repeat this several times. The pup will get the idea that the click and the food are paired (the clicker is now primed), which means you've completed stage 1.

Now you and your dog are ready for stage 2, during which you click only for the behavior you aim to elicit—in this case, sitting. It works as follows. Anxious for more food, the pup starts jumping up around your legs, sniffing and begging. Finally he gives up and sits spontaneously, which is the behavior you're looking for. Thus, you immediately click the clicker (just once, always once) and give him another food treat, also letting him know with kind, cheerful words that he has done the right thing—"Good boy!" (Keep it pleasant but clipped. Go overboard with the praise and you'll both lose the thread of the lesson.) After a couple more rounds of seeking and begging and, finally, sitting, he'll learn that it's the sitting that's making the clicker click and the food appear (served up with a helping of warm praise on the side).

Now it's time for stage 3—adding the voice cue "Sit." If you don't, he'll assume that every time he decides to sit, he'll get a click and a reward from you. It will be he who has trained you rather than vice versa. In fact, by this point he very well may be sitting like crazy to get the click and reward, but to no avail. Your next step is to say "Sit" and then wait for the desired response—sitting—to occur. He will finally sit, maybe in frustration, only to find he has again hit the jackpot. He'll very possibly try sitting again and again and again after the first reward for sitting fortuitously following your word cue, but he will see that nothing happens. Then you say "Sit" again and wait for him to follow through. Voilà—your puppy is learning his first word and the action you want him to associate with it. It may take a few days to become second nature to sit when you tell him to, but the seeds have been sown.

You can reinforce the behavior at those times when the puppy's motivation is high, say, before meals. Tell him to sit before you put down the food bowl before him. You'll be surprised at how quickly he learns to do your bidding (as long as it's reasonable) when there's something at stake. Before long, you'll be able to get him to sit just by saying the word and rewarding him directly, dispensing with the clicker. Then you can gradually cut back to supplying a food treat every other time you tell him to sit, then every third time, then randomly (although praise and perhaps petting along the side of his face will always be appreciated). The *possibility* that food will come will get him to comply more reliably with your cue. "It worked before," he'll think to himself. "It's *got* to work again. Perhaps I should try harder."

You can even reach the point where you almost *never* have to offer a food treat (although you should praise and pet now and then to keep the desired response firmly in place). But why go that far? Doesn't your dog deserve a food reward sometimes for doing what you ask? Don't you want to show him, at least occasionally, that you appreciate his good behavior?

NOTE: The clicker method does not require a clicker per se. You can click your tongue against the roof of your mouth or consistently use some other distinctive sound, like "Yes-s-s-s." Some people prefer such alternatives, arguing that a clicker is an unnecessary gizmo. If that's how you feel, fine. But the reason a clicker is so often used is that its sound is very distinct. There's little possibility of your dog confusing it with another sound and getting mixed signals.

Different Training Strokes for Different Folks

The clicker method is only one of several training methods for getting your dog to sit and follow other commands. We happen to like it very much because research has shown that as a secondary reinforcer (the food treat is primary), the clicker invokes faster learning and can be used to train a multitude of complicated behaviors. In fact, clickers have been used to teach all kinds of species all kinds of things, such as getting pigs to put wooden coins in piggy banks!

But it's not for everybody, or every dog, and there are other ways to go, as the following techniques for "Sit" illustrate.

Magnet Method

With the magnet method, also called the lure method, food is the magnet. Start by holding the treat right in front of your puppy's nose and then slowly draw it upward, in an arc, over the top of his face and his head. His eyes and snout will automatically go upward, and, as they do, his rump will automatically go down onto the ground. Presto—he's sitting, and he gets the treat along with a cheerful "Bravo!" from you. Refrain from letting go of the treat until his behind truly hits the deck (keep your fingers pinched tightly around it). He will learn that sitting on cue is what springs the reward.

"Sit" via
the magnet
method.

If your pup keeps backing up during this exercise, try it with his back in a corner. If he keeps jumping up, you're holding the treat too high. Once he has the drill down, add the word "Sit" to the routine, first saying it as he begins to lower his rump and later before he even makes a move. Pretty soon the verbal cue will elicit the behavior, and you can correctly assume he knows the word.

Capture Method

With the capture method, you capture the moment at which the puppy spontaneously happens to engage in the behavior you want to elicit. When you see him sit, say "Sit" and immediately reward him with a food treat and praise. The capture method can be used in conjunction with the clicker method, as described above. It takes a few times before the puppy realizes what is leading to the clicking and reward, but once he gets it, you're in business.

Placement Method

This method is somewhat controversial because it involves moving the dog into position rather than letting him learn for himself what is required, which could end up making life with your puppy more, not less, difficult. He could come to expect that it is your wish always to be hands-on about commands. We lean away from the placement method ourselves, but it can be employed as a means to an end. Some people find it works very well for them and their pup.

In the case of "Sit," you gently take your thumb and forefinger and slide them back along your puppy's back toward his hips. With a gentle squeeze (that we call "goosing"), you gently rotate his rear end back and down into the sitting position. After a couple of times doing this maneuver, then cheerfully giving him a food treat, you bring the word "Sit" into the equation, and the light bulb begins to go off in his head.

Which Training Method Is Right for You and Your Pup?

While we have had good results with the clicker method in lots of situations with lots of different dogs and their owners, you need to trust your own instincts and get a feel, too, for what works with your pup.

Note that even as you gravitate toward one method over another, you will not be able to use it in all training lessons. For instance, you obviously cannot use a hands-on placement method for "Come" or "Wait." The closest you'd be able to get to placement in those cases is to use a lead.

Fortunately, you'll get a sense pretty fast for what does and doesn't work with your pet. Since dogs, especially young puppies, learn so fast, you'll know within three to five days whether to try another learning tactic.

As we move on to other commands, we can't give you the specifics for every possible training method for each cue, as we have for "Sit." That would comprise a book in itself! We simply ask you to be aware that there is generally more than one approach for teaching your puppy a command. Stay flexible and willing to evaluate choices for training methods as you go along. As long as you keep it all happy and fun, your dog—and you—will benefit.

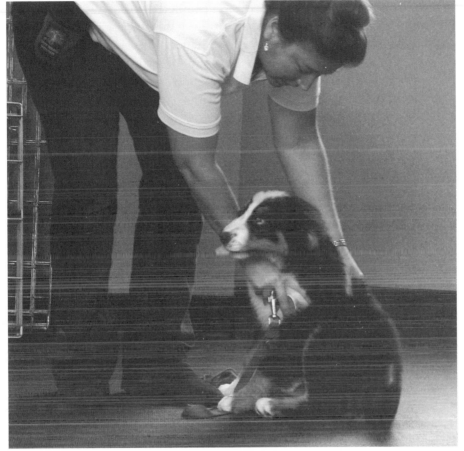

"Sit" via the placement method.

Down

"Down" means "Lie down," and it's pretty easy to get your puppy into position with the magnet method. Start the training session, as always, with a delicious morsel of food between your fingers and a heaping portion of goodwill. Then, with the puppy facing you while sitting (a position you can now get him into on command), hold the food right in front of his nose. Now, slowly lower the food to the floor, and subsequently draw it away from his nose. Think of the down-and-away motion as if you're making the letter *L*. Your pup will respond by lowering and then extending his neck to follow the treat. His front legs will also extend, and his body will lower itself to the ground. Pretty soon he will be lying down. Reward him by releasing the food from between your fingers and saying "Good boy."

Will Work for Love

Most puppies will train in exchange for food treats. But as a puppy matures into his second six months of life, you can replace some of the food during training with praise or petting. If you do, don't pet your puppy for an hour or so before the training session. Or engage in a training session when you've just returned from running errands for a while and he hasn't had your company. You need to shortchange him a little to increase his motivation to obey you when you give the commands.

After a couple of successful completions, you can preface the exercise with the "Down" cue. Soon he'll figure out that lying down on cue results in praise and other rewards. Rewards should initially be given for every successful exercise but then phased to an intermittent, random schedule, as with the "Sit" cue.

Leave It

This cue transmits to a puppy that you want him to keep his nose out of something (or someone). Using a lead works well here.

Start by putting a food treat on the floor but holding the lead so that the puppy cannot quite reach it. As he struggles to move forward, say "Leave it" as if the two words are one—"Leavit." He may continue to struggle for a while, but then he will give up. At that point say, "Take it" or "Release," and let him get to it. He will begin to understand that "Leave it" means just that and that if he complies, there's a chance of a reward. After a while, you'll be able to graduate to remote control—"Leave it" with no lead.

You can also teach "Leave it" by using the clicker method combined with a variation on the lure method. Hold the treat in your hand, but when your puppy goes to take it, keep the food out of reach. When he finally looks away or backs up, *then* click the clicker and put the treat on the floor.

After he gets the hang of that, simply put the food treat on the floor. When he comes to get it, put your foot over it and add the words "Leave it" (again, almost as if they're one sound). When he stops trying to get under your foot is when you let him have the food. He'll get the "Leave it" message after just a few tries.

Come

The most common refrain we hear at our Behavior Clinic is, "All I want my dog to do is come when I call." It's understandable. If your dog will come when you tell him to, you never have to worry that he will get into scrapes or otherwise cause himself—or others—trouble when he's outside and off leash.

"Come" is very teachable. It just takes more patience than other commands and a little more of a leap of faith on your part. After all, you can teach "Sit," "Down," or "Leave it" with your puppy right next to you. "Come" *has* to be done more by remote control.

Essentially it's the magnet, or lure, method that you'll make the most use of here. Your high praise and appreciative petting will serve as important adjuncts to the food magnet.

Start in a fenced-in yard or even inside your house or apartment. Let's say your puppy is across the living room as you enter from the kitchen. First call out to him. "Tino!" Once you have his attention, say, "Come! Good boy!" in an animated voice. (The reason you say "Good boy" *before* he comes is to let him know he's not in trouble.) Drop to one knee and open your arms so that your gesture is as animated as your speech. Look like you're ready for fun and offer a treat. When Tino makes his way to you, say, once again in a very pleased manner, "Good boy!" Hand him a wonderful food treat and stroke him nicely along the side of his face. As before, it is possible, even recommended, that over time you phase out regular food treats and exuberant animation and put such delights on a random schedule. That will assure a reliable response without your always having to be carrying food with you to make sure he comes when called. But remember, it's always a good idea to show him some recognition, however subtle, for his good work.

Never, *never* call your puppy to you and then show him that you're angry at him or frustrated. That's teaching him that coming to you could have unpleasant consequences. He will quickly learn *not* to come when you tell him to. Even if he has been playing knee-deep in mud and then tearing around and barking at a group of churchgoers on Sunday morning, you have to call to him happily and then praise him for coming over rather than snarl at him to "Come" and let him know how disappointed you are. You can accomplish only one thing at a time. Getting him back over to your side so you can put on his leash and keep him from any further running amok is plenty.

RAMPING IT UP

When you first teach your puppy basic commands, you're giving your lessons in a calm, quiet, extremely controlled setting—your living room with nobody else around, your backyard when your neighbors are not having a barbecue, and so on. But training necessarily becomes more complex as it continues.

"Come!"

For one thing, you can't stop reinforcing one command just because you move on to another. That is, when you teach "Down," you can't forget to throw a "Sit" or two in there, especially at first. In fact, your puppy will need intermittent reinforcement for the various commands you want him to learn throughout the entire first year of his life. It's a bit like spinning plates. You've got to keep the first plate spinning as you get others going.

And as you spin, you need to gradually make the circumstances surrounding each command a little more distracting so your puppy can learn to behave in real-life situations. After all, it's not truly crucial that he "leaves it" when "it" is the biscuit you put on the floor. But when "it" is a squirrel that's across a busy street with cars coming in both directions, "Leave it" takes on a whole new meaning. So does "Sit" or "Down" when you're on one side of the road and your puppy's on the other, and you don't want him to "come" until you've made sure traffic is all clear.

Older Dogs, Newer Tricks?

There's not a soul who hasn't heard the expression "You can't teach an old dog new tricks." Is it true? No. You absolutely can train an adult dog of any age to perform all the commands in this chapter — with the same methods that are recommended for puppies. The only difference is that it will take longer for the lessons to become ingrained. And there's a higher chance of refractory behavior. After all, the dog has already lived quite a while with some tricks of his own. But if, for example, you want to adopt an older dog from the pound, fear of not being able to train him should not stop you. In fact, time may be on your side. Since so many dogs have received at least rudimentary training, an adult dog may come to you already knowing "Sit," "Down," and other commands. You'll have a good chance of starting out ahead of the curve.

Start small with distractions during training, and initially, at least, keep them artificial—rehearsals for the real thing. For instance, if "Sit" is the goal, you can perhaps work with your puppy to sit when the doorbell rings. But don't just wait for the bell. Make a plan with someone to ring the bell at an appointed time, someone who will be prepared to wait outside until the puppy sits. The person may have to wait three to five minutes, ringing the bell several times, until your puppy understands that the faster he follows your command to sit when the bell rings, the faster he will get his reward. (You may very well have to practice "Sit" all over again once the door opens and the person becomes visible.)

With "Come," you'll really have to go gradually to get your puppy to come from a distance when you cue him. For instance, if you've just taught your puppy "Come" inside the house within the last couple of days and he then charges out of the backyard after a squirrel, do *not* yell "Come." You haven't yet gotten him to the point where he will comply. The squirrel is more enticing than your message is ingrained, and therefore, all you'll be doing is letting him know that he does not, in fact, have to listen to your command. Better first to acclimate him to "Come" when something distracting is going on in the next room—chicken smells wafting from the oven, for example, or a pillow fight between two small children that he wants to somehow get in on. *Then* move to situations outside, but again, make them situations that you control—a neighbor's dog on the other side of a fence or a person who "suddenly" steps out from behind the garage.

You can even hide behind a tree when your puppy runs ahead a little during a walk off leash and then checks behind his shoulder to see where you have gone to. Nervous about being without you, he will be more likely to come when you call him, stoop to the ground, open your arms wide, and praise him excitedly (and follow up with a delectable food treat and highly enthusiastic praise, at least at first). Whatever particulars you choose, only after you train your puppy to follow your commands by setting up situa-

Are Training Classes a Good Idea?

Generally speaking, we are fans of puppy training classes. They can provide some socialization for the dog (and you), and the setting comes with built-in distractions that puppies need in order to advance. In addition, there's always homework for you and your pet, so the classes will help keep you from slacking off on your training duties. (Just as a teenager can't learn to drive with a lesson once a week at driver's ed and no driving between times, a puppy can't learn to follow commands with just a single group lesson each week. His owners need to follow up at home.)

A couple of caveats for training classes,

however, are of the utmost importance. The first is that all the puppies in the class must have already had their initial vaccinations and be deemed by a veterinarian to be in good health and free of parasites.

The second, and this is just as important as the good health of your puppy's classmates, is that the trainer use positive methods, and positive methods only. A fair number of trainers, unfortunately, integrate negative, punishment-based methods that make dogs unnecessarily miserable and destroy trust between puppies and humans.

How do you make sure a trainer is the kind you're after? You have to do some

tions that are surprises to him will he be able to move on to listening to you during circumstances that neither of you anticipated.

For instance, if by chance one day he starts trying to chew through an electric wire, you'll be able to successfully tell him "Leave it" so that he doesn't risk hurting himself. (If he is not yet able to comply, gently remove him from the wire—or other object that he's not supposed to be chewing—and replace it with an item to chew that you deem acceptable. Safety before learning, always. When he does comply, food and praise are the order of the day.)

The ultimate aim is to get the dog to follow your cues 100 percent of the time in quiet surroundings and more than 85 percent of the time when distractions loom. No one's perfect, but 90 percent of the time in a quiet setting doesn't quite cut it, and neither does 65 percent of the time in a setting with distractions.

One hundred percent *can* be accomplished. One Border collie who was brought to our Behavior Clinic was extremely well trained by his owner, who even entered him into herding competitions. As the owner stood by the front desk, Dr. Dodman asked her to tell her dog "Down"—and the dog

---

Are Training Classes a Good Idea?, continued from page 174

probing, because anyone can hang out a shingle with the word "Trainer" (or even "Behaviorist") on it. There is no requirement for licensure or proper credentialing.

Here are the questions to ask. If the answer to any of them is yes, find another trainer.

1. Are you of the school that believes it's not right to punish a puppy but that for older dogs, physical punishments ("corrections") have a place?

2. Do you give corrections with the collar by jerking the lead?

3. Do you ever use choke or prong collars?

Do *not* ask if the person is a positive trainer, a term that gets bandied about as code for nonpunishing methods. Plenty of trainers call themselves "positive" because they use *some* positive training but resort to physical punishment as well. On the other hand, you might want to ask if the person is a member of the Association of Pet Dog Trainers, a group formed in reaction to the tactics of military-type trainers (see "Resources" for more information).

Beyond questions, you have to go with your gut. You should be able to get a sense of whether the trainer respects dogs and wants them to feel emotionally secure or looks at them as props to be controlled.

complied immediately, from a range of fifteen feet, and amid the clamor of a busy waiting room. Upon seeing that, Dr. Dodman wondered why such a well-trained dog needed to be brought to a behaviorist. The owner explained that all was fine as long as she was watching her dog. But if she took her eyes off him when outside in a public area, he would start to creep, and eventually run, to nip passing strangers (perhaps herding them like sheep). However, if she caught him mid-excursion, she could bark "Down" from any distance and the dog would hit the deck—sometimes only a few feet short of an intended target. The point here: even the force of a dog's nature can be overridden with good training. (Getting a dog not to follow his instinct when you're not watching is another story.)

TRAINING FOR OUTDOOR WALKS

Along with teaching your dog basic commands, you need to train him to wear a collar and a lead. There's no way out of it. Every dog has to be walked at least sometimes. Even dogs who live on farms occasionally go into town and have to act civilly. That is, you want your pup to walk *with* you—not drag you ahead and not keep you rooted in one spot because he feels he must sniff something for a very extended period of time. (Leaving time for *some* sniffing is only fair.) And you want to be able to control him should he decide to try to jump up on someone, bother another dog passing in the opposite direction, or try to run from you to chase a skunk.

Some pups are not at all bothered by collars or leashes. They habituate themselves naturally and quickly. Other puppies may need you to attach a leash to their collar and let it drag for a day or two, finally picking up the other end of the lead and then initially following the puppy around rather than vice versa. The point with such dogs is that you gradually phase in who is supposed to be walking whom. You don't just put on the collar and lead and go. (You'll know immediately whether your puppy is easygoing about being connected to you by a collar and lead or needs a couple of days to acclimate.)

There are three kinds of collars to choose from.

Buckle Collar

Traditionally, the lead, or leash, is attached to a basic flat nylon or leather collar, also called a buckle collar. That's the one most everybody is familiar with. We don't recommend it for physical control (though it's handy for attaching tags and ID). For one thing, a buckle collar is *harmful* to certain kinds of dogs: pugs and other brachycephalic (short-nosed) dogs, who have narrow airways, and toy dogs, who are prone to tracheal collapse. For another, it doesn't accomplish anything in a way that accustoms a dog to follow through on your expectations. Dogs will pull on leashes and choke and gag if they're after something; you can hear them coughing their way around the park each morning at dog-walking time. You may be able to keep a dog out of trouble by tugging at a traditional leash because you're stronger, but you won't feel good doing it, and the dog won't learn much from the experience.

Head Halter

Because buckle collars work in a way that makes both dogs and their people feel lousy, we recommend a different device. Called a head halter, it is never jerked and therefore can never cause the dog any pain. Rather, it uses sensitive areas on the dog's head and nape to send gentle but firm messages without causing any harm.

Head halters usually comprise two soft, adjustable nylon straps. One goes around the nose (which makes them difficult to impossible to keep on a brachycephalic breed), and the other rides high on the neck just behind the pup's ears—in front of his throat rather than under it. The neck strap is kept snug, with barely enough room to fit your pinky under it.

The nose strap sits at the base of the muzzle, close to the puppy's eyes (at the bridge of his nose). It's kept loose enough so that the dog can eat, drink, or pant with it on.

It's not completely clear how the head halter works, although it could be that it mimics the pressure a mother dog might apply to areas that are innately sensitized to receive signals of rebuke or relaxation. When you *gently* pull upward on the leash, the neck strap tenses, and perhaps that delivers a message like the one the puppy's mother sends when she picks up her young one by the scruff of his neck to lead or transport him. The puppy instinctively relaxes and is prepared to be led.

At the same time, gentle pressure exerted around the puppy's muzzle via the nose band conveys the same kind of firm but gentle rebuke, just like Mama would have done it, as the theory goes. That is, a head halter, apparently by providing pressure at biologically sensitive areas, signals a pup to calm down and reminds him who's in charge. No jerking of the collar or pain is involved (and no injuries have ever been reported to us).

Head halter.

Sometimes your application of tension to the head halter is unnecessary. Let's say your pup tries to walk ahead of you instead of at your side. Stand still. He can't pull you when you make like a tree. The tension on the nose strap will automatically cause his head to turn and make him look up at you. And in that situation, your dog must walk back toward you or wait until you catch up with him so that the tension is released with some slack and he can resume forward progress. He won't be able to struggle. If your pup is lagging behind, the tension will be delivered to his nape via the neck strap. In this case, to release the tension, the puppy must catch up with you—at which point you should tell him what a good boy he is! (You don't need your puppy to "heel" precisely beside your own feet like a little soldier. That's only necessary for show dogs who are to be entered into competitions.)

About half of all puppies take head halters in stride. Some sulk. Jolly such a pup out of his bad mood with treats and praise. Hold a good-tasting treat right in front of his nose so that he will get to thinking about and enjoying something, rather than focusing on being unhappy about the head halter.

Other pups don't sulk but struggle willfully to get out of the head halter. For one like that, apply steady upward tension on the leash so he gets the correct signals of control, and say "Stoppit." Maintain the tension until he relinquishes his struggle. It could take ten to twenty seconds—or longer—the first time. As soon as the pup gives up, release the tension and give lots of praise along with a wonderful food treat. He'll get the picture after just a few times.

To cut down on possible sulking or struggling, introduce the head halter as early in your pup's life as possible—*before* he grows to be strong enough to cause any real harm or develop a problem down the road. While it's relatively easy to acclimate a puppy to a head halter, adult dogs may put up a fight; they resent it.

Should You Hire a Personal Trainer for Your Pup?

We firmly believe that, if at all possible, people should train their own dog. It really strengthens the bond between owner and pet. Of course, a personal trainer can be helpful in showing you how to proceed. That is, he or she trains you!

Some people, although they truly love dogs and want one as a companion, are not meant to train, with or without professional help. Perhaps they lack the patience, or they can't keep their temper under wraps. In other cases, they simply may not like training—for whatever reason. In such instances, it may be better to go the route of a professional trainer as long as that person uses no physical punishment whatsoever. While training your own dog is best, nonpunishing training by a stranger is better for a puppy than unhappy training by an unmotivated owner.

You can find a petite head halter for a puppy as young as three months of age. Put it on for only five minutes at a stretch if your puppy is really miserable about it. (And keep the delectable treats coming to reward non-struggling behavior.) Small, manageable sessions will lead to longer ones.

Keep trading in your puppy's head halter for the next size up as he grows. You'll be glad you did. By the time your pup is six months old, you'll be able to use the head halter in all kinds of situations—to help reinforce, if necessary, the rule about not jumping on people who come to the door, to keep your puppy from acting overly aggressively toward other animals, and so on. Say the appropriate word and apply tension to the lead if the instruction is not followed. Once the desired behavior has been achieved, release the tension and praise or otherwise reward your pup's accomplishment.

Incidentally, a modification of the standard head halter by the addition of a single strap running from the neck strap to the nose strap—the Snoot Loop—is great for some brachycephalics and others dogs whose noses are not quite long enough to retain the nose loop.

Body harness.

Body Harness

For extremely short-nosed dogs—pugs and the like—even a Snoot Loop may be impractical, because it slips off. In such cases, we recommend a body harness. Body harnesses do not apply pressure to biologically sensitive areas, as a head halter is theorized to do, but they can still be used to deliver a meaningful message to a pup. They are well tolerated by most dogs and can work better than traditional collars and leads. The tension, or pressure, is applied around the chest—and released when the puppy does what you want.

Note that body harnesses are harder to get the hang of than head halters. You may need a few sessions with a trainer to help you learn to use one properly.

BEYOND THE BASICS

While "Sit," "Down," Leave It," and "Come" are great accomplishments of paramount importance, and while it is crucial that your puppy learn to follow your lead on walks, there is much more he can and should learn through training to make for a nicer life shared by the two of you. What follows are some commands that will go a long way to making things even more copacetic between you and your pup, but the list is by no means exhaustive. As we said at the beginning of the chapter, a puppy can learn dozens of words, or sound cues, that prompt him to engage in, or not engage in, various behaviors.

Quit It

This is a good command for getting your puppy to stop barking every time someone comes to the door. *Some* barking is acceptable. It's what dogs do, after all, and they have a right to say "Someone's at the door," just like you do. (You could even say a warm "Thank you" to your pup for a short burst of alarm barking to reward him for doing his duty by alerting you to the visitor.) It's the excessive barking, the kind that won't stop, that you have a right to curb.

A lot of puppy owners get in trouble at the door in the act of trying to calm down their young charge. They flail their arms, fairly trip over the dog, and yell for the barking to cease, which only makes the pup think his owner is barking, too, and that there's something to feel extremely agitated about.

> ## Adjusting Puppy to the Mail Carrier
>
> Many dogs go wild when the mail carrier comes. At first it may be on account of fear or territoriality. But your puppy may soon come to enjoy the experience on some level. After all, the arrival of the mail carrier inserts some action into what otherwise may be a relatively uneventful day.
>
> If you're home, you can go through the "Sit" routine or employ a "No bark" cue. But you can also take the opportunity to make your dog's day more pleasant. Why not leave a jar of biscuits by the door and ask the mail carrier to drop one through the slot upon arrival? That way, your puppy will realize that the mail coming is a good thing, and the anticipation will brighten up his morning or afternoon. What an easy way to give your canine friend something to look forward to six days a week.

A better alternative is to use the capture method, at first with the help of a friend on the other side of the door who may need to ring the bell or knock several times over the course of about five minutes for you to execute your training session. Here's how it works.

At some point after the first sign of a visitor, your puppy will stop barking for about three seconds, maybe to catch his breath. Exactly then, give

A well-trained puppy will be a civil host, able to greet company at the door without thrashing about or undue barking.

him a "shush" treat and tell him "Good dog!" He may soon resume barking, but then you'll get another opportunity to reward him for piping down for a moment. Then, when he starts barking a third time, issue the command "Quit it" before he stops to put silencing him on cue. You can even mutter, "Do you want a shush treat?" to keep him mindful of the reward in store. He'll quickly learn to quit barking when you tell him to.

Off

Don't confuse "Off" with "Down," which a lot of people do. They yell "Down" when their puppy jumps up on someone, but that leaves something of a disconnect in the dog's mind (not to mention the fact that yelling a command will make the dog less, not more, likely to comply). "Down" means "Lie down with your chest on the ground," which won't seem relevant to a dog who's jumping up on a visitor—or on you. That's why there's "Off." Like "Quit it," it can be easily taught with the capture method.

Let's say your puppy jumps on you in excitement when you come in from outside. Stand still. Don't do *anything.* Don't tell him "Stop it," don't pet him, don't laugh at how cute it all is even though you're not thrilled with the jumping, and don't push him off. Pushing him off as he jumps on you is construed by the pup as a game and will just reinforce the notion in his head that you're a big, squeaky toy. Instead, turn to stone. Your puppy will give up after a couple of minutes, or even less time, and stop jumping on you. When he does, come alive. Smile, pet him, and give him a reward (praise, petting, a food treat). You can use a clicker at first if you're clicker training. After two or three times, add the word "Off." He'll understand what produces the goods very quickly.

"Off" (as well as "Stoppit!") can also be used to train a pup out of humping. But turning to stone probably won't work. You may have to fit a head halter, either in anticipation of the humping or after initiation of the behavior, and apply tension to it to divert and correct this annoying, sometimes embarrassing, sexually derived, dominant-style behavior. And be sure to engage in a strong leadership program with the pup (emphasizing the "firm" in "firm," "fair," and "fun") if the humping is directed toward you.

No Bite

At around five months of age, perhaps six, your puppy is going to start mouthing. A little mouthing is not a bad thing. It's just part of development. But you don't want your pup calling the mouthing shots. As he gets older, his nipping can really hurt.

Don't pull your hand away and start exclaiming when he mouths. That will just make him think it's all a big game and that he's *supposed* to try again. Rather, lean forward and freeze. He'll let go, at which point you can reward him. Alternatively, you can say, "Ouch!" very startlingly, and *then* freeze. Your puppy will get the message that way, too, and after a few times, you can add the "No bite" command.

Stay/Wait

"Stay" and "Wait" (the first means stay put, the other means stop for a moment until I tell you to continue) are both reasonable commands to teach, but they're not absolutely necessary. "Sit" accomplishes the same thing —getting the dog to stay put or wait until you're ready to let him get going again with a command such as "Release." (Some people use "Okay," but others say that the word is uttered too commonly for a dog to be able to single it out as a salient cue.)

That said, there's a hand signal for "Wait" (and a few other commands) that's worth learning in case you and your dog are outside and he can't hear your cue—for instance, if he's on the other side of the road and you want him to stop because cars are coming, or if a jackhammer is muffling all communication.

Hand-Signal Commands

Teach these hand signals to your puppy as you teach him the words. That way, he'll be able to follow your command even if he can't hear you.

Sit: Extend your arm and hand in front of you with your palm up and your forearm at a right angle to the ground. Then raise your hand upward in an arc.

Down: Put your hand up in the air with your palm facing your dog, forearm at a right angle to the ground. Then lower your palm 90 degrees so that it faces the ground.

Come: Stretch one arm out toward your puppy, palm at 45 degrees to the vertical. Then bring your hand across your chest (signaling "Come—to me").

Wait: Flash your hand quickly in front of your dog's face, or quickly point a finger at him.

Successive Approximations (Also Known as Shaping a Behavior)

Sometimes you may find it difficult to train an entire behavior by capture or placement. Let's say, for instance, that you want your pup to go lie down in his dog bed several rooms away. Starting with "Go to bed" and then waiting for it to happen will take a long time. And placing him there yourself may not get the message across—and may not even be feasible, depending on his size and your strength and flexibility. A more effective method is to click and reward him when he crosses an imaginary line that is in the same direction as the bed. Then, keep moving that line closer and closer to his bed. (That's the successive approximations part.) When he finally reaches the bed itself and lies down on it, give him a bonus in the form of an even better treat than usual or triple rations. You'll soon be able to add the "Go to bed" command even when the bed is not in the same room as the two of you. Successive approximations can be used for all kinds of training that involve complicated responses, like fetching slippers or rolling over and playing dead.

ALWAYS A HAPPY ENDING

Regardless of the stage of training, all training sessions must end on a positive note so that the dog will look forward to learning from you the next time. That doesn't mean you should reward your pup at the end of a training interlude if he doesn't follow through. For example, "Down" does not

Hand signals (in case puppy is too far away to hear), *clockwise from top left:* "Sit," "Down," "Come," "Wait."

mean "Sit," so a puppy who sits but doesn't actually lie down in response to the "Down" command should not be rewarded. Yes, you want him to be happy, but not at the expense of his proper learning.

Failure to comply means that you should wait a few seconds and try it again. If it still doesn't work, go back to a simpler command, one that you know he will be able to follow. That way you can tell him what a good dog he is before the two of you knock off. Remember, your demeanor will determine how much your puppy can take in, and even how much he can learn at the next session. Lose your cool and you've torn down what you were building up. Remain calm, fresh, bright, eager, and patient in your collaborative effort and your puppy will, too.

9

Housetraining

IT MAY NOT BE IMMEDIATELY APPARENT, BUT A LOT OF DOGS ARE RELIN-
quished to shelters precisely because they don't learn to consistently do
their "business" outside. It's understandable. The last thing anyone wants is
to be living in a canine latrine.

The shame of it is that the failure to housetrain is almost invariably the
owner's. While housetraining takes some time, patience, and active over-
sight, it's something any puppy, and even an older dog, can get the hang of
in pretty short order. Within *days* a puppy will have the basics down if su
pervised properly, and within a couple of months she'll be accident-free.

Some people are led to believe they won't need to housetrain. A number
of breeders tell prospective owners that the puppies they raise are already
housetrained by the time they are adopted. And they may very well be. But
don't make the mistake of assuming you won't have to put anything into
housetraining if the breeder tells you the puppy has already been housebro-
ken at her original home. Your own housetraining should, in fact, begin
within a day of your puppy's coming to live with you. Why? Just because a
very young puppy has been housetrained in her original environment
doesn't mean she's naturally going to be able to transfer the skill without
any help. In addition, "housetrained" is a relative term. Puppies can hold
their urine only for so long. The bottom line: You have to make a concerted
effort to teach your pup appropriate elimination habits.

Following is everything you need to know about getting your young canine charge to learn to eliminate outside instead of indoors. It's all a bit intense at the start, as it is when you train a toddler to go to the bathroom without diapers. But your puppy really will go a long way toward having the drill down inside of a week, even by the end of a long weekend.

DESIGNATING AN ELIMINATION SPOT

You can't just open the back door and let your puppy out. She won't know what you expect of her. You need to choose a spot outside your house for your puppy to eliminate her waste and then escort her to it on leash.

The designated spot needs to be pretty close—maybe behind the garage or in a corner of the yard. The designated spot should not be your neighbor's berm—that narrow stretch of grass between the sidewalk and the road. While local pooper-scooper laws may require you to remove your dog's droppings, you cannot remove her urine, and urine kills grass.

You'll have a lot of opportunities to get your puppy acclimated to the spot you choose. As you'll recall from chapter 2, a puppy can hold her urine only for a few hours—her age in months plus one. Thus, an eight-week (two-month-old) puppy will have to relieve herself after just three hours, on average.

The thing to do is put on your puppy's leash, take her out to the spot, and use a consistent word cue, such as "Let's do it" or "Let's get busy." Then let the pup sniff for several minutes and walk back and forth as she needs. Do *not* use the spot to play or otherwise interact, or the puppy will lose focus and will have a harder time learning what the spot is intended for.

Give it a good five to ten minutes. If the puppy goes within that time, praise her lavishly and reward immediately with a to-die-for treat that you've taken outside with you and kept hidden. If you wait until you're back in the house to give the treat, your dog will think she's being rewarded for going back inside. Remember, she's paying attention to *her* sequence of events, not yours, and you can't communicate to her verbally that you're giving her a prize for a task she successfully accomplished a minute or two ago.

If your puppy does not eliminate when you take her to the designated spot, take her back to the house and put her in her crate, closing the door behind her. **This is not a punishment!** After all, her crate has some of her favorite toys in it along with a cushion on the bottom and perhaps some bumperlike cushioning along the sides. Confining the pup to her crate is simply a technique for making sure she does not have accidents indoors.

As you'll recall, a dog's crate is her den, or nest, and her instinct not to soil it is very strong. Thus, by putting her in it, you're making sure that she will not relieve herself in the house. (Make sure her collar and leash are off: they could accidentally get caught on the bars or some other part of the crate, and the dog could start choking.)

Wait just fifteen minutes after closing the crate gate. During that time, go about your business cheerfully. Do not express any annoyance or exasperation. Do not use any stern or warning words as you leave your puppy confined. That could only prove harmful—it is not your dog's fault that she was not ready to go to the bathroom. Your only aim is to let her build up an urge to "go" yet keep her from following through on that urge inside the house by putting to use her own sense of the sanctity of her den. (Give her a bowl of chicken soup if you want to hurry along the proceedings.)

When the fifteen minutes are up, let the pup out of her crate, but do not

On Crate Size and Housetraining

Earlier in the book we explained that the crate should be tall enough for your pup to stand up in, wide enough for her to turn around in, and long enough so that her nose and rump can't simultaneously touch both ends. That's the size that will make her feel snug and secure. An adult-size crate will likely be too large; this is why we suggest starting with a smaller crate and then buying a larger one later on. If that's too costly, the way to ensure that a full-size crate works as a prop in toilet training your puppy is to block off some of it with, say, a wooden divider. A puppy will never want to eliminate her waste where she rests or sleeps or sometimes gets food treats, but if there's too much distance from one end of the crate to the other, she may happily relieve herself at one end and then go back to snoozing or otherwise resting at the opposite end. That completely defeats the purpose of the crate in housetraining. The puppy will not be able to learn that eliminating takes place outside the house only.

Just as crate size is important, so is the length of time you confine a puppy to her crate. Let's say the puppy is only two months old but you *must* run out to do an errand, yet don't feel comfortable letting her roam about freely. If you keep the door to the crate closed for more than a few hours, she'll have no choice but to urinate in the crate. Not only will you have locked up the puppy for an unfair length of time with no company to help her feel safe, you will have seriously impaired the opportunity to housetrain her easily. Once a pup has soiled her own crate, she will no longer see it as sacrosanct.

show excitement that she is being allowed out. That only introduces the idea that the crate is not a good place to hang out but, rather, a place that's good to escape from. Then, crisply and still cheerfully, attach the puppy's collar and leash for the second time, take her back to the designated spot, and say the magic phrase. Again, if she "goes," praise her to the hilt and reward her with a delectable treat. If not, bring her patiently—and without any weariness on your part—back to her crate for another fifteen-minute stint. (It's good to start this process at the beginning of a weekend, when you have more time to pay attention to your puppy's needs.)

Most puppies get it pretty quickly—and are especially likely to "perform" if they have just eaten or woken from a nap. But some owners may need to put a tiny (and we do mean tiny) amount of urine or feces on the designated spot to give their pup the right idea; the odor gives the dog a cue.

WHAT A PROPER HOUSETRAINING SCHEDULE LOOKS LIKE

So just how many times a day do you need to take a puppy outside? A lot. Here are the basic times:

1. As soon as the pup wakes in the morning, which will probably be as early as five or six o'clock. (*You* stagger to the bathroom first thing in the morning, so why shouldn't your pup?)

2. Fifteen to twenty minutes after your puppy has had her first meal. (As we mentioned in chapter 2, a phenomenon called the gastro-colic reflex causes a dog's colon to start contracting when food hits her stomach; there's a good chance your puppy will eliminate solid waste shortly after she has eaten.)

3. Midmorning.

4. After the midday meal. (At twelve weeks of age, your puppy will still be getting three or four meals a day rather than two.)

5. Midafternoon.

6. After the evening meal.

7. Early evening.

8. Just before bedtime.

In other words, you want to be taking your puppy out to eliminate waste every two to three hours. If you're lucky, she'll sleep from about 11 PM to 5 AM, so you'll get something of a night's sleep. Reduced activity coupled

Owner and poodle mix stagger out for the dog's early morning piddle.

with no eating or drinking at night allows some puppies to go unrelieved longer than the age (in months)-plus-one rule suggests.

But some puppies can't make it till dawn. If yours is one of them, you'll need to set your alarm for 2 or 3 AM. Don't worry. This stage doesn't last more than a couple of months. It's not like the ongoing lack of sleep that's part and parcel of raising a human infant.

Other good times to take your puppy outside: When she is transitioning from one behavior to another. For instance, when a puppy wakes from a nap and starts to stretch, that's a good time to let her relieve herself. After she finishes chewing on a chew toy and lies or sits there looking like she's thinking is another good transition time. Let her "go" as soon as a car ride is over, too.

Your puppy will also cue you about her need to go. She'll start sniffing or circling. Thus, especially when your puppy is very young, it's a good idea to keep one eye on her while you keep the other on whatever you are doing. In fact, if your puppy seems to have a particularly reactive bladder and you're going to be remaining in one place for a while — at your desk or doing dishes at the sink — it's not a bad idea to keep her attached to your belt via her lead (unless you're unsteady on your feet). This so-called umbilical cord training allows you to continuously observe her for signs of "I need to go" behavior.

Of course, if you're housetraining your puppy but must leave her alone for hours at a time while you go to work, or if you go out for a long evening of dinner and a movie, it is your responsibility to find someone to take her for a walk while you're gone. Even a puppy who's *almost* old enough to wait for hours before relieving herself is not necessarily there completely.

When your puppy reaches five or six months of age and throughout her adulthood, you can cut back to taking her out about six times a day: first thing in the morning, after breakfast, two times during the day, after her evening meal, and before bed. An older dog can go longer than that, but why make her? You don't enjoy "holding it in" and neither does she. Besides, for dogs, it's about more than simply emptying their bladder and bowel. Going outside is social time, a fun and interesting time. It breaks up the day. Remember, your dog can't read a magazine or turn on the television to an interesting program. She needs those outdoors times to shake life up.

NOTE: Your dog can pretty much be counted on to urinate every single time you take her outside. Most dogs also eliminate solid waste sometime after they eat, but each has her own pattern. You'll start to recognize your own pup's pattern before long.

ACCIDENTS

No matter how assiduously you stick to a schedule, there *will* be some accidents in the beginning. Human children have accidents when first toilet trained, too.

Don't go ballistic. It won't do any good. If you find the pup has piddled or pooped while you were in another room and then let her have it, she won't have a clue what you are making a fuss about. Even if you take her to the mess and stick her face in it, she won't get it. Remember, dogs just don't sequence events in their minds the way humans do. Yelling about something even a couple of minutes after the fact will prove a total disconnect for her. Besides, as we've now said numerous times, yelling is counterproductive. It only makes a dog feel afraid of you. It doesn't teach her to obey you.

What you do have to do is clean up the mess—thoroughly. If a dog is able to sniff urine or feces at a particular spot, the odor will attract her back to the vicinity as a place to relieve herself as surely as a heat-seeking missile finds its way to a source of heat.

Urine odors can be especially hard to get rid of. You can't just treat the spot with a cleaner that has a strong fragrance, because while that fragrance may disguise the odor to you, it won't mask it for the dog. You absolutely should not treat the urine-stained spot with any product that contains ammonia, either. Ammonia smells like broken-down urine and will actually attract the pup to the spot.

So what are the options? You can use a product that contains live bacteria that feed on the urine chemicals and thereby destroy them or enzymes that break down the urine. It can be sprayed on the spot or made into a solution and then poured or dabbed on.

The difficulty is that while such products do a better job than those that simply mask the odor of urine, they tend to be slow acting and only partially effective. Also, products with biological ingredients like bacteria or enzymes are highly labile, degrading upon exposure to heat and other environmental influences.

One solution is to throw a damp towel over a spot treated with one of these products so it doesn't dry out before it has a chance to do the job. Or you can try a new class of product now on the market with a stable active ingredient. Shown by gas chromatography to neutralize molecules in urine that cause odors, it breaks down relatively slowly and therefore works more effectively (see "Resources" for more information).

Whatever product you use, apply it liberally. You may need to kiddiegate off a room until the odors are gone. Kiddie gates are not a bad idea in the first place. Since a puppy is going to have accidents upon arrival in your home, strategically placed kiddie gates at the entrance to rooms with wall-to-wall carpets or expensive area rugs can save you a lot of hassle going forward.

Consider that if you have rugs or wall-to-wall carpets and several areas have had urine deposited on them, you may have to have them cleaned professionally. Chances are it'll just be too much to tackle spot by spot.

If you must go the professional carpet cleaner route, do not choose among companies by asking if they treat pet-soiled spots. They will all say they do. Ask instead *how* the company locates pet odors. Some have a sort of divining rod—a pole with two electrodes on one end and a battery and meter on the other. When the electrodes hit upon a damp spot where urination recently occurred, a needle on the meter will deflect, indicating wetness, as an electrical circuit is completed. That tells where special efforts to clean are necessary. (Just laundering the rug or carpet in the usual way is not sufficient.)

Other carpet professionals use a black light, which is a source of ultraviolet light. If all the other lights in the room are shut off, pigments in the urine will fluoresce in the dark when the ultraviolet light shines on them. Stains will show up on upholstery with such a light, too.

NOTE: Large home goods stores sell hand-held black lights for use by nonprofessionals. They look like miniature fluorescent tubes.

WHEN URINATING INDOORS IS *NOT* AN ACCIDENT

There are essentially two reasons a puppy will urinate indoors on purpose. One reason is predicated on appeasement and affects mainly females. The other has to do with overconfidence, if you will, and is more common in males.

Submissive Urination: Identifying and Getting Past It

Sometimes a puppy is so insecure that she is overly respectful not only of strangers but also her caretaker. She will scrape and bow and prostrate herself on the floor to curry favor. Such an underconfident dog may also engage in squatting, rolling, and submissive urination when you come through the door at the end of the day or when a visitor arrives. Arguments among people in the household, scolding, loud noises, and even overly affectionate greetings can bring on indoor urinating, too. The pup may even run around with urine dribbling this way and that—it's called "excited" urination.

Your puppy is not being bad. She's simply showing that she knows a superior when she sees one. Her urination behavior has the same meaning as when a submissive dog displays deference by averting her eyes or rolling on her back. The worst thing you can do is get angry. That only makes the dog think, "I obviously didn't express myself well enough," and she'll squirm and soak the floor more profusely the next time.

Many puppies do stop on their own by the time they reach the age of about one. They gain in dominance, or confidence, and lose their juvenile super-submissiveness—although, admittedly, that's small comfort to someone who has to clean the kitchen or mudroom (and perhaps his or her shoes) every night for a year while waiting for the pup's maturity to arrive.

The way to move things along for such an overly deferent puppy is to treat her, as far as possible, with kid gloves. Work to avoid all circumstances that cause the pup to urinate while you build up her confidence. Go so far as to break the rule of consistent firmness, because this is one situation in which "firm" probably just won't work and will usually make things worse.

For instance, feed your overly submissive dog for any or no reason; free-choice feeding is not out of the question. Pet the pup if she asks for attention. Get a pull toy and let her grab it from you while you say in a high-pitched voice, "Oh, you win again." Allow her on the furniture, and so on. All these things will help build your pup's self-esteem and give her confidence.

To directly combat the indoors urination, when you come home in the evening do not talk to your pup, especially if you have a gruff voice, which most pups find intimidating (serious dog-to-dog admonitions are low-pitched growls). Do not look directly into your pup's eyes as you return home, either. And do not walk straight toward her. Instead, walk past her in a banana-shaped, curved-trajectory path. Then sit down so you're lower to the ground, and ignore your pup for a bit. This isn't cruel. It's allowing the pup to regroup and gain some control in the situation. She won't feel as threatened by you and will therefore be less inclined to urinate inappropriately to express her enduring respect.

If your puppy urinates in front of visitors, ask them to avoid greeting her when they come in or to crouch to the dog's level, avert their gaze, and gently encourage her to come over.

Suppose the puppy urinates prematurely when it's time to be walked because you have to reach for her scruff to attach the lead. If that's the case,

> ## Catching Puppy in the Act
>
> Once in a while you may see your pup in the process of urinating—or beginning to strain for defecation—on the floor. Do not yell at her or show anger in any other manner. That will only teach her not to go in front of you. It won't teach her not to go in the house. She'll just do it secretly.
>
> Instead, make a startling noise, by clapping loudly or banging a drawer. That will cause the pup's bowel and bladder sphincters to shut down, or pucker up, automatically. Then put her on her leash and take her outside to finish the deed.

always leave a training lead on her in the house to circumvent the need to reach down toward that all-sensitive area, the nape of the neck—where her mother used to grab her). That does away with one unnecessary challenge prior to taking her outside. (Training leads are loopless so they don't get tangled in the furniture and potentially choke the pup.)

When you do need to approach your overly deferent pup, crouch down low to pick up the leash, don't look straight at her, and speak in as high a voice as possible. That will help let her know that she does not have to grovel in respect for you. One man who came to see us had a cocker spaniel who was so scared of him we devised a system whereby the man crouch-walked *backward* toward his dog and caught the training lead by feel when it was time for the pup to go out. It worked. The dog gained confidence, and she and her owner developed a very good relationship.

Identifying — and Putting an End to — Willful Urination

Some dogs, almost always male, urinate in the house not to empty their bladder but to mark off territory or strut their stuff. They lift a leg, often against something vertical, and signal their "ownership" with a self-satisfied tinkle. Of course, when the vertical thing is a fire hydrant outside, it doesn't matter. But when it's a leg on your Louis XV armchair, it's a different matter entirely.

This can happen when a pup is as young as five months old. Since it's not a housetraining problem, it does not call for a housetraining solution. It calls for a marking solution. There are three of them.

1. *Castration.* As we explained in chapter 3, when you neuter your male dog, any marking problem he has usually declines to the point of being nonexistent within a month or so.

2. *Leadership strengthening.* When castration alone doesn't solve the problem, the correct treatment is to let the young sire know that no part of the house is his territory. It's *yours.* That means you need to redouble your efforts to firmly show the pup who's the real leader. Don't let him sit on furniture. Make him sit for his supper. Don't pet him when he asks for it but only when you decide to initiate it. In short, don't give an inch on whatever rules you have set. This is not cruelty; it's firmness, which a purposefully furniture-soiling dog needs.

3. *Medication.* There are some pups who, for whatever reason, feel they

need to prove something to everybody. They look like they have a super-strong ego but are actually expressing a weak one. To help stabilize the mood of such a pup and make sure he doesn't urinate on your valuables, your veterinarian might prescribe a mood stabilizer, like fluoxetine (Prozac). Buspirone (Buspar) sometimes works, too, by relieving anxiety.

CAN PAPER TRAINING EVER BE AN OPTION?

Paper training—laying out papers somewhere in the house where the pup learns to do her business inside before learning to do it outside—may work for some dogs. Still, we advise against it whenever possible, for a simple reason. Why not teach the right habit right from the get-go, as opposed to letting your puppy get the hang of something that you eventually want her to unlearn? Also, you could be setting yourself up for unintended accidents. If you paper train with newspapers, which many people do, and then leave the Sunday paper on the floor one morning as you go into the kitchen to pour yourself some coffee, you may find a urine-soaked, feces-festooned headline on your return. You *taught* the puppy that the newspaper is a toilet, right?

We believe that even toy puppies who will remain small into adulthood should be toilet trained outdoors. Even those whose owners pamper them and adorn them with bows and ribbons can be housetrained as well as larger dogs. And besides, to be graphically blunt, do you really want to be dealing with tiny Tootsie-roll droppings in your home throughout your dog's life?

That said, we are aware that paper training may be the only option in certain circumstances. A dog who lives on the twenty-fourth floor of an apartment building in a crowded city without any grass along the sidewalk may truly need to relieve herself without having to deal first with an elevator and a protracted walk to a park. A dog who is the beloved companion of a person with limited ambulatory mobility may also not be able to get outside for regular bathroom trips. And a puppy who's essentially ruining the house because she cannot get the hang of "going" outside might be better served, at least in the short run, by paper training.

The idea with paper training is similar to the rationale for using a crate. You confine the dog to a relatively small space in the house—a bathroom, perhaps, or the laundry room or mudroom—and spread a wide swath of newspapers at one end and the pup's food, water, and bed at the other end. Since even a young pup will work very hard not to soil the area in which she eats and rests, she will eliminate her waste as far away from her feeding station and bed as possible, which is to say, on the newspaper at the opposite end of the small room. Gradually, the area of the floor covered by newspapers can be shrunken down as she gets the message.

Alternatively, you can take the dog to the designated newspaper-covered spot in the house on leash when you believe it's time for her to relieve herself. Use the same tactics that you would outside. Don't distract her with games; in fact, essentially ignore her, but then praise her warmly and with treats when she does the deed. Your pup will get the hang of it pretty quickly.

A word to the wise: If you paper train your pup and then want to switch to regular housetraining, do it in one step. You will not be helping the dog by trying to change her elimination habits gradually. You'll just be confusing the heck out of her. She won't know what to do where.

A Litter Box for Your Puppy?

When we think "litter box" we generally think "cat," but Purina has come up with an alternative to paper training for puppies. Trade named Second Nature, it can be used not only by puppies but also by small adult dogs. It may be just the ticket for people who live in city high-rises and don't want to be rushing home every few hours to take their pup to the park.

Note: Pups do not take to litter boxes as well as cats and must be trained to use them in a manner similar to the method described for paper training.

WHEN A MEDICAL CONDITION INTERFERES

Actively and consistently apply the tactics we suggest in this chapter, and your puppy should be voiding exactly where you want her to in pretty short order. If she isn't, she may very well have one of a number of a medical problems rather than a behavioral one. For instance, a female puppy may exhibit postspaying incontinence—dribbling urine as a result of relaxed tone in the urogenital tract after she has been spayed. Removal of the ovaries eliminates them as a source of estrogen, a hormone responsible, among other things, for maintaining proper urogenital tract muscle tone. A typical manifestation is that the puppy may leave a small puddle behind her when she gets up from a nap.

The condition is generally treated successfully with medication. Some veterinarians prescribe phenylpropanolamine (PPA) to restore sphincter tone, while others recommend replacing the missing hormone with a small amount of its synthetic equivalent, diethylstilbestrol (DES). Don't worry. It won't cause health problems, as it did in women.

If these strategies fail, a surgery called colposuspension is called for. It entails approaching the vagina through the abdomen and repositioning it slightly by pulling it forward and suturing it (permanently) to the abdominal wall. That causes increased pressure where the urethra joins the vagina, improving urine retention.

Here are some other medical conditions that cause incontinence:

1. Cystitis — a bladder infection.
2. Polyuria/polydipsia — the puppy drinks a lot of water as a result of a medical condition, then urinates a lot.
3. Anatomical abnormalities — among the most common is a so-called pelvic bladder, a bladder inside the pelvis as opposed to inside the abdomen. It tends to be too small and may require a surgical correction.
4. Ectopic ureters — a condition in which one or both of the urine-carrying tubes — ureters — don't go from the kidneys to the bladder as they should but rather implant "south" of the bladder. That causes urine to trickle out, because the bladder and its valvelike sphincter are bypassed. The problem calls for a surgical solution.

If you have a good relationship with your puppy and she is not fearful or particularly willful, trouble housetraining her definitely warrants a trip to the veterinarian to rule out medical problems that could be causing her inability to wait until she gets outside to eliminate.

Rest assured, however, that such medical conditions are relatively rare and that housetraining generally goes fairly smoothly. Start on a Friday night of a holiday weekend, and by Tuesday morning you'll see significant progress.

10
Nipping Behavior Problems in the Bud

IT WAS THE SAME SCENARIO WHENEVER ELLIE AND GUNTHER MET UP AT the park. Ellie, a black Lab–Border collie mix, would lunge at Gunther, barking angrily while trying to block his every move. She would literally run in front of him each time he took a step. Gunther, a solid, massive bullmastiff, would position himself in a play bow before Ellie, which, instead of calming her, only made her more agitated. She'd bark more, move backward for a second, then charge forward again with renewed energy. Gunther would stay still for a minute or so while Ellie continued to bark, then finally walk away slowly, with Ellie chasing after him for a good ten to twenty yards until she called it a day and romped back to her owner.

On the face of it, it seemed that Ellie was the dominant dog and Gunther, the more fearful one.

It was anything but. Ellie was a sixty-pound scaredy-dog, and Gunther, calm and deferent, was dominant.

By dominant, we don't mean domineering. We mean confident. A confident dog has an "After you" approach to life. He feels good enough about himself and secure enough with his owner that he's comfortable playing and can let things slide. It doesn't mean he won't ever turn aggressive if he's truly crossed. But for the most part, he's happy simply to get along and have a nice day.

Another kind of behavior may also appear dominant but is not. It's exhibited by a dog who snarls, growls, and otherwise acts inappropriately aggressive, like Ellie. Why do we say Ellie is fearful rather than dominant? Fearful dogs, if they don't exhibit fear via cowering and the like, can act aggressively toward *others*—other dogs, other people. The barking is a dog's version of smoke and mirrors to keep danger away. (It tends to be worse when the dog is *on* a lead rather than off, because when escape is not possible, offense is the only strategy.) Another way of putting it: Some dogs use the language of aggression to try to change the world around them, but they are actually insecure.

Yet a third type of behavior also seems dominant—but isn't, quite. It involves *owner*-directed pushiness on the part of a pup. Such a pet has a flavoring of dominance, but in fact he's confused and anxious about where he stands in the family ranking order, maybe even to the point of being a little paranoid. Such a pup may growl if you go to pet the top of his head, for instance, or even lunge at you if you try to take his bone.

Ideally, by the time your puppy has completed the socialization period at twelve weeks of age, you will have kept him from developing both fear- and owner-directed pushiness through proper socialization and training. And if some tendencies you found undesirable did crop up, by always practicing the three Fs we described earlier—fun, fair, and firm—you should have been able to redirect unfortunate traits. But it always pays to keep in mind that dogs have the mentality of two- to five-year-old children. There's backsliding. There's forgetfulness.

There's human backsliding and forgetfulness, too—and human temperament to take into consideration. A cream puff of an owner (you know who you are) and a highly pushy puppy are going to have a hard time figuring out who's in charge. (It's *always* supposed to be the human.) Conversely, things may not go swimmingly for an anxious puppy and an owner whose strong suit is drill-sergeant leadership. That combo sometimes leads to submissive urination, which, as we explained in the previous chapter, can be mistaken for bad behavior when it is really deference on the puppy's part.

Then, too, not every puppy is *with* his owner from weeks three to twelve, when the learning window is wide open, or with a breeder who knows how to properly educate him. Some dogs are adopted during the second six months of their first year or even later.

That's okay. While preventing problems or dealing with them as soon as they crop up is preferable to treating them a little later on (select the dog who started life out right and you won't have as many behavior problems), there are things you can do to move pushiness or fear to the background in a somewhat older pup. He will still be reasonably malleable.

This chapter will detail steps you can take in a puppy's fourth through twelfth months of life (and, to some degree, even after that) to nip both pushy and fearful behavior in the bud.

Note that a dog does come with his own personality, which you should get at least a glimmer of when you first do temperament testing sometime around the end of a pup's second month of life. No matter how well you implement the leadership program and no matter how careful you are to socialize him properly during the sensitive period of learning, his underlying personality, or temperament, will always be there. That is, you can't eradicate a dog's genetic disposition to be willful or fearful. You can palliate it, and you can make a dog calm and even a joy to live with by altering your relationship with him (the sooner in a pup's life, the better—a six-month-old pup will be more susceptible to your strategies than a nine-month-old). But palliating inborn temperament is different from attempting the impossible: altering the inherent makeup of the dog. Another way of putting it: There are no extremes of cure. While you can modify a pup's behavior, even to a very large degree that will make you quite happy to have him around, you cannot excise his innate personality. You wouldn't want to, anyway. You chose your dog because he seemed like a cuddly sort or an independent sort, right?

Besides, dogs are rarely purely pushy or purely fearful in the first place, so you're probably not looking for an extreme solution to a personality difficulty. For instance, if you were to rate pushiness and fear on scales of 1 to 10, you'd be hard-pressed to find a dog that was a 10 for willful and a 0 for fear, or vice versa. You'd be much more likely to get, say, a 7:3 or a 4:6 ratio, or any other combination. The combination can add up to more than 10, too. You can even get a 10:10, a very pushy yet also very fearful dog, who likely won't be easy to rehabilitate, or even live with, in the first place. (Fortunately, a dog with high scores for both tendencies is rare.)

Because hardly any dog is all one thing, you'll want to read the sections on both pushiness and fear that follow to make sure you've got your puppy covered. You'll probably be *emphasizing* one approach over the other (if socializing your dog and training him haven't gotten him quite where you want him to be), but generally speaking, your "recipe" will contain at least a little of both.

It's important to keep in mind, too, that no matter what behavior you're curbing, *you're* the one in control. It's crucial to continue practicing good leadership by making the rules—and *sticking* with them through proper training. Just like a toddler seems to want control but really wants structure and guidance, so it goes with a puppy. A dog needs reassurance and is looking to you to call the shots, even if it doesn't appear that way.

Follow our instructions and we guarantee you'll end up with a much more secure dog—and a more confident one who is easier and more enjoyable to be around.

LEADING A PUSHY PUP

Generally speaking, puppies should be treated leniently. You should be aiming for reasonably permissive rather than strict—giving the pup attention when he cries, petting him a lot, and otherwise letting him know that you're thrilled to have him. That will not only go a long way toward letting him know that the world is not a place to fear. It will also allow him to develop confidence—and independence.

But some dogs are what we refer to as yuppy puppies. They are a little *too* confident, thinking everything is there for the taking and not developing appropriate deference to you and others. Is your puppy among them?

When the Behavior Is Not Pushy or Fearful but Predatory

While pushiness and fearfulness are modifiable character traits in a puppy, a predatory nature is considerably less mutable. For instance, herders, like Australian cattle dogs and German shepherds, are bred to, well, herd—a propensity that derives from predatory roots. If you don't want to deal with that quality in a dog (who might easily see the need to herd joggers or cars), you should probably not get a herder, as you will likely not enjoy his natural inclinations.

Hounds, too, have a predatory side, with an enhanced ability and motivation to follow a trail by sight or smell. Many scent hounds are so olfactorily driven that they appear to have attention deficit disorder when you are addressing them. They can't seem to get their nose off the ground, which could prove frustrating for some owners.

Then there's unadulterated predatory behavior, often exhibited at high intensity by terriers. If you have a fenced-in yard that is frequented by squirrels and you don't like carnage, it may be best to pass on a Parson Russell terrier, bull terrier, or the like.

204 : SIT! AND OTHER TRICKS

Does he show undue possessiveness over (guarding of) food or objects? Does he growl if you try to take his bone or tell him to move from a particular spot on the couch? Lift a lip if you pet the top of his head or pat him while he's relaxing? Then you can bet he has a fair level of dominance-like instinct, and not the good, confident, live-and-let-live kind of dominance, the largesse that you want a dog to have. Rather, it's the insecure, pushy, bossy, not-toeing-the-line kind of dominance. The Tufts technique for dealing with such a puppy is simple: no free lunch.

No Free Lunch

When you are trying to teach a puppy to stop growling at you, biting, or otherwise trying to rule the roost with some version of willful swagger, a no-free-lunch aspect of your leadership program becomes of utmost importance. Firm has to come out in front of fun and fair. That is, you have to make the pup understand that the *human* is in control, of resources in particular. The dog has to learn that nothing in life is free, including meals, petting, and treats.

How do you show that? You *make the dog work for all the good things in life.* For instance, if it's mealtime and the pup usually badgers you or shoves you aside as you put the food bowl on the floor, make him wait while you prepare breakfast or dinner. Then call your pup to you when you are ready, and instruct him to sit *where* and *when* you want—and stick to your guns. No sit, no food. You are not being harsh. You are simply showing that you are not a short-order cook at your puppy's beck and call but, rather, a "parent" who will not be walked all over.

You can't get a much better motivator for blunting an entitled streak as letting a dog know that he has to do what you say in order to receive valued assets, such as food. This isn't simply what we *believe.* Research with puppies even as young as nine weeks old has shown that potentially more dominant ones made to sit for their food begin acting less like the Donald Trumps of the canine world.

Take a similarly firm approach if your puppy comes over and wants his belly rubbed or wants to be petted. Don't automatically respond. Make him sit first. The puppy should work in order to play games he enjoys, too. If he comes over looking for some play action, don't just indulge him. Show him one of his toys. Make him sit for the toy. *Then* give it, but only if he has actually sat. Lying down instead of sitting, or sitting for half a second, doesn't cut it. Requiring him to comply for real, on the other hand, will make it clear that he's no longer in charge.

Here are three other tactics for curbing pushy, dominant-seeming behavior:

1. Do not respond to overbearing demands. Just as you shouldn't give a child a candy bar every time he asks for it, you shouldn't give a puppy whatever he wants whenever he wants it. A spoiled charge, either human or canine, is a rotten one.

2. Make a willful pup keep off high places—beds and furniture. This sends a clear message that you, not your dog, lead the pack in your house. Specifically, it prevents an uppity dog from being allowed to rule the roost from an elevated position, and it helps you maintain your edge.

3. Do not engage in rough play. While it's fun to have a tug of war with a dog over a stuffed toy or dishtowel, it sends the wrong message to an overconfident pup and may undermine your leadership role.

Remember, none of this means you should be mean to your quick-to-anger dog or unfairly controlling. You need always to remain fair. For instance, if your dog is sleeping, don't wake him and pet him just to show who's boss. Really do let a sleeping dog lie. Also, never yell at or spank your dog, with a rolled-up newspaper or otherwise. The most effective punishment is not actual, physical punishment but, rather, no reward (so called negative punishment). Just ignore your pup when you're not satisfied with his behavior. Dogs are pack animals who don't like to be separated from their pack's leader, even psychologically, so acting as though your dog is not in the room is extremely effective for getting him to change undesirable behavior. Note that forgoing confrontation when you are not happy with your puppy's behavior is not wimpy, as some owners—and trainers—mistakenly believe; it's smart.

As you redirect the bossy tendencies in your older pup, bear in mind that in the interest of controlling behavior, it's okay for a dog to be made emotionally uncomfortable sometimes by withholding attention or a coveted item. That doesn't make you a bad owner. It makes you a *good* owner, because it gives an unruly dog a way of meeting the challenge to truly fit into your household and make you glad to have him as a pet. By the same token, by clearly defining the hierarchy in the household, you're giving your dog the best chance of feeling secure and confident—able to enjoy you, other humans, and other dogs in his life.

SOCIALIZING A FEARFUL DOG

Just as "location, location, location" is the mantra in real estate, with fearful puppies it's "socialization, socialization, socialization." Leadership remains important, as it is for willful dogs, but it's the backdrop, not the centerpiece, of a strategy to make a scared dog less afraid.

Reinforcing the socialization of a fearful puppy can be trickier than setting a rule of no free lunch for a pushy one for a few reasons. First, it doesn't just happen; you have to work at it. Second, as we explained at the beginning of the chapter, fear can sometimes manifest itself as aggression and therefore may not *look* like fear. Third, there are three different kinds of fear, and they have to be dealt with in different ways. We refer to this triad as the Bermuda Triangle of fear.

The Bermuda Triangle of Fear

Both genetics and less-than-optimal training in the first three to twelve weeks of life lead some dogs to exhibit one or more of these three kinds of fear:

1. Fear of other living creatures — people, other dogs.
2. Situational fears — separation anxiety, fear of going in the car, fear of going to the vet.
3. Inanimate fears — fear of sound, flashing lights, slippery floors, thunderstorms, and so on.

No matter which type of fear affects your puppy, there are three things you should absolutely *avoid* doing:

1. Don't make light of it. Fear will not go away on its own, and if you don't deal with it, you'll end up with a more and more underconfident dog who will be thoroughly miserable, unnecessarily distressed, and perhaps unable to integrate well into various aspects of family life.
2. Don't inadvertently foster the problem by treating it as humorous. A little puppy growling at a stranger may look cute, and some owners encourage the inappropriate behavior by joking about it. But when a dog is fully grown and weighs fifty to seventy pounds — or more — the fear he expresses as aggression isn't so cute and may even lead to the pet's relinquishment.
3. Don't sympathize. We don't mean you shouldn't feel bad that your

dog is going through something. But if your dog is acting out through fear—growling at someone, pacing and panting during a storm, and the like—you should not say, "It's okay," and pet the dog reassuringly. That's "stroking" the fearful response. It's saying, nonverbally, "You did the right thing. You had the right reaction."

Instead, use the following strategies, all of which utilize *controlled* reintroductions to whatever the dog is frightened of. Your puppy is not going to become acclimated to whatever he fears with willy-nilly exposure just because you think he should. It's going to take a planned, gradual, and systematic approach, with a lot of stick-to-itiveness on your part. This is especially true when a dog's temperament predisposes him to be afraid. You have to step in and make the puppy less worried and more confident than nature slated him to be.

What it boils down to, no matter what fear you're trying to get your puppy over, is *systematic* desensitization (think stepwise habituation) with counterconditioning. You want to prepare your puppy for anything he may encounter in life by introducing it, or reintroducing it, in a gradual, non-threatening manner.

FEAR OF LIVING THINGS

"Your dog is frightened of children," a neighbor observes. "Take him to a Little League game to desensitize him."

Bad idea.

If your puppy is frightened of children—or people in general—and shows it either by barking at them aggressively or shaking in his paws, it is your job to *protect* him from sudden affronts by avoiding haphazard, in-your-face interactions. Trying to socialize your pup by throwing him into the deep end of the socialization pool will not work and may even make matters worse. All attempts at socializing a fearful pup should be carefully planned and supervised; it is up to *you* to make the puppy feel his environment is safe and to keep him away from all that he's frightened of *except* as part of a properly structured reintroduction program.

How do you supervise socialization for a fearful dog? Carefully engineer every interaction with a series of "stage-managed" exercises.

That's often not what happens. Let's say, for instance, that every time the doorbell rings, your puppy responds by running over to the front hall and

If the Pup Is Afraid of His Own Shadow

Some pups are so fearful, they consistently express their fear not as aggression but as actual fear: hiding under the bed, cowering, and generally acting scared to death. These are the natural omegas in the social hierarchy of dogs. Within a pack, there's the dominant alpha who holds the position of leader, several subordinates filling in the ranks at various levels below the alpha, and, finally, the lowest-ranking omega.

Dogs take that hierarchical approach to their human families, too, and while you want your puppy to consider himself of a somewhat lower status than all the human family members, you don't want him to be so shy or submissive that it hinders his enjoyment—or yours.

That's why, in such cases, you'll want to use a plan we developed at the Cummings School called the Reverse Dominance Program. Its aim is to increase the confidence of an overly submissive dog by rewarding confident and independent behavior while disregarding submissive or shy behavior. Ultimately, this changes the pup's perception of his owners in a positive way so that undue deference and overfearfulness are suppressed. It was reverse dominance we were recommending in the previous chapter to help a pup get over submissive urination.

The practical application, in general, goes like this: Do not acknowledge any submissive behavior from your dog, say, by trying to comfort him if he cowers from you or acts fearfully in a new situation. Also, resist the temptation to scratch your dog's belly if he rolls over on his back, and ignore submissive body language, which includes flattened ears, tail between the legs, and head hung low. If you pay attention to such moves, even negative attention, you will only reinforce the behavior.

Instead, wait to reward confident or relaxed behavior, such as direct eye contact and confident approaches. The way to elicit that kind of behavior is to show your scared puppy that *everything* in life is free. Make a point of allowing the pup on high places or spend more time down on the floor with him. When a dog is at eye level with a person, his authority is increased, which in turn increases his confidence.

In addition, let your shy puppy win tug-of-war games to build bravado, and play chase games during which he chases you—and wins. Give your pup the run of the house, too, if you can (or as much of it as you can). That privilege will translate to the dog as social status.

Finally, don't use body language your scared puppy will consider threatening. Express the benevolence of your leadership by avoiding initiating direct eye contact, and position yourself so the side of your body is facing him rather than the front.

Do not worry that using our Reverse Domi-

barking his head off. Perhaps you respond by angrily yelling "No" or "Stop that" while awkwardly trying to put distance between your pup and your guest. That's the worst thing you can do. Your pup will think you are joining in the fray and barking up a storm, too. Also, it shows that you yourself don't have control of the situation and are in no position to protect your charge, which only makes your pup more anxious.

By the same token, you're not helping your pup if you just let him run behind the bed every time someone knocks. You're allowing him to learn that hiding is the best strategy.

The solution, to start with, is to revisit some strategies from the socialization playbook. Ask visitors not to show up unexpectedly for a while. Instead, arrange for *particular* visitors at *selected* times during which you are able to devote the time and mental energy that are needed to put puppy socialization front and center.

Your first guest should be a gentle person who is comfortable around dogs (this will present the least challenge). Maybe choose a soft-spoken woman guest, then build up to a calm, composed man, then perhaps graduate to a child, whose sudden movements can be jarring and scary to a pup. After that, you may want to escalate to a fix-it man or other "tool-belt" person.

The whole process may take a few months, but along the way, the scenario should stay pretty much the same.

1. You sit with the puppy on a lead next to you, perhaps having him lie in a special safe-place dog bed or blanket and on a lead. A head halter is the preferred teaching tool. It will not hurt your pup; it will simply send the correct signals of your leadership when necessary. As you'll

---

If the Pup Is Afraid of His Own Shadow, continued from page 208

nance Program with your pup will be *too* successful, leaving you with a dominant, aggressive dog. In most instances, pups who need the program don't end up taking undue advantage. With the very small percentage of dogs who do get too big for their britches, growling if you take their toys and such, the solution is to back off from letting them know that everything in life is free and switch to the no-free-lunch approach, in which nothing can be taken for granted. The lesson of who's boss will come across pretty quickly.

recall, when you pull on it gently, it applies pressure around the dog's muzzle and over the nape of his neck. It's the same kind of maternal, finger-wagging-type signal the puppy's own mother would have given by grasping his muzzle or holding him by the scruff of his neck. The tactile sensations effectively transmit a signal that says, "Whatever you're doing, cut it out and listen to me."

2. The bell rings (at the appointed time) or there's a (scheduled) knock at the door. Escort your puppy to the door, applying gentle upward tension to the head halter if he starts barking or otherwise acting out. He will eventually stop remonstrating and be compelled to sit (when his head goes up, his butt goes down, through leverage). At this point you release the tension on the head halter, pet your pup firmly by stroking him from behind his eyes back over the top of his head while you look right at him (leadership signals), and then let in the visitor.

Greet the visitor calmly. "Hello. Welcome. I'd like you to meet my dog. By the way, please don't reach down to pet him because it frightens him. Instead, take this food treat from me and drop it onto the floor." Remind your guest not to stare at your puppy (this would be interpreted as a challenging gesture from a stranger), and encourage the person to walk in a curved path around the pup to defuse any potential threat or confrontation. (The more fearful the dog, the larger the personal space he needs around him—a bubble that's all too easy to prick.) Later in the desensitizing process, if you invite over a man with a loud voice, ask him to speak a little more quietly until the pup gets used to him.

3. Bring your guest in to sit with you in the living room, kitchen, or wherever you'd like. Keep your pup next to you and pay him attention when he is acting calmly. After a while, ask your guest to *gently* stand up and then sit down again *without* looking at the dog. That lets the dog know, "Okay, people occasionally stand up and move around. It's not a bad thing. I can handle it."

Say your guest wants to visit the bathroom. Perhaps hand her or him some sort of toy or treat to give to the pup upon returning—a tennis ball or a delectable morsel. If, as the person rises, the dog barks or lunges, apply steady, upward tension to the head halter and say nothing except a calm yet firm command like "Quit it." If the pup complies, release the tension and say, "Good pup!"

Little by little your pup will learn that people who come to the house are *your* visitors, not his, and that you control the situation. That takes a lot of pressure off the pup to try to protect himself. In pretty short order, your dog will learn not only that you'll make sure nothing bad happens but also that *good* things happen when people come over. You'll soon be able to let the bell ring without having planned it ahead of time.

Close Encounters of the Outside Kind

Just as you protect your fearful dog from unanticipated interactions with people indoors, you'll want to do the same outside. For starters, don't let him off the leash in a public place. That provides too much opportunity for un expected run-ins with humans or other dogs, and too much opportunity to let the dog make his own bad decisions (which sows the seeds for future bad decisions). Also, use a head halter or harness, *never* a choke chain, in case you need to gently remind the pup to stop what he's doing (lunging, barking, snarling) and listen to you.

Don't let people be intimidating to your dog even if they mean well. If someone asks, "May I pet your dog?" don't automatically respond by saying yes because you want to will the dog to be friendlier. Remind yourself how big and scary people must appear to a small pup, especially if they reach down and invade his personal space. Instead say, "Please don't pet him. I'm still training him to be calm around people, and that will make him nervous."

You *can* give the person a food treat to toss to your pup. Keep treats with you, such as freeze-dried liver, so the person you're talking to can casually drop some at the dog's feet without looking at him. Over time, that type of interaction will engender positive associations in the pup's mind. In addition, as best as you can manage it:

1. Don't let people stare at your puppy, which he will perceive as very frightening.

2. Don't let people walk straight toward you and the pup; instead, ask them to avoid a head-on approach. A circuitous route will be perceived as less threatening.

3. Don't let someone with a deep voice speak to the pup unless he's willing to raise his voice an octave or two.

Just as in the house, the puppy will come to realize that out of the house, too, you are making sure that bad things do not happen. Even better, your pup will see that humans, even outdoors, can be tolerated and are sometimes a source of good things. The slack you cut your dog (specifically, the length of free leash you permit) can get greater and greater until, eventually, some unsupervised running around can be permitted—that is, if your fearful pup can deal with other dogs, too.

It's a Dog-Meets-Dog World

Sometimes it's hard to know why a dog has become fearful of other dogs. It could be that he had a bad experience without your realizing it. Maybe he had a bad experience before he came into your care. Whatever the reason, use the same set of rules in desensitizing him as you would in desensitizing him to humans; work hard to prevent up-close interactions with other dogs unless they are fully orchestrated and controlled by you.

It is best to work it one dog at a time, with an owner who's *very* much in control of his or her dog. Think of the encounter you are about to set up as a controlled play date.

Start with a really nice cream puff of a dog. (For Ellie, the scared dog mentioned at the beginning of this chapter, that cream puff was Melville, a small, loopy Scottish terrier who seemed to mistake Ellie's aggressive fear for play behavior and kept coming back for more, until Ellie couldn't help but be won over.)

The initial meeting should occur on neutral territory, say, a park that neither pup has ever been to. With both dogs wearing head halters and on leash, start the introductions with the two at a safe (nonstressful) distance from each other, and gradually reduce the distance between them as the dogs' reactions permit. One way to do this is to walk your pup around the other dog in circles of ever-decreasing circumference (reversing direction occasionally so you don't get dizzy). Then have the other owner repeat the procedure, with the other dog being circled around yours. You may not be able to get the dogs very close on the first or second (or third) play date, and you may even lose some ground between sessions. But you will make steady progress overall.

Once the dogs can be near each other without barking and snapping, perhaps for an entire stroll around the perimeter of a small field or other area, walk them back to one of the owners' homes. You might even have one person walk both dogs, one on either side, to enhance the sense that they're "on the same team." Then get them used to sharing a home territory by feeding them together and playing with them together (perhaps in the yard to start with). Lavish plenty of praise on both for good, playful behavior. Be free with treats, high-voice praises, and compliments.

After the two dogs are truly used to each other, perhaps after several visits, you may want to give it a go off leash outside (you can leave long, lightweight "drag lines" attached so that either dog can be immediately apprehended in the event of a squabble). Take them to a park where dogs are allowed off their leashes, and see what happens. Remember to remain upbeat and positive; heap praise on the puppies for their friendly behavior toward each other.

Such a series of staged introductions should be arranged for each individual new dog friend. It may take multiple introductions to ten, fifteen, or even twenty different dogs to convince a fearful pup that not all dogs are bad. But your pup will finally get the picture, to the point that he will even be able to romp outside—and off leash—with dogs he hasn't met previously.

SITUATIONAL FEAR

The most common situational fear experienced by puppies is separation anxiety. It affects up to one in six dogs. Everyone has heard stories of dogs being so afraid alone at home that they rip up furniture, window shades, and storm doors, generally destroying the home as they go. But even dogs like that can be retrained, especially if they're less than a year old.

What's necessary with a "Velcro dog" who shadows his owners and cannot bear their leaving the house is independence training that teaches the puppy to stand on his own four feet. Retraining takes resolve and persistence on your part—but always without punishment, not even for destructive behavior that occurs in your absence. At the same time, you shouldn't cater to the dog's neediness with long, affectionate, worried goodbyes, which only serve to confirm that your leaving *is* a big deal.

Instead, a dog who starts to whimper, cry, pant, pace, or tremble within minutes of his owner's leaving needs a very matter-of-fact approach, one that gets the message across that temporary separation is not a catastrophe. Be casual about it: "See you later. Watch the house for me."

If the puppy is too anxious for that to work, try feeding him just as you leave.

That wasn't always the advice. In the old days, the recommendation for a dog with a high amount of separation anxiety was to ignore him for twenty minutes before leaving. But that has fallen out of favor—for good reason. It's rather harsh, and it doesn't work very well, anyway. Feeding the dog, on the other hand, may successfully distract him: "Hey, look what I've got!" Make it fun. It can be a very effective tactic, because the first five to ten minutes after you leave in the morning are the toughest for the puppy, and a meal can be just the thing to take his mind off his aloneness. If he doesn't eat the food you leave for him, pick it up immediately upon your return and feed the evening meal sometime later. A dog who does not eat his morning rations for a few days will get to the point that his hunger overcomes his separation anxiety. Appetite trumps fear.

Other bridges toward confidence and independence:

When you leave the house, put on an audiotape with your voice and household sounds to provide the dog with comfort in your absence (our preference), or leave the television or radio on.

Call your puppy on your answering machine from a neighbor's house or from work. Speak reassuringly, not sympathetically. (If you tell "the poor thing" that he's going through something awful, you will be directly teaching your pup that your leaving the house without him *is* something awful.)

Leave the pup his crate with the door open, near a window, so he can cocoon himself while watching the outside world. A glass sliding door in the kitchen or family room is great for this, because it allows you to keep the crate on the floor.

When you do return, do not be overaffectionate. If you make a big reunion out of every return, the puppy will end up on an emotional rollercoaster ride every time you come back from the supermarket, and the problem will be harder to resolve.

If the dog is extremely anxious about being apart from you and literally dogs your steps, you can do some training while you're at home. One solution is to make a point of *not always being available.* You may want to help a needy dog along some of the time, but it's not necessary—and is actually counterproductive—to respond to his neediness all of the time.

Another aspect of independence training involves teaching your pup to sit or lie down while you take two paces back, then work up to five paces, and, finally, leave the room. If the dog is able to stay put and not follow you, reward him with warm praise and a food treat. It's a way of saying, "See, you were okay," while praising the pup for his good behavior.

You'll also need to get such a pup out of your bed at night at some point and to teach him to cope on his own in the wee hours. For the first six months of a puppy's life, it's okay to cater to him, if necessary, by letting him sleep with you. But in the second six months, it might be time to teach a fearful puppy that he must learn to inhabit his own space, not yours. You can start by putting a dog bed next to your bed, then gradually moving it toward, and finally to the other side of, the bedroom door. Be persistent and don't waiver. Every time the dog gets up and comes back over to your bed, acknowledge that you know he's worried but tell him cheerfully, "Back to bed, you," and lead him back to his own spot. Then pleasantly but firmly tell the pup, "Lie down." If you stick to your guns, the puppy will learn over time that he can handle being separated from you at night. That's a huge step on the road to full independence.

Again, you're not being unkind. You're helping the pup adjust to the fact that you're not going to be in his presence every single minute of his life, and that being alone is nothing to get worked up about.

Fear of Car Rides

After separation anxiety, one of the most common situational trepidations is fear of car rides. How to get a puppy over it? As always, the trick is to acclimate your pup with baby steps.

You might want to start by feeding the puppy next to the car so that he associates the big "steel dragon" with something pleasant—his meals. Then

You can help desensitize a young puppy to riding in cars by playing with him in one.

you can graduate to feeding your pup on a step that's level with the floor of the car. From there you'll go on to give him the food *on* the floor of the car. Move from there to playing with him *in* the car.

In a study at Tufts that included hundreds of dogs, we found that at least 50 percent of those who had separation anxiety as adults came from the school of hard knocks—multiple owners, abusive owners, poor environment, and so on.

Once he's comfortable with that, turn on the engine but don't drive. When your pup can tolerate the sound, let the car roll backward a little to introduce the variable of movement. Then, when he's ready, drive—around the block. Provide lots of praise (not to be confused with sympathy) to augment confident (nonfearful) behavior. Next time out, go on a shortish ride that ends in a pleasant experience—perhaps at the home of someone your dog really loves or at a park in which he particularly likes to frolic. Over time, you will have adjusted your pup to the car to the point that he doesn't find car rides unpleasant at all.

Fear of the Vet

If your dog is afraid of going to the doctor, it pays to bear in mind that almost every visit to the veterinarian's office does result in something unpleasant: shots, the pup's mouth being forced open, his nails trimmed, and general poking and prodding. In other words, this is one fear that makes sense from a human perspective. The trick is to dilute the unpleasant experiences.

Start by bringing your pup to the vet's office but remaining in the parking lot, at the edge of the property. There, play with your dog. Bounce a ball, toss a Frisbee, give food treats, play other games. Then go home.

Next time, get a little closer to the entrance as you play. Your pup will be learning that wonderful things happen at that location.

The next time, perhaps, get your pup onto the front steps, and the time after that, into the waiting room. Try to get the staff in on it. Leave off food treats for them to hand out, and ask them to pet and make a big fuss over your dog.

If your veterinarian is amenable, ask him or her to come around the corner wearing a lab coat while all the fun is going on and give your pup a treat, say hello to him, and keep walking. Your vet might go for it, because puppy stress wastes time during a visit in the examination room. Some vets may even be willing to sit on the floor with your pup and play with him a bit, making it that much easier for the dog to learn that the vet is his friend, and the veterinarian's office, a good place to be.

FEAR OF INANIMATE THINGS

As with other kinds of fear, what's key here is reintroducing the puppy to whatever he's afraid of in a gradual, structured way—instilling confidence in the face of perceived adversity. Take storm phobia, part of which is about noise phobia—the most common inanimate fear among puppies.

You can't entirely prevent a storm-phobic pup from being exposed to the elements, but you can work to soften the experience.

In mild cases, you can take your pup to the basement, where the noise may not be as loud, and draw blinds or curtains while playing white noise to drown out the sounds of the storm. Don't sympathize or agonize over what your dog is going through, because this behavior transmits to the pup that what he's going through is unbearable. Instead, distract your little friend. Have fun by playing fetch or engaging in some other jolly routine. As the dog focuses on the fun, gradually increase exposure, maybe not to the first storm but to the third. Open the blinds a little. The next time around, leave the door to the kitchen open. Before very long, your dog will get the picture that a storm is nothing to be afraid of because it doesn't change the fun, relaxed atmosphere of the home. It presents no danger.

In more severe cases, you may want to buy a high-quality recording of the sounds of a storm—wind and rain crackling, occasional thunder, and so on. Start by playing the recording softly, then work up from there.

We want to caution you here that storm phobia is hard to overcome. With some puppies, even darkening skies will cause panic.

But there's hope. Ongoing research at Tufts Cummings School suggests that it's not always the sound of thunder that's the worst part of a storm for some scared pups, but shocks resulting from a buildup of static electricity. Think about the fact that during a storm, you'll often find a dog in the bathtub, pressed behind the pipe, or even in the sink—anywhere there are pipes that conduct electricity away. The reason, it seems, is that pups become "charged" during electric storms and thus are prone to getting shocked. Think how alarming this would be for a pup doing what a pup does—investigating his environment with his highly sensitive (in more ways than one) nose. Zing—ouch! (Big ouch!)

If static electricity turns out to be a factor in serious storm phobia, there appears to be a very simple solution: an antistatic, Superman-like cape. Don't laugh. In a study directed by Tufts researcher Nicole Cottam, MS, under the auspices of our Behavior Clinic, more than 50 percent of puppies whose owners equipped them with an antistatic cape at the beginning of a

An antistatic cape with a metallic lining may help puppy avoid the discomfort of shocks from static electricity during a thunder-and-lightning downpour.

storm become completely calm within about three storms. The underside of the cape has a flexible metallic lining that prevents the dog from becoming statically charged. Dogs not fitted with the cape usually get worse over time. (See "Resources" for information on purchasing an antistatic cape.)

Other Inanimate Fears

Other inanimate things puppies can end up fearful of include vacuum cleaners and various other noisy household items. You know what you have to do. Get your pup playing around the offending appliance when it's not on, and, by means of tape-recorded sounds of the machine, gradually increase the pup's exposure to the noise. Eventually, combine the sight and sound of the feared object. After a while, you'll be able to turn on the blender, coffee grinder, or vacuum cleaner without your dog going crazy.

Same with slippery floors, another common inanimate object that strikes terror into the hearts of some puppies. Perhaps start by putting down a runner to get the dog out onto the middle of the "ice." Once he's there, distract him with toys and treats. Take it one patient step at a time, and after a while your charge will be able to handle shiny walkways. (It should be noted that some floors really *are* slippery and may cause the pup to hurt himself by slipping, so don't try to adjust the pup to a floor when it's really the floor that needs adjusting.)

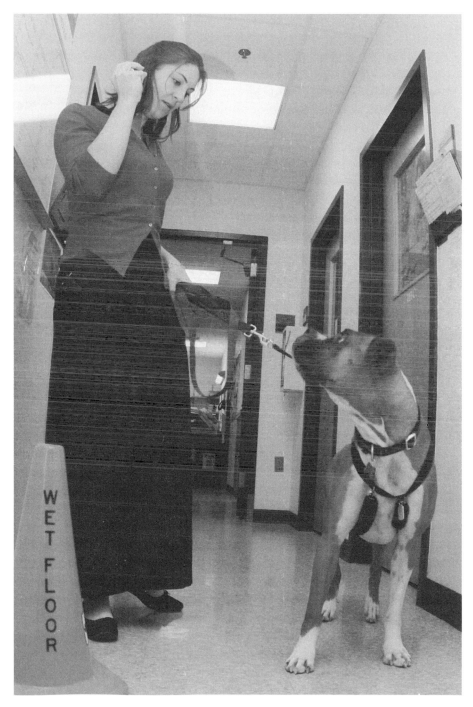

Some pups develop fearfulness of slippery floors.

WHEN IT'S TIME TO CONSIDER MEDICATION

Sometimes you end up stuck. No matter what you have tried to help a pup attenuate his fear—or aggression or other mood disorder—his genetics or unfortunate experiences prior to coming to live in your home have gotten the better of him. Nothing seems to work.

In such cases, a prescription for antianxiety medication from your vet may be the right way to go.

There tends to be a knee-jerk reaction toward giving a puppy behavior-modifying medication. There is no shortage of critics who say some veterinarians are too quick to reach for drugs. But drugs are a reasonable last resort, to be used when a puppy has been unresponsive to behavior modification techniques through socializing or training, and when his owners are saying, "This dog is so willful—or so frightened and skittish—that we are not sure we can keep him."

Since two out of three dogs who go into shelters do not come out alive, what do you have to lose by trying medication if all else has failed?

Nothing. In fact, short-term pharmacologic intervention can help a pup who hasn't been able to get a handle on life finally turn a corner so that behavior interventions *will* have an impact. That is, in many instances, drugs are a means to an end.

Consider the case of a Lhasa apso whose owners brought him to our offices because he became extremely bent out of shape with the arrival in the house of a new baby. The dog growled at the infant and began urine marking around the house to show his displeasure. The new parents were worried, not only that their baby would get bitten but also that the urine was making their home unhygienic. Dr. Dodman prescribed medicine, and both the growling at the baby and the urine marking stopped—immediately. The parents were then able to work behaviorally with the dog to help him get past his jealousy.

There are a number of mood-altering drugs. One class of medications, tricyclic antidepressants, stabilizes a puppy's mood and makes him feel better about himself by increasing brain levels of serotonin and norepinephrine. Tricyclic antidepressants may also prove effective in getting a dog who urinates submissively—or, like the dog described above, urine marks the inside of your home—through a behavioral impasse. That's because these drugs not only have mood-stabilizing properties; they also relax bladder muscles, increase bladder capacity, decrease the urge to void, and increase tone in the valvelike internal sphincter of the bladder. The three tricyclic antidepressants that may be used to treat inappropriate urination include amitriptyline (Elavil), imipramine (Tofranil), and clomipramine (Clomicalm).

More recently, fluoxetine (Prozac), a selective serotonin reuptake inhibitor, has been found to be efficacious in the treatment of a variety of anxiety-related disorders, including aggression, various fears and phobias, stress-induced urine marking, and compulsive disorders. It works as well as, if not better than, tricyclic antidepressants and has fewer side effects.

Another highly specific antianxiety medication, buspirone (Buspar), was first used at the Cummings School to treat severe, refractory, anxiety-based conditions. It is now prescribed for very anxious dogs as far away as Japan.

Dr. Dodman first used buspirone on dogs at the Tufts campus in 1987 — a year after it was approved for humans — with great success. One of his cases was Roscoe, a min pin (miniature Doberman pinscher) who suffered from worry and anxiety. Roscoe was the opposite of lighthearted, which is to say he was kind of sour and often growled at other dogs. His owner, who entered her charges in dog shows, was very knowledgeable about canine behavior problems and had already run the gamut of behavioral solutions: no free lunch, setting limits, realistic expectations. Nevertheless, Roscoe's sour mood persisted.

Finally Dr. Dodman treated him with buspirone, and it was as if Roscoe's cloud had lifted. He reverted to puppylike behavior: attention seeking, playful, and friendly. His owner was able to continue training him and reported, "He is *so* much better on Buspar . . . His growliness toward other dogs has gone, and that is very important to me. He was such a concern during dog shows with other dogs approaching."

Note that all of these drugs work as *background* treatments by adjusting the "thermostat" of anxiety and impulsivity. A puppy's underlying fear or uncertainty can break through if conditions are overwhelming. Also, most of these medications require one to two months to get up to speed; it takes a while for the requisite changes to occur in brain chemistry. For these reasons, you may need one or another supplementary medication as frontline treatment to handle acute fear — at least initially. Immediate-acting medications that will alleviate fear or anxiety include diazepam (Valium); a Valium-like drug called alprazolam (Xanax); and a beta-blocker called propranolol (Inderal).

You may need a frontline treatment for only a couple of months. But the plan should be to dispense with either or both treatments at the first opportunity once suitable learning has occurred. The reduction in fearfulness is

222 : SIT! AND OTHER TRICKS

often on the order of 50 to 75 percent, as opposed to 100 percent. But that's still a remarkable degree of success, and will be much appreciated by your pup! Thus, if your puppy exhibits intractable fear, such as extremely destructive behavior born of separation anxiety, talk with your veterinarian about the advisability of a prescription for antianxiety medication.

TWO STEPS FORWARD . . .

If you follow our recommendations for dogs who are either too big or too little for their britches, they will yield powerful results, even for a puppy who has you at your wit's end. But it's very important to keep in mind that nothing *always* works for all dogs. Be prepared for some trial and error, because you've got to figure it out to some degree as you go along. For instance, with some dogs who are scared of people, the best thing to do when the doorbell rings is *not* to take the dog to the door but to instruct the pup to go to his own bed, where he will need to be to feel safe. Likewise, for some dogs with submissive urination, the answer is to train your pup to stand when you come in the door so he can't assume the urinating position.

How do you know if you've taken the right tack? If you try something for three to five days (or on three to five different occasions) and the unfortunate behavior is not showing signs of abating, it's time to try something else. It generally doesn't take all that long for a puppy to respond to a strategy that he's going to respond to.

Bear in mind, too, that leading a dominant puppy or socializing a fearful one may be an ongoing pursuit. Just when you think you've got a problem licked, the wrong person could rekindle it, perhaps a repairman who's friendly but a loud, in-your-face type. That is, you might occasionally have to engage in some remedial training.

Take heart. It gets easier each time around. And the happier, more confident dog you get for life in return—who brings you a lot of pleasure—is well worth the effort.

11

Environmental Enrichment

IT SEEMED, ON THE FACE OF IT, LIKE SEPARATION ANXIETY. WHEN YUKON'S owners brought him to our Behavior Clinic, they explained that every time they left the house, he trashed it, chewing up couches and paper and pretty much anything else he could get his paws on. He also chewed his way through his crate, ripped through doors and window screens, and generally wreaked havoc by trying to escape. His aim certainly appeared to be to chase after his human folk. But this young, active Siberian husky–Border collie mix, while exhibiting behaviors that coincided with certain classic signs of separation anxiety, was not nervous about their leaving or about being alone; there was no dysfunctional bond between Yukon and his people. Rather, he simply was bored—and became even more bored when his owners left for the day. By breaking apart doors and screens, he was trying to get out of the house and *do* something.

Boredom is the scourge of dogs, particularly young dogs, across the country. Their owners take the time when they first get them home to housetrain them and engage them in some basic command training. They may even enroll them in a puppy training class. But by the time the pup is several months old, he's often left alone for several hours, or even the entire day, while the people in the house go to work and school. They may feel guilty about leaving their pet alone but put on the television or radio for stimulation and figure that those distractions, along with barking at the mailman and other passers-by, will be enough to keep the pup engaged. It's not.

While *you* might like sitting around a home with a stereo and TV and perhaps some plush furniture, those accouterments will have little appeal to a puppy. You have to "think dog" to keep your pup suitably occupied. It's crucial for two reasons. The first is that dogs, as they mature, have the mentality of toddlers or preschoolers, in many ways. Imagine leaving a preschooler alone all day with nothing, absolutely nothing, to do and no one to interact with and then just hugging her a bit and feeding her dinner when you arrived back home. It would be absolutely cruel, and so it would be with your puppy. She deserves better than that, both when she's young and throughout her life.

Second, idle doggie minds do mischief make, as Yukon's owners learned the hard way. Indeed, all too many dogs are given to shelters because their owners, who go out all day, label their pets "incorrigible" when they return to find their homes turned upside down. Even those dogs whose owners go the extra step of taking them to a veterinarian or trainer to find out what's wrong don't necessarily fare much better. Very well-meaning animal professionals sometimes misdiagnose lack of stimulation or engagement as separation anxiety, with the result that the dog is given medication when what she really needs is something to do.

Sometimes a dog is so understimulated that she goes from stir-crazy to crazed and really does need medication to help her cope. That's what happened to Hermione, a pointer whose owner consulted us because out of the blue she'd taken to phantom circling, pointing, digging, and hunting—not just in the yard but also indoors. We say "phantom" because there was nothing to hunt. The dog would just keep repeating the behavior with such frequency and intensity that she developed a true compulsive disorder. It had gotten to the point that she'd forget to eliminate when she was outdoors and couldn't focus enough to interact with her owners, resulting in significant disruption to her normal functioning.

Why did this happen? Hermione's owner was a hunter who often took his dog out with him, but he had to have knee surgery, which laid him up for a while, and so the dog was without her usual job. To cope, she invented one. To help Hermione conquer the compulsivity, we prescribed some medication on a temporary basis and came up with tasks she could engage in while her owner recuperated. It worked, and her problem resolved over time.

It's not just hunting and working dogs who need a job. Even adorable toy dogs who look great sitting on their owner's lap need a job to do to remain emotionally healthy. Consider that in the wild, the ancestors of today's domesticated dogs spent a considerable amount of time each day just procuring their next meal; no one brought them a day's nutritional allotment in a bowl.

Of course, if you're following the advice we have given in preceding chapters, your pup is already getting a fair amount of activity. She's frequently socializing with you, other humans, and other dogs. She's hard at work with training, learning how to follow your cues to sit, come, and perform other tasks. She's getting on the order of half a dozen walks outside each day, which allow her to relieve herself *and* explore her world. She's having regular meals and grooming sessions. And because you love her, she gets a fair amount of cuddle time, during which you stroke her and otherwise make her feel close and warm.

But eating, peeing, and cuddling are not enough. In fact, too much cuddling can foster undue dependency and even disrespect in certain dogs. You've got to purposefully and exhaustively keep your pup occupied. The more mindful you are about keeping your puppy busy, the better off not only will she be, but also everyone else in the household. An engaged dog is less likely to wonder what the cat tastes like, how good a chomping stick a chef's knife would make (it won't be long before a larger dog can reach the kitchen counter on her hind legs), or how far she can unfurl a roll of toilet paper.

What follows are ways to help keep your pup — and adult dog — occupied, with some suggestions for keeping her busy even when you or others might not be around.

HOW TO THINK DOG

By at least one estimate, adult dogs sleep an average of fourteen hours a day (puppies and very large adult dogs sleep even more), so there is a fair amount of downtime. But unlike people, dogs don't tend to get most of their sleep in all at once. They nod off between bursts of activity — exploring, smelling, tasting, and the like. (This is even more true for pups than adult dogs.)

The best way to satisfy your puppy's penchant for bursts of activity: Approximate the way she would keep active if she lived on her own. That means building into her life opportunities to run, jump, hunt, bite, chase, chew, mouth, tumble, wrestle, and so on. Just how can you do that if you live in, say, a suburban cul-de-sac or on the tenth floor of an apartment building? In large part, with the right toys.

Plush, Squeaky, Chewy

A puppy should have toys with different textures and games built into them to accommodate her various natural instincts and keep things interesting. For instance, there are several **toys that make a job of procuring food.** These contraptions render eating a very mouthy, teething, sucking experience—just right for a young dog. One of them is called a *Kong,* which is a hard rubber toy that's hollow in the center with a small opening near one end. Into that opening can go a young puppy's kibble, which she has to work to retrieve. When the pup reaches the age of five or six months, you

Plush, Squeaky, Chewy. The chewy thing on the right is a Kong.

can graduate her to different Kong treats, such as a bit of peanut butter or cream cheese or grated carrot mixed with water and then frozen. Vanilla yogurt works, too. Just put a bit of yogurt into the Kong and then let the whole thing sit in the freezer for a while. Frosty Paws, frozen dog treats available in some supermarkets, can be slightly thawed, then put in the Kong and refrozen, too.

Boomer balls also make absorbing work out of eating. These are hard plastic balls that may have holes drilled into them. That's where the kibble goes,

Is Playing Tug the Right Way to Go?

Puppies tend to like to tug on rope toys now and again. The texture is sometimes just what they need for teething. But many trainers advise against playing tug with your pup. It has long been thought that tug-of-war games make puppies more aggressive. Research has shown that it's not so cut-and dry, however.

In fact, games of tug that allow a meek pup to win can help her build self-confidence. And some dogs benefit from tug games because they teach them to give up to their owners whatever might be in their mouth. It works as follows. When a pup presents a toy to initiate a game, her owner can say, "What've you got?" The pup proudly shows her booty, the owner takes it (with a "Give it" cue), praises her, then returns the toy to initiate a game of tug.

This teaches the dog who calls the shots because it switches the commencement of the game from the dog to the owner after the dog *asks* to play by presenting and then relinquishing the object, say, a rope or chew toy. That is, instead of the pup goading her

owner into a kind of chase game, the owner shows genuine curiosity in what the pup is showing and the dog is thereby cued to *share*. That way, when the pup starts mouthing and carrying off something that her owner doesn't want her to have, she will be able to share and relinquish, at which point the owner can praise her compliance and then refocus the pup's attention onto something more acceptable.

The bottom line: Tugging games can be useful. To go a step further, tugging is a natural behavior for dogs that you need to acknowledge and allow for. But you need to acknowledge it intelligently. Use the specific tactics described here in combination with common sense. No matter what lesson you are trying to instill, if you engage in a tug game with your dog and she becomes too aggressive or overwrought, stop. You might decide to try it again another day, but sense a reasonable limit and stick to it. If the pup *always* gets controlling, possessive, and too feisty, it's probably best not to play tug with her at all.

and many puppies love rolling and pushing the ball to make the food come out. *Buster cubes* work along the same lines. The dog has to get the food to come out of various geometric shapes cut into the cube. You can make it harder or easier depending on just how big you want the openings of those shapes to be.

Twist & Treat toys also allow pups to express some of their mouthing instinct on reaching their food. The top screws down, and you can make the gap between the top and the bottom as narrow or wide as you want, depending on how difficult you want to make it for your dog to get her food. Your pup will bat the thing around, chasing and attacking it until some food falls out.

Most dogs enjoy food toys. Dogs who are more naturally wired to work for their food—including those with high predatory tendencies, such as terriers; herding and hunting breeds; and northern breeds like malamutes and Siberian huskies—may be particularly apt to get something out of them. For such breeds, wrestling with the toy will be as much of a reward as getting the food out.

Plush toys are great for when your pup is feeling particularly feisty and mouthy. Puppies investigate the world with their mouths, and all dogs have at least some predatory biological imperative. Supplying plush toys helps to redirect a pup's instincts onto acceptable objects rather than human flesh, cashmere socks, or valued household treasures. We especially recommend plush-within-plush toys. The outer toy has a Velcro closure that the puppy has to pry open with her teeth and paws. Once inside, she finds another plush toy with another Velcro closure. Inside that smaller toy is a replaceable squeaky toy that the dog bites until she punctures it. Great fun! Dogs seem to like the sound of the Velcro, and they'll work hard to open it and get to the prize. (Sometimes you can substitute a food treat for the squeaky toy inside.)

Velcro plushes are much better, in our opinion, than plush toys whose pouches are stitched together with thread. Once the puppy reaches the squeaky toy inside a stitched plush object, you'll end up throwing the whole thing out. Who's going to sit there and keeping sewing up the pouch? Better you spend that time engaging with your pup.

Along with food toys and plush toys should come *chew toys,* such as dried chew sticks. Plush toys and many food toys are great when the puppy is raring to go and full of energy, and a Kong might be good not only for those times but for "nursing," when the pup is tired and needs something to help her fall asleep. A chew stick can be good to gnaw on when the pup is not so tired but needs a bit of downtime, as you do.

All the toys you buy your dog (and there are more than we can delve into here, including ones that move on their own) can be used to redirect her energy and keep her out of trouble. Some chewy toys can even be scented with various aromas to entice not just scent hounds but all kinds of dogs. For instance, many dogs love the smell of vanilla or anise. Others are really curious about hunting lure odors (obtainable from sporting goods departments of large stores). If these odors are added to an otherwise boring toy, perhaps a rope chew toy, it will suddenly have new attraction. Then, if you see your pup mouthing your socks, or a silk tie or scarf, you can replace your valuables with the more interestingly scented alternative. If your fur ball of

The You Factor

Never underestimate your own role in your puppy's environmental enrichment, and not just because you must be there to rotate toys. Today's dogs are very people-oriented, depending greatly on their owners not simply for varied activities but also for a sense of family in general.

This was not always the case. Recent molecular studies indicate that dogs were domesticated from wolves in East Asia at least fifteen thousand years ago, and those predomesticated wolves saved their sociability for *each other*. Domestic dogs in the here and now, on the other hand, were bred to be with people—and not only to work with and for them. Via breeding, we have also increased dogs' need for *social* interaction with humans. Some dogs, in fact, like to socialize with humans more than with other dogs.

That's true now more than ever, because the working relationship between dogs and humans is largely a thing of the past. Currently, a dog's ability, even biological need, to respond to human communication signals is played out not on the farm, on the hunt, or in other work spheres but purely in the social arena. In other words, your role as companion, as opposed to work boss, is more central than ever to a dog's inclination to interact with you. You truly have to be an integral part of your canine friend's life for her biologically driven social and emotional needs to be met.

Indeed, some research has even suggested that a dog may be better at interpreting—and responding to—her owner's communication signals than people often assume. The body language that accompanies our words (pointing, of course, but also mood-defining body language that expresses whether we are tense, relaxed, fearful, or anxious) helps them along.

a cat is tired of being chased, you can get your pup interested in your custom-scented furry toy—or in a ball or other object that rolls or bounces around and keeps getting away from her just as she pounces.

Keep in mind that none of these distractions takes the place of *you*. Even a fairly young pup will learn how to open something like a Velcro plush toy within minutes, so you've got to be there to keep interacting, rotating toys, and generally taking on the role of the best, most fun "preschool" teacher there is. A toy chest chock-full of goodies is no good without someone to share the fun.

The best bet is to keep some items out at all times but tuck away some favorites so that the pup learns to ask for—and earn—the cool stuff. That will help keep her life more interesting. Too many puppies have free access to all of their toys—and end up bored.

NOTE: Certain toys are not safe for certain dogs unless you are there to supervise. For instance, bull terriers and other strong-jawed breeds are serious chewers and should not be left alone with objects they could tear into small pieces (or sizable chunks) and then potentially swallow. Plush toys (and rawhide bones) are among those objects that are easily ripped apart

---

Puppy Day Care

We cannot stress enough that if you have a puppy at home, you should be home, too. Leaving a pup alone for several hours at a time is going to result in a very frustrated, anxious dog whom you don't much enjoy being around even though it was you who raised her.

Of course, in today's world, staying with a puppy all day is easy to say and hard to do. But there's more than one way not to leave a puppy alone.

Whether or not you're a stay-at-home owner, some pups thrive on the environmental enrichment conferred by several hours a day of puppy day care. Those who have the

temperament for it enjoy the interactions with other dogs and with the human caretakers who look after them. They like the romping, the play time, and the socializing.

If you decide to use doggie day care, either because you simply want your dog to have different kinds of activity or because you *must* return to work outside the home, choose a place wisely. There's no accreditation for dog-sitting enterprises, so you need to visit a few places and get a feel. Are the people nice? Does the establishment have an unpleasant odor? Do the pups seem, in general, happy?

Make sure, too, that enough people are

and can get lodged in the throat or cause other GI problems. Dogs, puppies in particular, should also not be left alone with toys that have small parts attached, such as bells or eyeballs, which can end up causing dangerous obstructions, even death. Finally, make sure that balls and other fun things are not the right size for getting stuck in a puppy's throat — or swallowed whole.

TRICKS FOR TREATS

Beyond keeping a good toy chest, you can teach your puppy tricks. This is a little different from training, which keeps your dog safe, under control, and mannerly. Tricks are just for the fun of it.

Dogs love tricks. They *like* to think, they *like* to challenge themselves, and they *like* to succeed, and learning new tricks speaks to all those instincts. Owners like tricks, too. They're one more opportunity for bonding with their pets, one more chance to find out just how intelligent and cooperative their little charges can be.

Part of the reason for a pup's intelligence coming through with tricks is that an owner's body language tends to be more relaxed and happy — more

---

Puppy Day Care, continued from page 230

there to supervise the dogs — and separate them should a problem break out. Also be certain that the dog groups are kept small. Some day care facilities may be tempted to take in large groups of dogs for financial reasons, but that can make it too easy for a dog to become overstimulated, which can lead to aggression.

Your puppy should also not be put only with adult dogs; there should be other puppies in the mix. And be certain that the workers don't use any counterproductive punishment techniques, such as hitting, and that the dogs are divided by temperament, not size. If you happen to have a vizsla who's a scaredy-dog, she should be with other timid dogs, not with confident hulks.

Finally, a dog in day care needs rest periods. A facility might advertise fifteen acres of beautiful grounds for your pup to run with other dogs, but unless there's downtime for your pup to rest and regroup, your young charge can become overly stressed. (Think of a preschooler who plays through nap time, not realizing she's tired, and who then gets crankier and crankier.)

That's a fair number of caveats, but if you choose the right day care situation early on, you'll have a place for your puppy to be comfortable if you want to be out of the house for much of the day, or if you want to travel, once she matures.

positive—when teaching tricks than when issuing an obedience cue. That positive body language, which dogs really pick up on, makes them even more willing to work with their owners. Another attraction is that tricks encourage motion rather than inhibit it, as obedience cues tend to do. Of course, teaching tricks helps keep owners from making the mistake of carrying their little puppies around in their arms *all* the time—a constant cuddling that, as we said before, is not good for pups (or their people).

What kinds of tricks can you teach your dog? The list is as long as your imagination. Some people like to teach their dogs to jump through their arms, or a Hula-Hoop. Others get their dogs to make a figure eight between their legs. Still others engage their pups in games of hide-and-seek (a particularly good indoor choice for the puppy in inclement weather). It takes two people, each with treats, starting out by standing a few feet apart. As the dog gets the hang of it, you can call her name from behind chairs, then from separate rooms, and finally from separate floors of the house. Everyone has a great time, and the pup learns a couple of valuable lessons to boot. That's because part of the play, when the pup finds you, is taking hold of her collar to give her the food reward before encouraging her to find the other human participant, who repeats the exercise. Thus, the dog figures out that coming over to you when called and having her collar grabbed (which may have to happen, on occasion) is a good experience, and one that doesn't mean the game is over.

Teaching your puppy tricks won't just keep her occupied. It will invest her with the sense that she's part of your family. By doing tricks with her, you're reinforcing the idea that she's living in, and belongs in, a human world with human rules and interactions. Then, too, the tricks will keep *you* from getting bored with your responsibility as a pet owner. Taking that point one step further, if you find your puppy fun to be around, chances are you'll end up interacting with her that much more.

MATCHING THE ENVIRONMENTAL ENRICHMENT TO THE BREED

Along with engaging your puppy yourself at home and perhaps taking her to day care, you can enroll her in various structured activities to which her breed, or at least her personality, is particularly well suited. That is, you can help a dog approximate what she has been bred to excel at—or what her ancestors did in the wild—with various strategies.

Teaching dogs tricks is a great way to enrich their lives. They like doing tricks just as much as we like watching them.

Think of it like gym for dogs. People now have to contrive physical activities like jogging and going to the fitness center to take the place of the physical work of hunting and gathering our bodies evolved to do but no longer engage in. In the same way, dogs need structured activities that let them act on their own need to be engaged physically. This is extremely important now that dogs don't have an opportunity to work out their instincts for physicality through jobs such as herding, pulling, and hunting.

In this section we offer some suggestions, along with some generalities about which breeds enjoy which type of activity. Bear in mind that this is a broad-strokes approach. Just because we say a breed tends to like a certain activity doesn't mean *your* dog will. And just because we don't happen to mention your breed in connection with a particular activity doesn't mean your dog wouldn't like it. You've got to play it by ear a little, whether your dog is a particular breed or a breed mix, assessing her not just as part of a group but as the individual she is. If you observe your puppy closely as you raise and train her, it shouldn't be too difficult. You'll learn whether your pup likes to work independently or prefers to engage in physical activity *with* you, and that will help guide your choices.

Also important to keep in mind is that almost all the activities we suggest require that your pup has been through basic obedience training—"Sit," "Down," and so on. That will keep your dog safe and controllable as she learns the new moves. In some cases a pup must be almost out of puppyhood to do the activity in earnest. Consider that if you try to engage a very young pup in something like a sheep-herding class, she could end up hurt—or worse.

On the other hand, we have found on the Internet agility classes for puppies as young as four months old, with puppy-size equipment. In fact, almost any activity can be geared toward young puppies, as long as you scale down the equipment and don't overtax the dogs. Overtaxing them is not good for their growing bodies. Also, while it may seem that puppies have more energy than adult dogs, they tire more quickly. They can't take all that much action in one go.

Rally-O Classes

Rally-O classes ("O" for "obedience") may prove enjoyable for dogs who like to work with their owners—dogs from the sporting group, like Labrador and golden retrievers, herding breeds like shepherds, and some nonsporting breeds, such as poodles.

Rally-O classes are a fun way to take obedience training one step further. The first sign says "Down Walk Around Dog." (The "Down" is for the dog, of course.)

Rally-O obedience classes allow a dog and her owner to work at becoming as precise and well oiled a machine as they can be. A dog and her owner make their way through a course that has been set up with signposts. (There are Rally-O competitions, too.) At each post, you do what the sign tells you. You might be instructed to walk your dog to the first post, have her halt in a sit, take one step backward, turn 90 degrees, then proceed to the next post. At the next sign, you may be told to slow your pace; then, at the next, to speed up; and then, perhaps to weave through some cones.

Rally-O courses, which can be found in the suburbs of most large cities, serve to make training a little more interesting than some of the more traditional beginner obedience training (once the pup has mastered basic training cues). They also get the dog out of the house with you, which is an environmental enrichment strategy in itself.

Agility Classes

Beginner agility classes can potentially work for a pup from any breed. Some herding breeds and terriers tend to excel in classes that go beyond beginner, as do athletic dogs who can move like the wind and overexuberant pups who have gone through socialization but are just not ready to concentrate on standard obedience commands and who, along with their owners, become frustrated easily with "Sit," "Down," and the like. Other pups for whom agility classes might work well: skittish, insecure ones who may have developed some fear aggression. Agility exercises help those dogs gain confidence. Breeds that are inclined to thrive on agility training include Border collies, Australian shepherds, Parson Russell terriers, and poodles. Dobermans, too, are often absolutely crazy about it.

Agility classes are an extension of jumping through hoops or doing figure eights at home. A pup may have to scale an A-frame at an incline or walk a seesaw. She starts on the bottom at one end, walks to the middle, and then pushes down the other side as she walks to the far end. There are chutes and tunnels, too. (With a chute, the dog starts at the opening on one side, runs through, then shoots or pushes through a tarplike material at the other end.) Other props: weave poles, tire jumps, and hurdles. You start out with your pup on a leash, not only to keep her safe but also to keep her from running amok and to teach precision. This inhibits the dog's style up front, but it's better to progress gradually.

Puppy's first agility course.

Frisbee Canine Disc Competitions

Border collies are big on these, as are Labrador and golden retrievers, although the competitions are often enjoyed by any of the sporting and herding breeds. Of course, you can always just go out in your backyard and throw a Frisbee around for your dog to catch, but competitions take the activity one step further.

Flyball

Flyball classes are good for any dog who likes balls and likes to run. They're particularly suited to dogs with lots of energy and who are good with other dogs and a lot going on at once.

Flyball classes tend to be set up as follows. There's a series of four hurdles, ten feet apart from each other. The dogs act sort of as a relay team—four dogs to a team. The first dog jumps all four hurdles, then steps on a spring-loaded pedal sitting on top of a box. That releases a ball that the dog catches, upon which she turns around and races back through the four hurdles in reverse. Then the next dog goes, and so on. It all goes very fast, with each owner racing the dog through as fast as possible so that it's a fun frenzy of dogs running, jumping, and catching balls. (Flyball, for obvious reasons, does not tend to work well for dogs with fear or with fear aggression.)

Musical Freestyle

This requires very intense training, so it's good for people and their dogs who work well as a team when it comes to commands. It's also good for owners who aren't very quick or athletic but who love music and have been very good at training their dog in general.

Musical freestyle is, literally, dancing with your dog. Classes and competitions are becoming more popular, although they're still hard to find in more remote areas. The whole thing amounts to choreographing a performance through fine-tuned training.

We have been flabbergasted at the performances some human-dog duos have put on. At one demonstration we saw, a woman and her Border collie danced to *Boléro*. Dressed up in a matador costume, the owner twirled in place and the dog circled around her. Then the owner did high kicks and the dog jumped over her legs. Finally, the dog stood on his hind legs and put his front paws on the woman's hips as they danced together!

Flyball is great for dogs with energy to burn.

You don't need a cape to engage your dog in musical freestyle dancing, but you do need a very well-trained dog who is attuned to your cues.

This briard enjoys herding sheep in his herding class.

Herding Classes

These are good for—you guessed it—herding dogs: briards, Border collies, Old English sheep dogs, Australian shepherds, Australian cattle dogs, corgis, Bouviers des Flandres, and so on.

Different herding breeds were bred to deal with different livestock—corgis with cattle, for instance, and briards with sheep—but if you live reasonably close to a rural area, you can usually find a class to suit your particular dog. For instance, there are sheep-herding classes and cattle-herding classes, and in some places you may even be able to sign up your dog to herd geese. You can graduate to herding trials, or competitions, if your dog is really into it.

Herding classes are a prime example of doggie gyms. A herding dog who lives in a suburb or city is not going to get a chance to do her thing—herd as real farm work—so she might benefit from going to an outlet that lets her herd for sport.

Lure Courses

These are intended primarily for sight hounds with high predatory instincts, such as Rhodesian ridgebacks, salukis, greyhounds, basenjis, and whippets.

At many lure courses (your veterinarian's office might know where one is available, or check local availability on the Internet), a plastic bag is attached to a machine. In a fenced-in area, the dog is let off leash to track the bag as it's pulled along on a long line, zigzagging, like prey trying to escape. This allows your pup to give in to her genetic inclinations in a safe manner.

Earth Dog Courses

These are intended primarily for small terriers and some hounds.

The complexity of the course varies from simple ten-foot-long tunnels to longer tunnels with twists and turns. Each course has a particular odor strewn along a path, finally leading the dog down a hole to a mock den in the ground to the source of what she's smelling (sometimes rats in a cage that the dog can see and sniff but not touch). She'll then dig for a period of time. There's usually a lot of barking going on. Norfolk terriers are just maniacal about earth courses.

Like herding and lure classes, these courses serve as gyms for dogs who can't otherwise act on their innate tendencies.

Tracking Classes

Tracking classes are enjoyed by scent hounds, including bloodhounds and basset hounds, and by German shepherds and some other athletic breeds. We are not talking about real search-and-rescue training or man-trailing training (as in, the prisoner has escaped and must be tracked through a swamp), which are wholly different ballgames. Rather, this is sniffing purely for sport.

The setups can be simple. The teacher sets a trail and deposits, say, a glove somewhere along it for the dog to track. It's different from earth dog courses, which simulate going down a hole to kill a varmint.

Therapy Giving

This activity is most appropriate for dogs at least one year old (just exiting puppyhood) who are social, enjoy being around people, are confident,

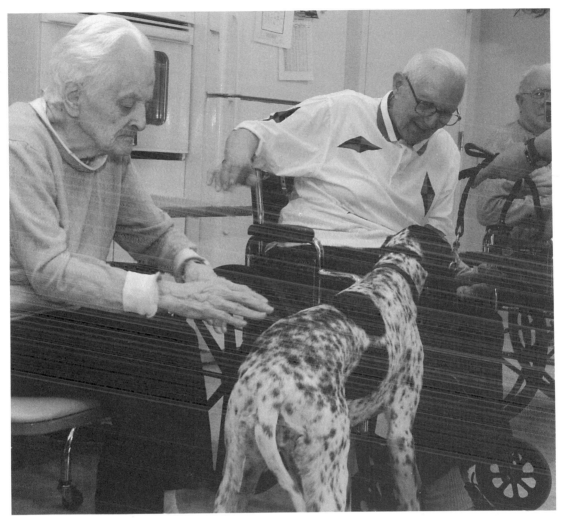

A therapy dog does a good job, as the people's gestures and faces demonstrate.

and can handle contingencies like shiny floors, metal crates, wheelchairs, walkers, and elevators.

Before they are allowed to practice their "profession" and enrich their environment by providing company to people who can't get out on a regular basis, therapy dogs must be approved by one of various organizations that can gauge whether they pass the AKC (American Kennel Club) Canine Good Citizen test. Therapy Dog International is the oldest of these groups, but the Delta Society and many local agencies across the country also provide screening services.

Once a dog is approved, her owner takes her to an assisted-living facility or nursing home in her locale, where she makes people happy while getting plenty of attention for herself in return. She enriches the environment of the residents by making them healthier, too. Studies have shown that holding or petting an animal releases strain and tension and can draw out a person from loneliness or depression. Holding isn't even necessarily part of the equation. While some people want to pet the dog, others just seem pleased by her presence.

Dog owners of all ages enjoy this activity, but therapy dogs might be just the thing for some elderly owners who live independently but are not agile enough to take their dogs on long romps or otherwise engage them in athletic pursuits. Calm toy dogs are well suited as "therapists" because they're not intimidating, but we know of one seventy-eight-year-old woman whose German shepherd, Annie, loved to visit people at area nursing homes and was adored by those she called on.

ENRICHING OUTSIDE THE BOX

For environmental enrichment that goes beyond playing with toys or teaching new tricks, you don't necessarily have to take your puppy to a class. Some dogs like doing whatever it is *you* enjoy doing, especially if you choose your pup with your leisure activities in mind. For instance, if you like swimming and indulge your hobby in a lake (as opposed to a pool at a gym), consider a dog who loves the water, like a retriever or a Portuguese water dog. If you like to take long walks, consider pairing yourself with any active breed from, say, the sporting or herding group. Hounds, terriers, and some working breeds like walks, too. (A dog from a toy breed might be active, but what she considers a long hike might be a very short walk for you.) Some dogs can even be trained to enjoy running or walking on an indoor treadmill with their owners.

For Yukon, the dog mentioned at the beginning of this chapter, the solution to his trashing the house every time his owners left was found in mushing—dog sled racing. The dog's owners loved it, and Yukon, with his Husky roots, loved it too. In summer, they indulged his penchant for dragging large things behind him by hitching him to a cart and having him carry around tools, brush, and other things in the yard.

You can't keep a puppy occupied every single minute she is awake, just as you do not constantly hold or otherwise occupy an infant who isn't sleeping. But the more you put into enriching your dog's environment up front and even in her second year of life, the easier you'll have it during your dog's adult years.

Granted, you'll always need to keep life interesting for her. While many adult dogs who have had appropriate and fulfilling environmental enrichment as puppies can comfortably bear to hang out all day while everyone else in the house goes to work or school, out-of-the-house families should still seriously consider doggie day care or, if that proves too expensive, perhaps a professional dog walker once or twice a day or a stay-at-home neighbor who can pop in to entertain the dog. And outside intervention or not, the dog must get some real exercise each morning before everyone leaves – a romp or at least a longish walk —rather than simply be taken outside to eliminate. (If you can get to a park or field as opposed to just neighborhood sidewalks, a thirty-foot leash or retractable leash allows the pup to really romp, because she can circle and cover a lot of ground as you go along at your own pace.) Leaving a frozen-food-filled Kong near the crate and a couple of safe toys out isn't a bad idea, either. And upon returning home on weeknights and when around on weekends, owners have to make sure to engage their pet in some fun and absorbing activities.

Still, an adult dog who was kept busy as a pup will probably be able to handle downtime much better than a pup who was underemployed. And the ability to cope with downtime, in its own ironic way, will ultimately *increase* a dog's environmental enrichment. A pet who can stay calm and go with the flow will be much more likely to be taken by you to your friends' homes, on shopping expeditions, on errands, and so on. In other words, a dog who receives appropriate environmental enrichment early on will fit so much better into the environments in which you stage your life as the years pass.

PART 5

In the Event of Illness

12

Is It a Medical Emergency?

Your puppy vomits on a sunday night, when the local vet is not available. Do you:

   1. Take him to the nearest veterinary emergency room?
   2. Give him some fresh water or a bowl of milk to settle his stomach?
   3. Offer him a square meal for his stomach to "work on"?

All of a sudden your puppy is limping, yelping in pain with every step he tries to take and refusing to put any weight on his leg. Do you:

   1. Carry him straight to the car and go get an x-ray to see if there's a fracture?
   2. Wait it out and see if he starts to feel better on his own?
   3. Attach a splint to his leg for a couple of days and see whether restricting his movement improves the situation?

Your pup tends to drink a lot of water, but for the past day or two he's drinking like there's no tomorrow. Do you:

   1. Assume he just happens to be really thirsty and keep replenishing his water bowl?

2. Rush him to the vet's office immediately?

3. Add some water to his dry food to see if that helps?

Believe it or not, the only definite emergency here is the copious water drinking, which could be a sign of a life-or-death illness and requires immediate attention. The other situations call for a wait-and-see approach rather than a de facto $140 visit to the emergency room.

But how can you tell? What's the way to distinguish between a sick and a healthy dog, or a sick dog with a garden-variety illness and one who is gravely ill? A lot of people assume you feel the puppy's snout to make sure it's cold and wet. But the state of the dog's nose has nothing to do with his well-being. Your pup could be perfectly healthy with a nose that's warm and dry.

Here are the six most common signs of illness in a puppy and how seriously to take them; unusual situations in which your pup *must* be rushed to the vet's office or a hospital; and how to take your dog's vital signs, such as heart rate and temperature.

SIX COMMON SIGNS OF ILLNESS

These six signs of illness in your pup or older dog should generally prompt you to call your vet, and that, in turn, may or may not prompt your vet to tell you to come in. Obviously, it can be hard to determine over the phone how serious a medical condition is, no matter how carefully you explain things and no matter how much the situation *seems* like something diagnosable and perhaps workable at home. Thus, your vet's office may tell you to come in for a clinical exam even if they're not sure the problem requires their attention. If they do, go! It's always safer to err on the side of caution.

Behavior Change

Your puppy is just not acting himself. He's either unusually agitated or unusually lethargic; if you excitedly tell him, "Let's go outside," he won't even lift his head. Call the vet's office. You will probably be advised to get your dog in there as soon as possible. Granted, such marked behavior changes are very nonspecific signs. You can't tell, for instance, what's wrong just because Fido isn't himself, but something could, in fact, be very wrong. Severe lethargy, in fact, is the most common reason we see emergencies at our clinic, proving symptomatic of everything from a mild infection of the GI tract to life-threatening acute kidney failure.

Vomiting or Diarrhea

These are *really* common problems in puppies, but they don't automatically necessitate a visit to the emergency room. A little vomiting or diarrhea probably just signifies that the pup got into the trash and nibbled on something he shouldn't have. He'll eat or drink again when he's ready.

While waiting, you shouldn't put him on baby food, and you definitely shouldn't start giving him milk. Baby food is pretty rich stuff for a puppy who is sick to his stomach, and milk will likely disturb an upset stomach even more. We've seen far too many dogs whose owners gave them one or both of those in the mistaken belief that they would help—and only made things worse.

Some people (including some veterinarians) suggest reintroducing the pup to food with a little chicken and rice or hamburger and rice, but it's not medically necessary (although it might placate owners who want to feel that they're "doing something"). The dog will do just fine on his own chow. As for water, if the pup can hold it down, keep the water bowl filled, as usual. If not, restrict water to small amounts given frequently.

Where, however, do you draw the line between "a little" vomiting or diarrhea and "let's go right to the vet's office"? Here: If the dog throws up more than a few times and is acting sick (a dog may vomit but show no other signs of illness), get him into the car. Sometimes persistent vomiting is a sign that the pup has swallowed a sock or a ball, which has become lodged in his GI tract. That is, you could have a surgical emergency on your hands. (We perform several surgeries every month, many of them on puppies, to remove swallowed socks, balls, and other objects.) Other times the vomiting is so copious that the pup must be kept in the hospital to be given supportive care and intravenous fluids so that he doesn't become dehydrated.

It's the same with copious diarrhea, not a discrete bout or two but uncontrollable runs wherein the puppy must go to the yard every couple of minutes and even then, can't necessarily hold it in until he gets outside. The cause may be a viral disease that simply has to run its course, but a dog under such distress may require carefully calibrated fluid infusions so that his illness doesn't become complicated by dehydration.

Limping

Don't automatically rush into emergency mode if your puppy starts limping and acting like he will never walk another step. Chances are that he has not broken his leg but, rather, simply hurt himself a little. Keep in mind that puppies have not yet distinguished major from minor pain. An adult dog who bangs his leg will simply say "Ow" to himself and get on with it. A pup, on the other hand, will scream bloody murder, so to speak—but, more often than not, be running around again inside half an hour. Puppies do break limbs and get bad sprains, of course, but our advice is as follows: if your puppy (*not* older dog) suddenly is hobbling around in pain and won't put any weight on his paw, give it a half hour. If after that time the pain persists, bring him in. Even with that advice, however, we should mention that only about one in five puppies we see with leg pain has sustained a fracture.

Coughing

A single cough or even a single bout of coughing is nothing to worry about. But any *persistent* coughing that lasts more than a day should engender a visit to the vet. It could be a sign of pneumonia—a common illness in puppies. Consider that as many as one in twenty puppies (a not insignificant 5 percent) ends up with pneumonia or some other respiratory issue—often within a month or two of his owner's bringing him home. Such problems require immediate attention. The longer you wait, the sicker the pup is going to get, and the harder it will be for him to recover.

Not Eating/Not Hungry

Anorexia in a pup, just like marked behavior changes, is a nonspecific sign of illness. If your dog's eating pattern is way off for more than a day, it's hard to say what's wrong, but something most probably is, and it could be anything from an infection to organ failure. Get him to the doctor.

Drinking Lots of Water

We're not talking about lapping at the water bowl after some active playing outside on a hot summer's day. This is about drinking much more water than usual for no discernible reason. If that's the case, call your vet's office and get your puppy in there. Excessive water drinking can indicate a problem with the liver or kidneys, both of which filter waste from the dog's body and have to be in top working order for the puppy's survival.

We talked about basic water needs in chapter 4, but if you want to calculate a little more closely approximately how much water your dog should drink each day, multiply his weight in kilograms (1 kilogram = 2.2 pounds) by 40 for the volume in milliliters (240 milliliters is about 1 cup). For example, a dog weighing 20 kilograms (44 pounds) should drink 20 × 40 = 800 milliliters (3+ cups) of water per day.

To measure how much your dog is actually drinking, add a measured amount to a large water bowl and determine what's left after twenty-four hours. (Don't forget to keep toilet lids down during this time!)

Keep in mind that the precise amount a dog drinks depends not only on how hot the weather is and how active he has been but also on what he eats. Dogs who eat wet food drink less water than those on dry rations because they get water in their provisions.

OBVIOUS EMERGENCIES

The preceding signs are the common ones. There are also some unusual circumstances in which you *must* get your dog to a veterinarian's office as quickly as possible. There is no wait-and-see wiggle room.

• **Severe trauma, such as being hit by a car.** Even if your dog looks okay, take him to the emergency room—and then continue to keep a close watch on him even if he is released. He could have life-threatening internal injuries that might be missed despite an entirely thorough workup. One of our clinicians once examined a dog who had been run over by a car and, to his surprise, detected no apparent injuries. The dog looked absolutely fine—he wasn't limping, behaved normally, was breathing normally, had normal heart sounds, normal x-rays of his back and abdomen, and normal blood work. He was therefore sent home. The next morning his owners found him dead. His stomach and intestines, which were in place at the time of the examination the day before, had poked through a tiny hole in his diaphragm caused by the accident and impaired his breathing. The condition is called a diaphragmatic hernia, and even with a chest x-ray it gets missed on rare occasions.

The moral here: Following any serious trauma, a dog should be watched like a hawk for at least twenty-four hours, even with appropriate emergency room treatment.

- **Difficulty breathing.** Like a person who is having trouble breathing, a dog who can't breathe right must be seen immediately.

- **Seizure.** A seizure can result from disparate causes ranging from epilepsy to a metabolic disease, such as liver or kidney failure. Both the liver and kidneys filter toxins from the body. When those organs fail to do their job, poisons build up in the body, including in the brain, and may cause seizures. An inability of the liver or kidneys to do their job properly is the most common metabolic reason for seizures in puppies and usually requires serious medical intervention, even surgery. Often, the problem with the liver is that an anomalous blood vessel shunts blood away from that organ. Thus, the liver is unable to "clean" the blood, and surgery is needed to reroute blood flow *through* the liver. A puppy of any breed can have this condition, but breeds that tend to be afflicted more than others include Yorkshire terriers, Bernese mountain dogs, Irish wolfhounds, Cairn terriers, Maltese, and golden and Labrador retrievers.

Yet another reason for seizures in puppies is hydrocephalus, a congenital condition in which fluids in the brain don't drain properly. This problem, which affects Chihuahuas and English bulldogs more commonly than any other breed, is treated with both medication and surgery but is harder to manage than seizures caused by a failing liver or kidneys.

Sometimes seizures are caused by puppies getting into things they shouldn't. Toxins can include lawn and garden chemicals, antifreeze, and lead paint (from chewing woodwork). Your veterinarian will evaluate these and other possibilities while exploring the cause of your dog's seizures. (More on poisonings in a bit.)

- **Distended, tense abdomen.** The dog may also be anxious and uncomfortable and unable to settle down, and perhaps vomiting white foam as well. This is most likely a sign of a disease called gastric dilatation and volvulus (bloat and twist), a life-threatening emergency. The stomach fills with air and flips over, literally twisting upon itself and thereby knotting up important blood vessels, kinking off the esophagus on the top end of the stomach and the small intestine on the bottom end.

The problem, which occurs all of a sudden (but usually not in dogs less than one year old), usually affects large, breed, deep-chested breeds, such as Great Danes, Irish setters, Greater Swiss mountain dogs, Akitas, German shepherds, and any other dogs with a deep chest as part of their conformation. You can't miss the problem. It will look like someone inflated a giant balloon inside your dog's abdomen.

The sooner you recognize it and get your dog to the vet's office for surgery, the better the chance for recovery. During the surgery, the stomach is flipped back over and permanently secured to the inner wall of the abdominal cavity via a procedure known as a gastropexy, which prevents the stomach from flipping again.

Unfortunately, it's more common than you might think. At our hospital, we perform about sixty-five emergency surgeries a year to correct gastric dilatation and volvulus—more than one a week.

If your dog is a female, your vet may talk to you, depending on her breed, about elective gastropexy while she is being spayed. (A Great Dane, for instance, has a very high one-in-four chance of falling victim to gastric dilatation and volvulus.) The surgeon is working in the abdomen when performing a spay, anyway, and there's something to be said for putting the dog under anesthesia once instead of possibly twice. Elective gastropexy may even be considered in male dogs at the time of castration.

Canine Influenza: An Emerging Problem

Around 2004, dogs in locales across the United States started coming down with canine influenza, caused by a mutant of an equine influenza virus. (The illness was first identified on greyhound racetracks.) In most dogs, the problem presents as nothing worse than a mild cough. But about 10 percent go on to develop life-threatening pneumonia. (All things being equal, puppies—and old dogs—are more susceptible to viral diseases than other dogs.)

As of this writing, there is no vaccine for canine influenza, although one could be developed anytime. In the meantime, at least rest assured that there is no threat to people. In addition, Internet discussions of whole kennels dying of canine influenza are not based on fact. The disease is serious, but it does not become epidemic in a particular area.

If your veterinarian suspects your dog has the disease, he may send off a blood sample or a mucus sample from the respiratory tract for diagnostic testing. Beyond that, there's not much that can be done at this time. You and the dog just have to wait it out.

Vital Signs

While the coolness and wetness of a puppy's nose don't provide any clues to his well-being, other physical signs do, and they're good to be aware of if you suspect something may be wrong. In fact, they can goad you to call the vet's office if you're on the fence.

1. Check the inside of your dog's lip, or gums. They should be bright pink. Even in breeds like chow chows and Akitas, who have a lot of black pigment, you should be able to find some pink. If the inside gums are pale or muddy-colored, it could be a sign of shock.

2. Take your dog's temperature (with a separate rectal thermometer that you keep on hand just for your canine friend). "Normal" is not a single number. It's a range: approximately 100 to 102.5 degrees Fahrenheit.

3. Check your dog's pulse. You can usually feel the beat on the inside of his thigh if you cup your hands around his rear leg and gently press your fingers into the depression in the center of his groin, as shown on the left. Most dogs' resting heart rate is between 80 and 120. If your dog's is above 140 beats per minute when he is in a calm, resting state, it should be cause for concern.

4. Check your dog's breathing. Panting is normal, but if the dog is struggling or making a lot of noise to take in and breathe out air, something is very wrong.

An owner checks the heart rate of her Havanese.

• **Profuse bleeding.** If your dog bleeds from a small wound and you can stop it quickly with mild pressure, you can deal with it at home. But if mild pressure doesn't stop the hemorrhaging—or even if you have managed to stop the bleeding but the wound is gaping—you need to take your puppy to the vet. Do *not* apply a tourniquet, which can cut off circulation. For the trip to the doctor's office, apply pressure with gauze that you keep in place with tape or with an Ace bandage.

• **Choking.** Choking, obviously, is an emergency. If you can't breathe, you can't live. The most common things dogs choke on isn't food. It's balls—ones small enough to pick up in their mouths but large enough so they become lodged in the back of the throat.

One of our clinicians encountered a dog who had inhaled a ball-like acorn. The dog loved to toss acorns into the air and then catch them, but mistimed it once. The acorn lodged in his airway, causing him to gasp for breath and then faint. At that point, the acorn rolled forward and the obstruction was relieved. The dog regained consciousness and stood. Then the acorn rolled back down his airway again, and he obstructed and fainted again. The process was repeated over and over. But once the acorn was removed via a procedure called a bronchoscopy, the dog was fine.

You may not always have to take a choking dog to the vet's office immediately. First try the Heimlich maneuver. Pick up your pup so he's on his hind legs, with his head up. Grasp your hands around his middle, below his rib cage. Then pull toward you and up, very forcefully. For a toy dog or a small puppy, simply hang the dog upside down and shake him.

NOTE: Even if it works and the obstruction seems cleared, take your dog to the vet's office for a professional all-clear.

• **Poisonings.** Literally dozens of substances can poison your pup. Here are some of the most common, in addition to the foods we mentioned in chapter 3:

Citronella candles
Swimming pool treatment supplies
Fly baits containing methomyl
Slug and snail baits containing metaldehyde

Medications (painkillers, cold medicines, antidepressants, vitamins, and
   diet pills are potentially lethal even in small doses)
Antifreeze
Ice-melting products
Fabric softener sheets
Mothballs
Christmas tree water (which could contain fertilizer from the tree)
Batteries

Poisoning effects range from gastrointestinal discomfort for a day or two
to death, depending on the substance ingested, the amount, and the size of
your pet. For instance, antifreeze, even in very small amounts, can be fatal
to a dog, whereas lapped-up Christmas tree water may cause nothing worse
than a transient GI problem. Either way, if you think your dog may have
been poisoned, get him to the vet's office right away.

HAVE A FIRST-AID KIT ON HAND

Keeping certain materials on hand can mitigate damage in the event of an
emergency, including, sometimes, a poisoning emergency. That is, if you
have the proper first-aid supplies, you may be able to forestall complications
in a dog who has to be rushed to the vet's office. Sometimes the right supplies can ward off an emergency altogether. Here are the first-aid materials
any dog owner should have in the house:

Gauze, sterile pads, and vet wrap, a self-clinging elastic wrap—all can be
   used to wrap a wound prior to transport to the vet.
Scissors.
Styptic pencil or powder to stop a nail from bleeding if it has been cut
   too close.
Tweezers or forceps to remove splinters, ticks, etc.
Triple antibiotic ointment to inhibit bacterial growth and infection, to
   be applied to wounds upon direction by a vet.
Antiseptic to help prevent infection in minor cuts and to disinfect
   minor wounds.
Hydrocortisone cream to reduce itching caused by insect bites and
   allergies.
Diphenhydramine, an antihistamine for allergic reactions.
Cold pack to reduce swelling.

Eyewash to rinse foreign objects or dust out of the dog's eyes.

Hydrogen peroxide (10 percent strength, easily available over the counter) to induce vomiting in case of poisoning. Your vet or poison control center should be able to tell you the correct dose. (Either one should also be able to tell you whether induction is appropriate; sometimes it can worsen the poisoning, depending on the toxin.)

Antiseptic wipes, to clean your hands as well as a cut on the dog.

Alcohol prep pads to clean scissors and tweezers before use. (They should not be used directly on a wound.)

Muzzle (a scared dog in pain may bite even a loved one).

Latex gloves.

A ready list of emergency health-care-provider phone numbers.

ALL SET

There you have it—everything from what you need to have on hand to assist your puppy through a medical problem to the foods to feed, the vaccination appointments to make, and, just as important, the way to show your dog your love and respect as you teach him to respect you back. (Do everything right and his love will flow back to you naturally.)

Of course, we can't possibly anticipate every contingency that may occur. Nor would you want it that way. One of the best parts about raising a puppy is discovering through some serendipity his natural proclivities, his level of intelligence, the things about your interactions that best support and enhance the bond between the two of you. But with our recommendations put into practice, you absolutely will get your dog off to the most positive start possible. And going forward, your dog will get the best chance of having a wonderful life with you, as the appreciated companion you always hoped he would be. Enjoy.

Resources

THE FOLLOWING RESOURCES SHOULD BY NO MEANS BE CONSIDERED AN EX-
haustive list of where to find further information about, or buy gear for,
puppies. But it will help you get started as you bring a new pup or older
dog into your life.

Note that any mentions of product manufacturers should be thought of
as guides to get you on your way; they should not be construed as endorse-
ments of one brand over another. Note, too, that Web sites for various organizations and companies come and go. If we've listed one that no longer
exists when you try to find it, you may be able to locate it at another site
with your search engine.

Chapter 1. How to Select a Puppy

For more detailed information on breed groups and all the breeds within
each group, check out the Web site of the **American Kennel Club, www
.akc.org.** It also provides contact information for breed rescue groups—organizations devoted to saving puppies or older dogs of particular breeds
that may have been abandoned or given up, then making sure they end up
in the homes of people who will offer them the kind of dog's life they deserve. The American Kennel Club even offers an Online Breeder Classifieds
Service.

You can also search for a purebred puppy, or a mixed breed, via **www
.petfinder.org.** Be sure to click on "Baby" as opposed to "Young," "Adult," or
"Senior" if it is indeed a puppy you seek. Pictures of the breeds and useful
blurbs on each can be found as well at **www.dogbreedinfo.com,** and **www
.petplace.com** supplies additional information about some of the heredi-
tary conditions of purebred dogs mentioned in the chapter.

For people whose puppy, older dog, or other pet has died, Tufts offers a
Pet Loss Support Hotline at 508-839-7966. The hotline is staffed by veterinary students who have had extensive training with a licensed psychologist.
Its ultimate goal is to support callers with the knowledge that they are not
alone and that they are not silly or ridiculous for having strong feelings over
the loss of the their pet. To learn more about the hotline, where phone
callers may speak as long as they wish, visit **www.tufts.edu/vet/petloss.**

Chapter 2. Getting Puppy Settled In

For automobile/vehicle barriers for your traveling older pup or adult dog,
surf to **www.hunterk9.com** and click on "Cargo Area." For a selection of car
safety accessories for dogs, visit **www.petsafetybelts.com.**

For crate bedding and other crate accessories, check out **www.petdreams
.com** or call 1-866-PET-DREAMS or 1-866-738-3732.

Chapter 3. Puppy's Physical Well-Being: Preventive Medical and Health Care

The **American Veterinary Medical Association,** while in the main an or-
ganization for veterinarians, also offers information for pet owners on
everything from vaccinations and household hazards to canine influenza.
The Web site also posts interesting news tidbits, including the fact that consumer spending on pets more than doubled from $17 billion in 1994 to an
estimated $38 billion in 2006. Go to **www.avma.org.**

The largest pet insurance company in the United States is **Veterinary Pet
Insurance (VPI),** which can be found at **www.petinsurance.com** or 1-800-
872-7387. Available in all fifty states as well as Washington, D.C., VPI offers
a policy that allows owners to take their pets to any licensed veterinarian,
specialist, or animal hospital they wish. **PetCare Pet Insurance (www.pet
careinsurance.com** or 1-866-275-7387) is the second largest pet insurance
company in the United States (and the largest in Canada). Policies start at
less than $10 a month.

The **American Heartworm Society** (**www.heartwormsociety.org**) can tell you everything you want—and need—to know about heartworm, including the fact that dogs are the most definitive hosts for it (although thirty other species are also affected). Clinical signs of the disease, along with diagnosis and treatments, are given, and frequently asked questions are answered.

Chapter 4. The Best Puppy Diet Ever

The **American College of Veterinary Nutritionists** (**www.acvn.org**) offers links to Web sites for pet owners interested in learning more about their dog's nutrition from veterinary nutritionists and from experienced veterinarians who specialize in pet nutrition. The **American Academy of Veterinary Nutrition** (**www.aavn.org**) lists veterinary schools and other respected organizations that offer phone consultations for pet owners with specific concerns. (Click on "Nutrition Resources.") And articles on the site address such topics as managing your pet's weight.

Chapter 5. The Socialization Period

The "Puppy Center" at **www.petplace.com** offers information about the socialization of pups.

Chapter 6. How Puppy Perceives the World Around Him

A worthy account of the sensory abilities of dogs can be found in the behavior textbook *Domestic Animal Behavior for Veterinarians and Animal Scientists,* 4th edition, by Dr. Katherine A. Houpt (Malden, Mass.: Blackwell Publishing, 2004).

Goggles for dogs to wear during car rides in order not to get hit in the eye by pebbles and stones that fly up can be purchased from **Doggles,** made by Midknight Creations in Diamond Springs, California. Call 1-866-DOG-GLES (or 530-344-1645).

Chapter 7. Young Dogs and Young Children Under the Same Roof

An excellent book that goes into some depth on how to adjust children and dogs to each other is *Child-Proofing Your Dog,* by Brian Kilcommons and Sarah Wilson (New York: Warner Books, 1994). Also, in his book *The Dog Who Loved Too Much* (New York: Bantam Books, 1996), Dr. Dodman has written a chapter entitled "Two Dogs and a Baby," which describes how to interpret and handle the various reactions that dogs may show to children.

Chapter 8. Training Your Pup

The **Association of Pet Dog Trainers (www.apdt.com)** promotes positive, no-punishment training only and may be able to help you locate a positive trainer in your area.

You may also want to check out *Clicking with Your Dog: Step by Step in Pictures,* written and illustrated by Peggy Tillman (Waltham, Mass.: Sunshine Books, 2001).

Chapter 9. Housetraining

A product called **Zero Odor** appears to be effective at removing urine odors from carpets, couches, and the like. It keeps pups from going back to the same spot to do their business. Surf to **www.zopet.com.**

Chapter 10. Nipping Behavior Problems in the Bud

Storm Defender antistatic capes can be researched and purchased at **www .stormdefender.com.**

Chapter 11. Environmental Enrichment

The **American Kennel Club** Web site, **www.akc.org,** has links to information about environmental enrichment courses ranging from agility to Rally-O sessions. Type in the kind of enrichment you are looking for and see what comes up.

Chapter 12. Is It a Medical Emergency?

The **Animal Control Poison Center** of the ASPCA (**www.aspca.org**) has a hotline open twenty-four hours a day, 365 days a year, for people who think their pet may have ingested a potentially poisonous substance. Call 1-888-426-4435. (You may be charged a $55 consultation fee.) The Web site also offers articles with poison prevention tips and related information.

Acknowledgments

A BOOK TAKES A VILLAGE, DESPITE HOW FEW NAMES MAY APPEAR ON THE cover. We'd like to thank our "village" for their help. First, a note of appreciation to our immediate past dean, Dr. Phil Kosch, who advocated tirelessly for veterinarians to play a role in assuring that the public has easy access to accurate health information about pets, and who was a supporter of projects such as this one throughout his deanship. We thank here, too, Dr. Tony Schwartz, former associate dean for academic affairs, who helped develop and promote the idea of a book written specifically with new puppy owners in mind and who provided the administrative support necessary to move *Puppy's First Steps* beyond the idea stage.

The many friends of Cummings School of Veterinary Medicine at Tufts University, including Bill Cummings and the Cummings Foundation, provided invaluable support, and efforts such as this book would not be able to get off the ground without them.

To our students and faculty, whose talent, compassion, and dedication assure that the future of our profession, and of the animals we care for, is in very good hands—a deep bow.

A bow (and a hug), too, to Cummings School administrative assistant Ronni Tinker, who always managed to "patch us through" no matter how far afield we were.

A special note of thanks to Cummings School Media Services director

Andy Cunningham, who brought good things to life for this book. Also to Dogs for Deaf and Disabled Americans (www.neads.org), which trains dogs to assist people who are deaf or hard of hearing as well as people who are physically disabled, for helping us to arrange puppy photo shoots. Likewise, we thank the folks at Especially for Pets on Route 9 in Westborough, Massachusetts, who graciously let us use their pet store training facilities to photograph puppies but who, we gratefully point out, don't sell puppies, as puppies cannot be raised properly in a retail environment.

Much appreciation goes as well to our book agent, Wendy Weil, who makes things happen like no other, and to our editor at Houghton Mifflin, Susan Canavan, who believed in this project and lobbied for it from the start.

Additional gratitude goes to dog training expert Brian Kilcommons, for his insights on how to make fast friends of dogs and children and for his take on various breeds.

Contributor John Berg, DVM, would personally like to thank and express his love for his wife, Gail, and his daughters, Cara and Sidney, whose love of animals — including but not limited to cats, horses, hamsters, goats, baby opossums, foxes, mice, frogs, toads, hermit crabs, fish, and *especially* puppies — is truly boundless.

Contributor Alice Moon-Fanelli, PhD, CAAB, conveys deep appreciation to all the wild and domestic canids that have shared their lives with her: "They have been my truly greatest teachers." A heartfelt thank-you, also, to her mother, Gene Earnshaw, who piqued her interest in dog behavior and genetics in the first place. Thanks as well go to her PhD faculty advisor, Dr. Benson Ginsburg, who gave her a once-in-a-lifetime opportunity to study wild canid behavior. In addition, with great love and devotion she acknowledges her husband, John Fanelli, who "spent a month wooing me by sitting on my living room floor howling in order to win the trust of my coyote-beagle hybrid, Henry." ("Now that's how to pick a husband," she says. "Let your dog do it!") Last but certainly not least, Dr. Moon-Fanelli thanks her mentor and colleague, Dr. Nicholas Dodman, for the opportunity to study and treat companion animal behavior problems and for generously including her in his quest to identify animal models for human obsessive compulsive disorder.

Contributor Scott Shaw, DVM, expresses his gratitude to Larry Berkwitt, DVM, who was his mentor during his internship and residency at the Veterinary Referral and Emergency Center of Norwalk, Connecticut. "Larry taught me more about veterinary medicine than anyone else, and without his guidance and support, I would not be the veterinarian I am today." Dr. Shaw also owes a debt of gratitude to "my wonderful wife, Pamela, who puts up with my long hours and erratic schedule so I can do the job I love."

Editor Nicholas Dodman, BVMS, MRCVS, expresses love and appreciation to his wife, Linda, and his four children: Stevie, Vicky, Keisha, and Danny.

Writing collaborator Larry Lindner thanks pack members Doug Lindner and Quinlen Anderson for spreading the puppy love; Richard and Gary Lindner for never-ending cheer and support; Anne Fletcher, Tom Hawke, Christopher Hendel, Fay Reiter, Anne Simpson, and Gail Zyla for their encouragement — and for everything else; his son, John, for filling his heart to bursting; and last (and first and in between), his wife, Constance, for whom no words could ever suffice.

Illustration Credits

Index

Page numbers in italics refer to illustrations and sidebars.